JOE BROWN'S ARMY

An engraving of the seal of Confederate Georgia, with its distinctive sun-burst, which appeared on state commissions during the war. (Courtesy of Special Collections, University of Georgia Libraries, Athens, Georgia.)

Joseph E. Brown, governor of Georgia, 1861-1865. (From an 1861 photograph. Courtesy of the Atlanta Historical Society.)

JOE BROWN'S ARMY

The Georgia State Line, 1862–1865

WILLIAM HARRIS BRAGG

*The publication of this volume
was made possible in part
by a grant from
the Watson-Brown Foundation,
Atlanta, Georgia*

MERCER

ISBN 0-86554-262-7

The paper used in this publication meets
the minimum requirements of American National Standard
for Information Sciences—Permanence of Paper
for Printed Library Materials, ANSI Z39.48–1984.

Library of Congress Cataloging-in-Publication Data
William Harris Bragg.
Joe Brown's Army.

A revision of thesis (M.A.)—Georgia College.
Bibliography: p. 161
Includes index.
1. United States—History—Civil War, 1861-1865—
Regimental histories.   2. Confederate States of
America. Army. Georgia State Line—History.   3. Brown,
Joseph E. (Joseph Emerson), 1821-1894.   I. Title.
E559.4.B73   1987   973'.458   87-1548
ISBN 0-86554-262-7   (alk. paper)

CONTENTS

For Wanda

PREFACE

Unique in origin and service, the two regiments of the Georgia State Line were conspicuous among the local defense forces raised in Confederate Georgia. Indirectly brought into being by the Great Locomotive Chase of 1862, the State Line was raised to protect Georgia and serve only within her borders. Its military career began with coastal defense in February 1863 and continued until the surrender of Georgia's forces in May 1865. During their tour of duty the Line's men served both as bridge guards and construction crews on the Western and Atlantic Railroad, fought alongside the Army of Tennessee during the final four months of the Atlanta Campaign, and saw action under Lieutenant General William J. Hardee during Sherman's March to the Sea. Finally, men of the State Line fought at Columbus, on one of the last battlefields of the war.

On the political and domestic fronts, the State Line was deeply involved in the internecine squabbling of the Georgia and Confederate administrations regarding conscription, as well as in dealing with North Georgia's twin problems of desertion and disloyalty.

But despite the State Line's relative prominence in Confederate Georgia, the organization was largely forgotten after the war. Its history went unrecorded; its existence was mainly vouched for by scattered references among the official manuscripts and publications of Governor Joseph E. Brown's administration, occasional contemporary newspaper accounts, and certain obscure memoirs.

While most writers on Georgia in the Civil War have touched very briefly on the Georgia State Line in their accounts, few have mentioned more than the organization's creation in 1862, and none have called it by its unusual name.[1] In fact, the inconsistency with which the distinctive

---

[1]I. W. Avery, *The History of the State of Georgia from 1850 to 1881* (New York: Brown & Derby, 1881) 263; Joseph Tyrone Derry, *Georgia,* vol. 6 in Clement A.

styling "Georgia State Line" was used during the war probably helped the
force—along with its unique significance—to become lost in a welter of
other state organizations. All shared the same bewildering characteristic;
they were often identified without qualification as "Georgia State Troops."

For purposes of clarification, briefly surveyed below are the six organizations most often confused with the Georgia State Line: the Georgia
Militia, the three state armies raised in 1861, the Georgia State Guard
(1863-1864), and the Georgia Reserve Force (1864-1865).

Of these organizations only the Georgia Militia predated the Empire
State's secession from the Union; militiamen had participated in "the Rev-
olutionary War, the War of 1812, and the various Indian uprisings until
1840." At the time of the Civil War, the Georgia Militia comprised all able-
bodied white males between eighteen and forty-five. At the local level, in
county militia districts, these men were formed into companies; statewide
there was organization into regiments, brigades, and divisions. Theoreti-
cally, the militiamen met regularly for drill but were to be called out only
during emergencies; otherwise, they were free to go about their business.[2]

After the war broke out, many militiamen joined volunteer companies
for Confederate service. But as volunteering dwindled, Governor Brown used
the militia organization to raise the troops necessary to meet Confederate manpower requisitions. Confederate conscription legislation in
April and September 1862 technically absorbed the militia by calling out
for service those men within the militia's age range. But by early 1864
Governor Brown had reorganized the militia to embrace all white males
from sixteen to sixty not in Confederate service. This new organization was

---

Evans, ed., *Confederate Military History,* 12 vols. (Atlanta: Confederate Publishing Co., 1899) 108; Charles Edgeworth Jones, *Georgia in the War, 1861-1865* (Atlanta: Foote & Davies, 1909) 36; Albert Burton Moore, *Conscription and Conflict
in the Confederacy* (New York: Macmillan & Co., 1924) 156; Frank Lawrence Owsley, *State Rights in the Confederacy* (Chicago: University of Chicago Press, 1925)
35-36; Louise Biles Hill, *Joseph E. Brown and the Confederacy* (Chapel Hill: University of North Carolina Press, 1939) 88 n. 48—the most comprehensive description; T. Conn Bryan, *Confederate Georgia* (Athens: University of Georgia Press,
1953) 88; Joseph H. Parks, *Joseph E. Brown of Georgia* (Baton Rouge: Louisiana
State University Press, 1977) 226-30, 290.

[2]Alex M. Hitz, "Georgia Militia Districts," *Georgia Bar Journal* 18 (February
1956): 1; Richard Peters, ed., *The Public Statutes at Large of the United States of
America* (Boston: Charles C. Little and James Brown, 1848) 271; Allen D. Candler,
ed., *The Confederate Records of the State of Georgia,* 6 vols. (Atlanta: C. P. Byrd,
State Printer, 1909-1911) 2:208-11 (hereafter referred to as *CR*); James Horace Bass,
"Georgia in the Confederacy, 1861-1865" (Ph.D. dissertation, University of Texas,
1932) 83-84. Service in the militia had become voluntary rather than compulsory
by 1860, and the system had fallen into a state of disorganization. Brown initiated
a speedy rejuvenation. Herbert Fielder, *A Sketch of the Life and Times and Speeches
of Joseph E. Brown* (Springfield MA: Press of Springfield Printing Co., 1883) 163-
64.

almost immediately disrupted by the last conscription act, which took militiamen from seventeen to eighteen and forty-five to fifty years of age. Nonetheless, Brown was able to create a sizable militia force by mid-1864: Major General G. W. Smith's First Division, Georgia Militia. Drawn mainly from exempts (many of them the thousands of state civil and military officers) and from boys younger than seventeen and men older than fifty, this force fought during the Atlanta and Savannah Campaigns.[3]

In 1861 three bodies of state troops were raised in Georgia, all created by prewar legislation. The first, grandiosely called the Georgia Army, was actually two regiments called for by the Secession Convention at Milledgeville in January 1861. According to the ordinance creating the force, it was intended for "defensive service" within the state.[4]

Although the governor secured the services of William J. Hardee and W. H. T. Walker as commanders of these units, both officers resigned before the war began and soon entered Confederate service. On 20 March 1861 the convention turned over control of military operations in Georgia to the Confederacy, and it soon tendered the two state regiments for service in the Provisional Army. Those companies formed by that time were consolidated into the First Georgia Regulars. Commanded by Colonel C. J. Williams, this regiment was transferred to Virginia in the summer of 1861.[5]

In mid-March 1861 Governor Brown began raising state troops under an act of the 1860 General Assembly empowering him to raise 10,000 troops "for the defense of the State." It being impracticable to raise the entire force, Brown created instead a small army: the Fourth Brigade, Georgia Volunteers, commanded by Brigadier General William Phillips. This force included two infantry regiments plus rifle, artillery, and cavalry battalions. Before it could enter active state service, the entire organization, numbering some 2,500 men, was tendered in early August 1861 to the Confederacy.[6]

Under the same legislative authority he had employed in organizing Phillips' brigade, Brown set out in September 1861 to form another army.

---

[3]Bass, "Georgia in the Confederacy," 213-14; *CR*, 2:192-93; Bass, "Georgia in the Confederacy," 228, 233, 240, 242, 246-48, 252-53.

[4]*CR*, 1:710.

[5]Nathaniel Cheairs Hughes, *General William J. Hardee: Old Reliable* (Baton Rouge: Louisiana State University Press, 1965) 70; W. H. T. Walker to Henry C. Wayne, 11 March 1861, Adjutant General's Incoming Correspondence (hereafter referred to as AGIC), Georgia Department of Archives and History (hereafter referred to as GDAH); *CR*, 1:726, 737-38; Derry, *Georgia,* 16; *CR*, 2:92.

[6]*CR*, 3:101-102, 2:90-92.

While it was the first state brigade raised, Phillips' organization was enumerated fourth; the state had been divided into four districts for raising toops, and the men who volunteered came from the fourth district. The remaining three brigades comprised the state army raised in the fall of 1861.

By December he had a three-brigade division of approximately 8,000 six-month state troops stationed at Savannah under Major General Henry R. Jackson. Most were still in service when the first conscription act was passed the following April, and were consequently turned over to the Richmond government.[7]

More similar to the militia were two other local defense forces raised in the state, the Georgia State Guard and the Georgia Reserve Force. Both were organized under the auspices of the Confederate government, and both were commanded by Confederate Major General Howell Cobb. The short-lived Georgia State Guard was raised for the Confederacy in the summer of 1863 by Governor Brown, drawing mainly from exempts and men older than conscription age. Brown's 3,000 militia officers helped raise the force and were given furloughs to join. Once organized, the men were to serve, during emergencies only, from 1 August 1863 to 1 February 1864. Once called out, however, many were not released until the six-months' enlistment expired. Brown claimed to have raised 15,000 men for this force; General Cobb and Secretary of War James Seddon calculated their numbers to have been much lower.[8]

In April 1864, a few months after the disbandment of the Georgia State Guard, General Cobb began organizing the Georgia Reserve Force—often more accurately called the Confederate Reserves. Members of this organization were men from seventeen to eighteen and forty-five to fifty, along with Confederate soldiers detailed from the army to work in munitions factories and elsewhere. Since they were to constitute "a reserve for State defense and detail duty," the Reserves would not be compelled to serve outside Georgia—although some did so briefly during the Savannah Campaign. Several factors, including lack of cooperation from Governor Brown, prevented Cobb from raising more than a "nominal force" of about 6,000 men. Although it was originally intended that they be called out only during emergencies—akin to the plan for the militia and the State Guard—many of the Reserves remained on active guard and garrison duty (most at Andersonville and Macon, respectively) for the remainder of the war.[9]

The State Line differed in one way or another from all of the aforementioned organizations. It drew from all classes of men, exempted or not, re-

---

[7]Ibid., 2:93, 249-52, 3:188.

[8]Ibid., 2:456-62, 3:618-19, 538, 637. There was much controversy surrounding this force. Hill, *Joseph E. Brown*, 165-81.

[9]*CR*, 3:503-504; *War of the Rebellion: Official Records of the Union and Confederate Armies* (Washington DC: Government Printing Office, 1880-1901) ser. 4, vol. 3:178, 474. (Hereafter referred to as *OR*. Unless otherwise noted, citations are from ser. 1.) Horace Montgomery, *Howell Cobb's Confederate Career* (Tuscaloosa AL: Confederate Publishing Co., 1959), 115-16; Howell Cobb to Charles C. Jones, Jr., 12 September 1867, Charles C. Jones, Jr. Papers, Manuscript Department, William R. Perkins Library, Duke University, Durham, North Carolina.

gardless of conscription legislation; it served for the duration of the war, not for a brief enlistment or only during crises; and it was only loaned, never surrendered, to the Confederate government.

All of these local defense troops, whether state or Confederate, were very much a part of the story of Georgia in the war. Recounting the State Line's role in that story is the purpose of this study.

ACKNOWLEDGMENTS

The history of the Georgia State Line could not have been pieced together without the assistance of several institutions and many individuals. For their helpfulness I especially wish to thank the staffs of the Library of Congress and the National Archives, Washington, D.C.; the Georgia Department of Archives and History, Atlanta, particularly Miss Charlotte Ray of the Civil War Section (who has cheerfully given years of valuable assistance), Mr. J. Harmon Smith, and Miss Gail Miller; the Georgia Historical Society, Savannah; the William R. Perkins Library, Duke University, Durham, North Carolina, especially Mr. Robert C. Byrd of the Manuscript Department; the University of Georgia Libraries, Athens, particularly the staff of Special Collections; University of Georgia Cartographic Services, particularly Mr. Jim Ingram; The Library, Manhattanville College, Purchase, New York, especially Mrs. Donna L. Nickerson of Special Collections; and the Robert W. Woodruff Library, Emory University, Atlanta, particularly Mr. Richard H. F. Lindemann, formerly of Special Collections. The Woodruff Library was also extremely generous in extending borrowing privileges to me.

I am indebted also to the staffs of several local institutions: the Washington Memorial Library, Macon, Georgia (whose Genealogical Room is an excellent research facility); the Stetson Library, Mercer University, Macon, Georgia; the Mary Vinson Memorial Library, Milledgeville, Georgia; and Georgia College's Ina Dillard Russell Library, Milledgeville, particularly Mrs. Nancy Dyer and Mrs. Sue Gladin.

In allowing me to use privately held papers and genealogical information, descendants of some of the study's principal figures were especially helpful. I am in great debt to Mrs. Albert Anderson, Mr. Beverly Evans, Dr. Jabez Galt, Mrs. Natalie Redfern, Mr. Lamar H. Roberts, Ms. Mattie Saffold, and Mrs. Suzanne Shockley. All of these people contributed immeasurably to my research; none placed restrictions of any kind on my use of the materials provided.

I am also indebted to Mr. Charles J. Brockman, Mr. Lee Joyner, Mr. Byron O. Merritt, III, Mr. William G. Moffat, Mrs. W. L. Walton, and Dr. Willard Wight, who offered help, suggestions, and insight. Of great assistance with the photographs were Mr. Richard A. Daniel, Mr. Edwin Hodges, Mr. Keith Bohannon, and especially Mr. Jim Enos of Carlisle, Pennsylvania, who worked several wonders. Mr. and Mrs. John L. Tatum made an invaluable contribution to my research by hospitably allowing their home near Atlanta to be used as a base for numerous assaults on the Georgia Archives. And Ms. Merilyn Davis went beyond the call of both duty and friendship by working many hours typing numerous muster rolls.

In shorter form this study was my Master's thesis at Georgia College. As such it benefited greatly from the perceptive comments and valuable suggestions of Dr. Frank B. Vinson, Dr. O. W. Taylor, and Dr. Eugene Alvarez. To my thesis director, Dr. William Ivy Hair, for his patient help, esteemed advice, and above all, his example, I am greatly indebted.

Finally, I must express my gratitude to my parents, who educated me and indulged my enthusiasm for history and books, and to my wife, Wanda, without whom I could not have researched or written this study.

Any errors of fact or interpretation are the responsibility of the author.

A STATE LINE CHRONOLOGY

1862

April 11: Fort Pulaski surrenders.

12: Andrews' Raiders strike the State Road.

16: Word of the Conscription Act's passage reaches Governor Brown.

May 12: The Railroad Bridge Guard begins duty under Capt. E. M. Galt.

June 6: The House Committee on the Western and Atlantic Railroad advises creation of another Bridge Guard company.

July: Capt. Albert Howell's Company B, Bridge Guard, begins duty.

August–September: Controversy between the Bridge Guard and the conscription officers.

November 6: Governor Brown calls for the Bridge Guard to be increased to two regiments.

December 13: The General Assembly passes legislation creating the State Line.

17: General Orders, No. 23— the governor's call for volunteers.

29: Governor Brown advises President Jefferson Davis of the creation of the State Line.

December 1862–
January 1863: The raising of the State Line companies.

1863

January– February: Galt's expedition to Dahlonega.

February 20-21: The State Line companies hold regimental elections; election of Galt and Storey as regimental commanders.

February-April: The State Line forms part of Savannah's garrison and is sent briefly to Charleston SC in early April.

April: The expedition to Walker County.

April–June: Controversy over agricultural leave.

May 3: Forrest defeats Streight's Raiders; the State Line sent briefly to Rome.

May 1863–May 1864: The State Line's service on the State Road.

May-July: The State Line companies alternate training and guard duty.

June: Col. Storey's resignation;
Col. Wilson's election.

July: All State Line companies
are distributed to points along the road.

September: Northernmost posts of the State Line are evacuated during the Chickamauga Campaign.

September 19-20: The Battle of Chickamauga.

September 1863–
May 1864: The State Line guards posts from Resaca to the Chattahoochee, falling back with the Army of Tennessee.

1864

December 1863–
April 1864: First Regiment controversies over detached companies at Marietta.

January: The Wilson-Saffold controversy
in the Second Regiment.

February: The expedition to Cherokee County.

April: Creation of the State Line cavalry;
expedition to north-central Georgia.

May: The First Regiment joins the Army of Tennessee; skirmishing near New Hope Church.

June: The Second Regiment joins the Army
of Tennessee.

June 22: The Battle of Kolb Farm.

July 9: The withdrawal across the Chattahoochee.

20: The Battle of Peachtree Creek.

CHAPTER I

State Rights, State Troops

In December 1861 Confederate Secretary of War Judah P. Benjamin sent President Jefferson Davis a formal report of his department's activites, accomplishments, and problems. Prominent among the problems was the policy of several Confederate governors on raising state troops. Although careful to ascribe these governors' motives to a "natural desire of aiding in the defense of their own State," Benjamin nonetheless termed these local defense attempts as "shortsighted," "unwise," and "disastrous." He noted that the Confederacy's sole hope of victory against "so powerful an enemy" was in a "concentration of the common strength under one head." These governors, he explained, were raising their own armies, withholding arms and ammunition, and enrolling volunteers for short enlistments, "alluring them by proposals to arm and equip them and retain them solely for service within the State."[1]

Conspicuous among these governors was Joseph E. Brown of Georgia, who had energetically pursued the policy Benjamin condemned. But the Secretary's account did not fully describe Brown's actions or motives, for the governor had made great contributions to the common defense, always meeting the Confederacy's troop requisitions. He did withhold some men and arms for state use, but the number of men and amount of materiel withheld were relatively modest, particularly in comparison to the men held back by some other Confederate governors. Brown acted as he did for a reason well known to Benjamin: insufficient trust in the Davis administration—that "one head" which was to gather and deploy the nation's

[1] *OR*, ser. 4, vol. 1: 795.

troops.[2] Whether well-founded or not, Brown's suspicions of the Richmond government greatly outweighed his faith in it, and he was not alone in seeing Davis's regime as dictatorial, incompetent, and biased against Georgia.[3]

Yet the governor's state rights philosophy, which underlay so much of what Brown did, was also important in explaining his actions. Along with the old Tertium Quid, John Randolph, the governor evidently believed that asking a state to surrender part of her sovereignty was "like asking a lady to surrender part of her chastity." And, like many of his fellow Confederate governors, Brown considered his right to keep "troops of war" to be the *sine qua non* of his state's sovereignty; consequently, he thought of state rights in terms of state troops. Therefore, as chief executive of a state that the Confederate constitution described as being of a "sovereign and independent character," he felt that it was his responsibility and his right to protect his state when the Richmond government could not or would not.[4]

In addition to this philosophical view was Brown's apparent belief that he shared personally in the state's sovereignty. This might seem paradoxical at first glance: simple in his tastes and somber in his dress, the abstemious governor did not at all resemble in appearance the stereotypical sovereign. Yet beneath his plain exterior was a personality as monarchical as that of the Sun King. Inevitably, Brown—"self-willed, argumenta-

---

[2]Thomas Robson Hay, "Joseph E. Brown, Governor of Georgia, 1857-1865," *Georgia Historical Quarterly* 13 (June 1929): 92-93; Bass, "Georgia in the Confederacy," 138; Clement Eaton, *A History of the Southern Confederacy* (New York: The Free Press, 1954) 253. Among those governors withholding troops from the Confederacy, Brown was actually one of the lesser offenders. During 1861-1862 the governors of South Carolina and North Carolina each withheld as many as 20,000 troops, while Georgia held back only about 8000. Even after conscription began, the Carolinas seem to have kept about 17,000 local defense troops each, while Georgia was withholding only about 10,000. Owsley, *State Rights in the Confederacy,* 26-28, 30, 40, 41, 68.

[3]Alexander C. Niven, "Joseph E. Brown, Confederate Obstructionist," *Georgia Historical Quarterly* 42 (September 1958): 234-35, 237; Rudolph von Abele, *Alexander H. Stephens: A Biography* (New York: Alfred A. Knopf, 1946) 207; Henry C. Wayne to Colonel William R. Boggs, 9 January 1862, Adjutant General's Letter Book No. 5, GDAH. Adjutant General's Letter Books hereafter referred to as AGLB.

[4]Russell Kirk, *Randolph of Roanoke: A Study in Conservative Thought* (Chicago: The University of Chicago Press, 1951) 55; Owsley, *State Rights in the Confederacy,* 53; *OR,* ser. 4, vol. 1: 136; *CR.* 2: 93; Janet E. Kaufman, "Sentinels on the Watchtower: The Confederate Governors and the Davis Administration" (Ph.D. dissertation, American University, 1977) 434.

tive, jealous of his prerogatives"—would clash with Jefferson Davis, who was also "a born controversialist."[5]

The issue of state troops would be but one of many points of conflict between two men whose philosophies were fundamentally opposed. On one hand was the governor who, unable to see past his state's interests, seemed to consider Georgia as simply an ally of the Confederacy, whose government was a mere creature of the states. These states, he would hold, could find a suitable model for union in the German Confederation—a bastion of particularism where central authority was severely limited. On the other hand was the president, a nationalist pragmatically seeking to achieve the Confederacy's independence at any cost—even to the extent of creating an immensely powerful and intrusive central government that effectively "jettisoned state rights."[6]

The collision of these two leaders over Georgia's defense embodied that fatal internal conflict which helped foredoom the Confederacy's fight for independence. How could independent states, absolute in their sovereignty, wage war successfully without surrendering—at least temporarily—some of their rights and powers to the central government? The answer, as far as Brown and other doctrinaire state rightists were concerned, was that such diminution of sovereignty was impossible and absurd; it would merely subsititute a tyranny in Richmond for one in Washington, thus negating the reason for fighting in the first place.[7]

A showdown over the issue of troops for Georgia's defense became unavoidable even before the firing on Sumter. In February of 1861, while Georgia was still an independent republic, the Provisional Congress had given President Davis "control of all military operations" in the Confederate states, control which the state Secession Convention ratified the next month, after Georgia joined the Confederacy.[8]

---

[5]Avery, *The History of the State of Georgia,* 16, 48-49, 290; James Horace Bass, "The Attack upon the Confederate Administration in Georgia in the Spring of 1864," *Georgia Historical Quarterly* 18 (September 1934): 228-29; Hay, "Joseph E. Brown, Governor of Georgia, 1857-1865," 94; James Ford Rhodes, *History of the United States from the Compromise of 1850 to the End of the Roosevelt Administration,* 9 vols. (New York: The Macmillan Co., 1928) 5: 476.

[6]Owsley, *State Rights in the Confederacy,* 27-28; Niven, "Joseph E. Brown, Confederate Obstructionist," 255; *CR,* 3: 700; *CR,* 638; Richard E. Beringer et al., *Why the South Lost the Civil War* (Athens: The University of Georgia Press, 1986) 65, 291, 402.

[7]*CR,* 2: 738-739, 853-854; E. Merton Coulter, *The Confederate States of America, 1861-1865* (Baton Rouge: Louisiana State University Press and the Littlefield Fund for Southern History, 1950) 402; Hill, *Joseph E. Brown,* 258-259; Kaufman, "Sentinels on the Watchtower: The Confederate Governors and the Davis Administration." 432-34.

[8]*OR,* ser. 4, vol. 1: 117; *CR,* 1: 726.

In spite of this legislation, the Constitution of Georgia made the governor "Commander-in-Chief of the army and navy" of Georgia "and the militia thereof," with the Code of Georgia empowering him to call out the militia. And the Confederate constitution gave the state some militia powers, as well as the implied right to keep troops in time of war. Georgia's right to have local defense troops was, then, at least debatable, and the governor liked nothing better than a verbal confrontation. He never lost an argument because, like Dr. Samuel Johnson, if his pistol misfired he simply beat his opponent down with the butt end of it.[9]

Soon displeased with Davis's troop deployments, Brown wrote to the Secretary of War in May 1861, when coastal Georgians were clamoring for protection from Yankee raids: "While I still recognize the authority of the President. . . , I demand the exercise of that authority in the behalf of the defenseless and unprotected citizens of the State." If Davis would not act, Brown would. He seems to have decided at the outset that he would provide the Confederacy with troops while simultaneously raising, arming, and training state forces.[10]

Consequently, during the first year of the war—before the Richmond government sought to assure a dependable manpower source through conscription—Brown raised two state armies, both of them forerunners of the State Line, the "miniature state army" which would be the only regular force that Brown created after constription began. Brown's experiences with these precursors of that force would determine in large part his local defense policy for the rest of the war, as well as harden his attitude toward the Davis administration on the issue of state protection.[11]

During early June 1861, acting under the legislature's authority, Brown organized his first body of state troops. This force, a reinforced brigade commanded by William Phillips, was raised exclusively for Georgia's defense. But before the troops could be deployed, Brown offered to transfer the unit to the Confederacy for the duration of the war, promising two ad-

---

[9]*The Constitution of the State of Georgia* [March 23, 1861. Savannah, 1861], 10; R. H. Clark, T. R. R. Cobb, and D. Irwin, *The Code of the State of Georgia* (Atlanta: Crusader Book and Job Office, 1861) 210-11; *Constitution of the Confederate States of America, OR,* ser. 4, vol. 1:140 (Article I, Section 8, Paragraph 16) 142 (Article I, Section 10, Paragraph 3).

[10]*CR*, 3: 69.

[11]Hill, *Joseph E. Brown,* 88. Like the two regiments ordered raised by the Secession Convention, the State Line regiments were considered to be "regular troops," a distinction not shared with Georgia's other local defense forces. *CR*, 1: 710; *CR*, 3: 650; Brown to Andrew Johnson, 20 May 1865, Joseph E. Brown Papers, Felix Hargrett Collection, Special Collections, University of Georgia Libraries, Athens, Georgia. Hereafter referred to as Hargrett Collection. For purposes of this discussion, Phillips' Brigade is identified as Brown's first army since—unlike the Secession Convention's Georgia Army—it was created during the war.

ditional armed regiments to induce Davis to accept the brigade as organized. This would have been tantamount to allowing Brown to appoint a Confederate brigadier general; and, to the governor, this probably was a compelling reason for the tender. Such a move would increase Brown's military and patronage powers at the expense of the president's. The move was also said to violate a Confederate law stating that the government could accept no organized unit larger than a regiment, meaning that Brown could appoint no Confederate officer higher than a colonel. The crux of the matter was that Davis wanted the troops, and Brown wanted a Confederate brigadier general's commission for Phillips.[12]

In early August Brown finally relented, breaking up the brigade in the manner specified by Richmond. Although Phillips accepted a colonelcy and led a portion of his brigade to Confederate fame as Phillips' Legion, this incident would prove harmful to Georgia's relations with the Confederacy.[13]

Brown created his second state army only a little over a month after surrendering his first. A September 1861 inspection tour convinced the governor that Georgia's coast still was not being properly protected by the government. Having diligently filled Georgia's troops quotas, he made his own requisition of the Richmond government—apparently regarding the Confederate armies as a sort of manpower bank available for withdrawals as well as deposits.[14]

Although this novel approach was unsuccessful, Brown had already begun the creation of the First Division, Georgia Volunteers—three brigades of state troops. This allowed him to appoint numerous staff officers,

---

[12]Parks, *Joseph E. Brown of Georgia,* 152-55; Hill, *Joseph E. Brown,* 62-63. At the same time Davis was refusing Brown's request for a Confederate commission for Phillips, he was giving Confederate generals' commissions to several of the state generals under Governor Isham Harris of Tennessee. This was done when Harris's state army was transferred to the Confederacy. Thomas Lawrence Connelly, *Army of the Heartland: The Army of Tennessee, 1861-1862* (Baton Rouge: Louisiana State University Press, 1967) 32, 37.

[13]Parks, *Joseph E. Brown of Georgia,* 55. As Brown wrote in a confidential letter prior to his reluctant capitulation to Davis, disbandment of the brigade would "cut Phillips's head off and give all his enemies the advantage of him. Nor is this all: it would be injustice to me and to the State." Brown to "Dear Sir," July 10, 1861, Hargrett Collection. Over three years later Brown pointed to this episode as evidence that Davis was requisitioning the Georgia Militia so that he could disband it and "appoint his own partisans and favorites to command." *CR,* 3: 652-53.

[14]*CR,* 2: 93; 3: 128-29, 142.

as well as a major general and three brigadiers, two of whom were general officers lured from Confederate service.[15]

This state army never came under enemy fire, but was nonetheless useful to both the state and the Confederacy. Brown suggested close co-operation with the Confederate forces on the coast, commanded by Brigadier General A. R. Lawton, and the evidence shows that the relationship was fairly harmonious. No less a Confederate officer than General Robert E. Lee was pleased with the presence of the state troops. Lee, at that time charged with defending the Atlantic seaboard from South Carolina to Florida, appreciated these reinforcements; he suggested work the state army could do, such as building boats, constructing fortifications, and obstructing waterways.[16]

Ironically, the six-month enlistments of many of Brown's state soldiers began to expire in April 1862, just as the Federal attack the governor feared suddenly became a reality. The blow fell where it had long been expected—near Savannah. A Federal expeditionary force had closed upon the port city's major downriver defense, Fort Pulaski, placing powerful artillery on nearby Tybee Island. Although the fort had been considered impregnable, the Yankees' innovative rifled cannon breached Pulaski's masonry walls, resulting in the fortress's surrender on April 11. As panic spread through Savannah, the governor hastened to the beleaguered city.[17]

Yet Savannah was not destined to be Brown's only concern. As Pulaski fell, a Federal plot was reaching fruition at the other end of the state. On April 12 a daring band of Union saboteurs led by James J. Andrews stole the locomotive "General" above Atlanta and sped northward, planning to break track and torch trestles as they went. Only the incredible perseverance of the Confederate conductor and engineer, leading the celebrated "Great Locomotive Chase," thwarted the raiders. The state-owned railroad was thus saved from what could have been catastrophic damage.[18]

Undoubtedly upset by the fall of Fort Pulaski, Brown must have been equally disturbed by the attack on the Western and Atlantic Railroad. Created with public funds in 1836, this line had brought modern commerce and transportation to the governor's section of the state, "Cherokee

---

[15]Ibid., 2: 52-55, 59, 70-71; Gilbert Sumter Guinn, "The Coastal Defense of the Confederate Atlantic Seaboard States, 1861-1862: A Study in Political and Military Mobilization" (Ph.D. dissertation, University of South Carolina, 1973) 293-96, 300. Returning to state service was W. H. T. Walker, who had resigned his Confederate commission and was appointed a state brigadier general.

[16]Bryan, *Confederate Georgia,* 68-70.

[17]Parks, *Joseph E. Brown of Georgia,* 193-94; Alexander A. Lawrence, *A Present for Mr. Lincoln* (Macon GA: The Ardivan Press, 1961) 52-54, 62-63.

[18]Eugene Alvarez, "Peter James Bracken: The Forgotten Engineer of the 'General,' " *Atlanta Historical Journal* 24 (Winter 1980): 41-42; *Milledgeville Southern Recorder,* 15, 22 April 1862.

Georgia," and had finally become profitable during Brown's first term. In his quests for reelection, Brown could always point to the increasing railroad revenues that annually poured into the state coffers because of his efficient supervision. And the road itself, as a rich source of patronage, was calculated to be worth 20,000 votes as early as 1857.[19]

An attempt to wreck the Western and Atlantic would distress Brown for another important reason: as a major line of Confederate communication and supply, the State Road was extremely valuable to the war effort. One authority has asserted that no rail network, excepting possibly Virginia's, was "more vital to the cause of Southern independence" than Georgia's network. And in the state's rail system, the Western and Atlantic was the vital link connecting the Confederacy's two major lines of communication. One line passed from Richmond to Vicksburg, Mississippi, through Chattanooga, Tennessee—the State Road's northern terminus; the "second but incomplete route" stretched to Richmond from Meridian, Mississippi, by way of Atlanta, southern terminus of the road. Men and war materiel were shipped over the road, as were provisions for the Confederacy's troops and coal, ore, and metals for Georgia's foundries and factories.[20]

With Brown still reeling from Pulaski's fall and Andrews' aborted raid, yet another blow fell. Before the governor could leave Savannah to inspect the railroad, Davis delivered what Brown and other Georgians considered a tyrannous stroke; and the uneasy alliance that had existed since the war had begun was irretrievably broken.[21]

On April 15, Brown received a telegram notifying him of the passage of a conscription act. In Savannah, the recent military disaster had already produced great anger and consternation; both were doubtless compounded by news of the act, which served not only to make most of the state army subject to Confederate service, but also placed the majority of the Georgia Militia within Richmond's control.[22]

---

[19]Ulrich B. Phillips, "An American State-Owned Railroad," *Yale Review* 15 (November 1906): 259,271,277; Hill, *Joseph E. Brown,* 26-29; Horace Montgomery, *Cracker Parties* (Baton Rouge: Louisiana State University Press, 1950) 201. Brown was fascinated by railroads; he enjoyed traveling by rail and had a lively appreciation of the profit potential of rail systems. Having offered to lease the State Road for a decade during his first term as governor, he headed a firm which did take over control in 1870, thus ending state operation. Parks, *Joseph E. Brown of Georgia,* 67; Phillips, "An American State-Owned Railroad," 276, 282.

[20]Robert C. Black, III, "The Railroads of Georgia in the Confederate War Effort," *Journal of Southern History* 13 (November 1947): 511-13; Brown to Jefferson Davis, 25 May 1863, Governor's Letter Book, 1861-1865 (hereafter referred to as GLB), GDAH.

[21]Parks, *Joseph E. Brown of Georgia,* 196; Hill, 79, 83-84.

[22]*CR,* 3: 186-88, 197; Lawrence, *A Present for Mr. Lincoln,* 66.

At first, however, Governor Brown was amazingly subdued and helpful in his dealings with the Confederate authorities. Although many of his state troops fell within the eighteen-to-thirty-five age range of the legislation, he kept them in their organizations at the request of the Secretary of War, making it easier for the state soldiers to be taken from him.[23]

Brown's initially even temper is partially explained by his hope of having the state force transferred intact to the Confederacy, with all state generals receiving Confederate commissions. Foremost among these officers was Henry Rootes Jackson, a friend and political ally of Brown who had given up a Confederate commission to become major general in command of the state division. If his organization had to enter Confederate service regiment by regiment—as had been the case with Phillips' brigade—Jackson was without a command, and he and his subordinate generals held worthless commissions.[24]

To Jackson's cost, Brown found Davis even more adamant than before. Jackson's resignation of his Confederate commission was undoubtedly a contributing factor in the president's refusal to reinstate him, but a contemporary of Jackson felt that another reason was Davis's personal animosity toward the general dating from the time they had served together in the Mexican War.[25]

At any rate, Davis refused the services of this able, popular officer; Jackson was not utilized by the Confederacy for some time. Consequently, the rancor Brown felt over this refusal, this slight of a favorite must have added vigor to the assault the governor soon launched on the Conscription Act. Brown's most recent biographer has described his request as "reasonable" and has noted that "by failing to grant it, Davis gave evidence of as much obstinancy as Brown."[26]

With the close of the war's first year, Brown had succeeded in meeting all Confederate troop levies while also raising and equipping two state armies. The first he had voluntarily surrendered to Davis; the second had been taken from him by the Conscription Act. In addition, his Georgia Militia had been greatly reduced in numbers by the legislation. Brown had lost face as well as men. As he later wrote a friend, "In the present state of things my position resembles that of a nominal governor of a province more than the governor of a sovereign State." Brown's military status, the state's adjutant general asserted, had been undercut as well. "Having turned over to the Confederate Generals the State Troops and exclusive control of Military Matters," he wrote, "and the Conscription Law having pretty effec-

---

[23]*CR*, 3: 187-189; Brown's Proclamation "To the Officers and Soldiers of the State Troops," dated 16 April 1862, *Milledgeville Confederate Union*, 22 April 1862.

[24]*CR*, 3: 208.

[25]Avery, *The History of the State of Georgia*, 240.

[26]Derry, *Georgia*, 428; Parks, 206.

tually abolished the Militia, the title 'Commander in Chief' in connexion with that of Governor is but an Empty Sound."[27]

After accepting Jackson's resignation, turning over the state troops to General Lawton, and lingering briefly to quell the "almost mutinous" mood of the conscripted state soldiers, Brown left for northwest Georgia. Soon he conceived an idea that promised to turn to his advantage the recent occurrences on the State Road and in Savannah.[28]

From the ease with which Andrews' men had carried out their railroad raid, it was obvious that the Western and Atlantic was in need of a permanent defense force. Brown therefore determined that, despite the conscription legislation, he would take steps to protect his rail line—using whatever men he pleased. Considering that he had previously dealt with state brigades and divisions, Brown made an unusually modest start. He decided to create a company to be known as the Railroad Bridge Guard; and he resolved that no one would take it from him.[29]

---

[27]Brown to Judge James Hillyer, 27 June 1862, Hargrett Collection; Henry C. Wayne to Alfred Tyler, 23 April 1862, AGLB No. 8, GDAH.

[28]*CR*, 3: 190; H. H. Waters to Mark A. Cooper, 22 April 1862, Executive Secretary Letter Book (hereafter referred to as ESLB), vol. 5, GDAH.

[29]*CR*, 2: 257.

CHAPTER II

The Railroad Bridge Guard:
Nucleus of the
Georgia State Line

In early 1862 Union sympathizers had burned two State Road bridges over Chickamauga Creek. With Andrews' Raid following only a few months later, the necessity for increasing the security of the Western and Atlantic was undeniable. Consequently, by early May the governor had raised a bridge guard company from conscription-age men. Although creating a state company seemed to be a small step, it was a step on the road to raising yet another state army; subsequent events showed that this small unit represented to the governor the nucleus of a larger force to be organized when circumstances allowed.[1]

In creating the company, Brown avoided contact with the General Assembly, acting without its sanction. The legislature was not in session and, in any event, was dominated by adherents of Eugenius Nisbet, whom Brown had defeated in the 1861 gubernatorial election; the governor could expect little help from that quarter. Moreover, despite the authorization for a 10,000-man force in 1860, no legislature had as yet sided with Brown against Davis on the issue of state troops. Consequently, the governor took the responsibility of raising the company himself under his powers as president of the State Road, placing himself "immediately in charge."[2]

---

[1]*CR*, 2: 256; *Report of the Superintendent and Treasurer of the Western and Atlantic Rail Road, to his Excellency, Joseph E. Brown, Governor, October 1, 1862* (Atlanta: Office of the Daily Intelligencer, 1862) 4.

[2]*CR*, 2: 256; Avery, *The History of the State of Georgia*, 212; Bass, "Georgia in the Confederacy," 221-22; Henry C. Wayne to Colonel John Dunwody, 5 September 1862, AGLB No. 11, GDAH.

Under these circumstances, no election of officers was necessary. Staff and line positions were filled by the governor, thus modestly rebuilding those patronage powers he had lost with his state armies.[3]

To the post of Bridge Guard commander Brown appointed Edward Machen Ballenger Galt. Although a resident of Dalton, Whitfield County, Galt came from a prominent family in Brown's home town of Canton in Cherokee County; and Galt's family was related to another local family, the Grishams, into which the governor had married. Surviving correspondence, however, shows no particular warmth between Galt and Brown. Brown's letters are brusque and businesslike; those of Galt—who at forty-two was almost two years the governor's senior—show that he was not especially awed by the governor and presumed a certain amount of influence with him.[4]

Galt's father was Canton's leading merchant, and the son seems to have been involved in family enterprises during part of the decade prior to the war. But by 1860 he was a farmer, with a wife and six children, who owned four slaves and employed a couple of day laborers. With the opening of the war, Galt became involved with a group seeking to manufacture gunpowder for the state. Perhaps because of this involvement, Brown offered Galt a captain's commission and the position of assistant to state Quartermaster General Ira Foster. Galt's actual title was chief of ordnance, and his task, for which he was admittedly unqualified, was to supervise the forging and turning of gun barrels in a state factory set up in the State Road's Atlanta machine shop.[5]

Galt, therefore, was already a state officer when on 7 May 1862, he was tendered his Bridge Guard commission. His company, recruited by him in counties bordering the state railway, was "about full" by this time; Galt and his men went on duty on or about May 12.[6]

---

[3]Brown to Joseph G. Watson, 29 December 1862, Hargrett Collection.

[4]Wayne to Edward M. Galt, 7 May 1862, AGLB no. 8, GDAH; Lloyd G. Marlin, *The History of Cherokee County* (Atlanta: Walter W. Brown Publishing Co., 1932) 253; Galt to Brown, 14 May 1861, Joseph E. Brown Papers, Telamon Cuyler Collection, Special Collections, University of Georgia Libraries, Athens, GA[hereafter referred to as Cuyler (Brown)]; Brown to Galt, 21 May 1861, Hargrett Collection. Galt seems to have dropped the "Ballenger" from his name by the time of the war; he normally signed his name "E. M. Galt."

[5]Galt to Brown, 24 October 1861, Governor Brown's Incoming Correspondence (hereafter referred to as GBIC), GDAH; Marlin, 253; Lamar H. Roberts to author, 12 July 1979; U. S. Bureau of the Census, Schedule 1, Free Inhabitants, Whitfield County, Georgia, 1850, 1860; U. S. Bureau of the Census, Schedule 2, Slave Inhabitants, Whitfield County, Georgia, 1860; Galt to Brown, 14 May 1861, Hargrett Collection; H. H. Waters to Galt, 20 November 1861, ESLB, vol. 5, GDAH; Galt to Brown, 24 October 1861, GBIC, GDAH; *CR*, 2:109.

[6]Galt to Brown, 20 May 1862, Cuyler (Brown).

An interesting aspect of the commission Brown offered to the Guard's company officers was an "anti-drinking clause" born of the governor's antipathy for alcoholic beverages. Although a Baptist lay preacher, Galt bridled at this constraint. "I must abide the whiskey restrictions in my commission," he wrote the governor, "though it seems like signing away 'one's Liberty'."[7]

Because of their later prominence in the State Line, two other Bridge Guard officers deserve mention. The first, Lieutenant Francis M. Cowen, a lawyer from Cobb County, had earlier represented Milton County in the state senate. Like Galt, he had been an assistant quartermaster with captain's rank; Cowen, however, had served with the second state army at Savannah.[8]

Grateful for this second appointment, Cowen did not balk at his commission's stricture against strong drink; on the contrary, he fulsomely praised the governor and his political philosophy, making Biblical allusions which must have pleased Brown:

> I had rather have a lieutenancy from the champion of state rights than a captaincy from the fathers of conscription, or to express it in a more emphatic style, I had rather be a door keeper in the House of Joseph than to dwell in the tents of Jefferson.[9]

The second of the two officers had been even more closely connected to the governor in the past; he was Brown's twenty-three-year-old brother, Captain John Mackey Brown. John, along with brothers Aaron and George, had served with the Confederate army in Virginia. John had been a private in the 23rd Georgia, Aaron an assistant surgeon for the 2d Georgia; George, whom the governor was having educated in South Carolina when the war came, had joined the Hampton Legion as a private.[10]

At twenty—the youngest of the thirteen Brown siblings—George was probably directly responsible for John's return to Georgia and eventual appointment to a state position. George survived being wounded at First Manassas only to die of typhoid in Richmond in December 1861 with his two brothers at his side. According to the governor, his mother was incon-

---

[7]Ibid.

[8]Cobb County Probate Court, Returns of the estate of F. M. Cowen, File no. 701; Ralph A. Wooster, "Notes on the Georgia Legislature of 1860," *Georgia Historical Quarterly* 45 (March 1961): 29; Brown to F. M. Cowen, 6 February 1862, Hargrett Collection; Cowen to Wayne, 22 November 1861, AGIC, GDAH. Cowen was a kinsman of Mrs. Joseph E. Brown. F. M. Cowen to "Cousin Lizzie," 29 December 1861, Hargrett Collection.

[9]Cowen to Brown, May 10, 1862, GBIC, GDAH.

[10]Lillian Henderson, ed., *Roster of the Confederate Soldiers of Georgia*, 6 vols. (Hapeville GA: Longino & Porter, Inc., 1959-64) 1:374; ibid., 2:1013; *Milledgeville Southern Federal Union*, 24 December 1861.

solable; George was, "on account of his being her youngest, probably more dear to her than any of her other children." The governor's mother apparently influenced him to have her youngest remaining soldier son return home to Georgia, where he entered state service.[11]

In John's case, the governor interceded directly with Secretary Benjamin. First, he had Benjamin transfer young Brown to Savannah to the state regiment of Colonel E. W. Chastain. Then the governor requested that Benjamin discharge John; he had been given a captain's commission and a state commissary post, and would be needed for the rest of the war. As it turned out, provisioning the Railroad Bridge Guard would be his first responsibility.[12]

Brown also pulled his brother Aaron, aged thirty, into state service by appointing him assistant surgeon in Chastain's regiment. Such nepotism was not unusual during the period, but the hard work and responsibility the governor demanded from his brothers perhaps were. As will be shown, Brown did not allow his brothers to treat their positions as sinecures; he held them to high standards and was mortified by their shortcomings.[13]

An excellent example of Brown's stringent attitude toward his brothers is found in one of the few surviving letters to John, written the first week the bridge guards were on duty. It also well illustrates Brown's penchant for heavy-handed sarcasm:

> Captain:
>   . . . General Foster sent you the quartermaster stores for the Bridge Guards by my direction. You ask me to consider whether or not you will need a "surgeant." I confess to my inability to give you an opinion, as I do not know what a "surgeant" is. I at first supposed you might be of the opinion there was some military officer or *assistant* with that title, below the rank of captain but as I could see no possible use which a captain could have for such an officer, to help supply 125 men on a line of R. Road, and as I am unable to find any such word or title in any military dictionary at my command, and as I know of no piece in "draughts" called a "*surgeant*," I incline strongly to the opinion you can get along very well as Quartermaster and commissary for the Bridge Guards without one. Should the task become too laborious you will please inform me of the fact, and I will apply the *proper remedy*.[14]

---

[11]Brown to Judge J. H. Lumpkin, 18 December 1861, Hargrett Collection; Brown to Mrs. Sallie C. Bird, 31 January 1863, ibid.

[12]Brown to Judah P. Benjamin, 30 January 1862, Hargrett Collection.

[13]H. H. Waters to Drs. A. Young and A. P. Brown, 23 November 1861, ESLB, vol. 5, GDAH. The governor did not shield Aaron from conscription when Chastain's regiment was drawn into Confederate service in April 1862. Brown to Colonel A. W. Reynolds, 23 August 1862, Hargrett Collection.

[14]Brown to Captain John M. Brown, 15 May 1863, Hargrett Collection.

Captain Brown supplied food, tentage, and other articles to the guards, who were divided into squads and stationed at the bridges along the road. No uniforms were distributed; instead, the men furnished their own clothing and were reimbursed with an annual commutation of $50. The state armory provided some rifles, but there was a general scarcity of arms.[15]

As to medical care, the state Surgeon General supplied medicine, and Galt could engage a doctor to tend to his troops when necessary. The chronically ill, however, were sent home to recover.[16]

During the first week of service, several questions arose among the men and were relayed to the governor by Galt. Could the men provide substitutes for themselves if they no longer wished to serve? The answer, which remained in force for the State Line, was "no"; the men had "joined voluntarily and must serve unless disabled."[17]

Would the men be allowed agricultural furloughs? The response was at first a qualified "yes"; the practice was approved as long as only one man per squad was furloughed. Eventually, the number was left to Galt's discretion— as long as he left no bridges vulnerable. The governor moved to offset the effect of such leave by allowing the force to be increased to one hundred and fifty men. But grave damage had been done. Capitulation to Galt in this matter was later to cause much trouble in the State Line.[18]

On June 6, 1862, the House Committee on the Western and Atlantic Railroad sent the governor a letter much to his liking:

> The undersigned members . . . beg leave to say, that they think the military force you now have guarding the bridges over the Road is inadequate and as they learn you have been contemplating an increase of that force, they . . . think it should be increased forthwith to the extent of at least one full company. . . .[19]

This unanimous recommendation, the governor wrote back the next day, met with his approval. He would immediately proceed to carry out the committee's wishes.[20]

Within a month's time Brown's selection for captain, Albert Howell, was raising Company B, Bridge Guard, mainly in Catoosa County. A youth of

---

[15]Galt to Brown, 14 May 1862, GBIC, GDAH; Wayne to Galt, 22 May 1862, AGLB No. 9, GDAH. If Galt approved, the money could, however, be paid proportionately following each two months of service.

[16]Wayne to Galt, 22 May 1862, AGLB No. 9, GDAH.

[17]Galt to Brown, 14 May 1862, GBIC, GDAH; H. H. Waters to Galt, 20 May 1862, ESLB, vol. 5, GDAH.

[18]H. H. Waters to Galt, ibid.; H. H. Waters to Galt, 29 May 1862, ibid.

[19]*Report of House Committee on Western and Atlantic Railroad* (Milledgeville GA: n.p., 1862) 17-18.

[20]Ibid., 18.

nineteen, Howell was the son of Fulton County jurist and farmer Clark Howell, owner of Howell's Mills on Peachtree Creek. Young Howell had served until November 1861 with the 1st Georgia in Virginia. Confederate service apparently impressed him indelibly, for he spent most of the remainder of the war trying to reenter Richmond's forces with a body of state troops. He had first attempted this in February 1862 when he was a major in the state army at Savannah. He was refused, and it is noteworthy that he somehow escaped conscription two months later. He did, however, request transfer several more times while he was an officer of the Bridge Guard and, later, of the State Line.[21]

Howell's company, like Galt's, ultimately reached a strength of one hundred and fifty men. It guarded the bridges above Ringgold while Galt's men took charge of those below, including the Chattahoochee Bridge near Atlanta. Galt's company guarded a total of nine bridges and had its headquarters at Dalton, conveniently near Galt's home. Headquarters for Howell's company was located at Graysville, just below the Tennessee border. About sixteen miles of the State Road were within Tennessee, as were five of the seven bridges entrusted to Howell.[22]

Despite rumors that Governor Brown had a plethora of guns, there was difficulty in arming Howell's men; indeed, it was first thought that lack of arms would prevent expansion of the Bridge Guard. But the company's major problem had to do with alcohol. In early September 1862 Brown wrote Howell:

> I am pained to hear the report that you have not suppressed the drinking of ardent spirits in your company and that probably some of the officers occasionally indulge. This I cannot tolerate. . . . [Any offenders] will be delivered to the enrolling officer as a conscript and will receive no further protection from the State.[23]

Fortunately for the offenders it was discovered that the anti-drinking clause had been omitted inadvertently from the commissions of Company B. Brown was advised that it might seem arbitrary if any soldiers were turned over to the enrolling officers under the circumstances; a court-martial was considered more effective. In this only known court-martial for the bridge guards, a lieutenant was found guilty of drunkenness and forfeited

---

[21]Robert H. Norris to Brown, 3 July 1862, Cuyler (Brown); *Atlanta Constitution,* 25 August 1927; H. H. Waters to Albert Howell, 22 October 1862, ESLB, vol. 7, GDAH; Howell to Wayne, 25 February 1863, AGIC, GDAH.

[22]Brown to Howell, 5 September 1862, Hargrett Collection; Howell to Brown, 18 October 1862, Cuyler (Brown).

[23]Brown asserted that he had "turned over the balance of the State arms with the troops" in April. Brown to G. B. Lamar, 16 June 1862, Hargrett Collection; Brown to James Hillyer, 27 June 1862, ibid.; Brown to Howell, 5 September 1862, ibid.

his commission. Despite this example, however, alcohol remained a problem in both the Bridge Guard and the State Line.[24]

At about the time Brown was threatening drunken state soldiers with enrollment, the conscription officers began to show interest in the three-hundred-man state force and its numerous conscription-age men. In late August, Colonel John Dunwody, Confederate enrolling officer for Georgia, advised Captains Galt and Howell that a number of their men would be enrolled, then sent to a camp of instruction and on to Confederate service. The governor had personally informed Dunwody in late May that he would not permit enrollment of either the Bridge Guard or his militia officers. Outraged, he charged that Dunwody was not happy unless he was "attempting to create collision with the State government." He added that Dunwody's actions were in direct violation of the policy of the Secretary of War, who had written Brown that the enrolling officers were to avoid conflict with state authorities; in case of state interference, enrolling officers were to do no more than protest and refer the case to the Secretary.[25]

On September 1, after having threatened the bridge guards with conscription, Dunwody belatedly wrote to Georgia's Adjutant and Inspector General, Henry C. Wayne, requesting information on the state companies. Wayne somewhat disingenuously protested that he had little knowledge of the unit, adding, however, that at the governor's direction he had instructed the company commanders not to permit their men to be enrolled.[26]

This last was an understatement. Wayne's letters to Galt and Howell stated that since Brown regarded their companies as "absolutely necessary to protect valuable State property . . . , he will not permit any of your men to be taken by an officer of any other Government." If an attempt at enrollment was made, they were to advise the Confederate officer of Brown's position on the matter. If that officer persisted and attempted to conscript by force the men in question, the company commanders were to "repel force by force."[27]

---

[24]Wayne to Brown, 16 September 1862, AGLB No. 12, GDAH; Wayne to Second Lieutenant William T. Day, 20 September 1862, ibid.

[25]Brown to Wayne, 26 August 1862, GLB, GDAH; Wayne to Dunwody, 15 September 1862, AGLB No. 12, GDAH. Dunwody claimed to Wayne that he had not been told the Bridge Guard was not to be enrolled. But Dunwody's letter of 26 May 1862 to Confederate Adjutant General Samuel Cooper notes that Brown specifically told him the Guard was to be exempt from conscription. *CR*, 3: 230. Dunwody's attempts to enroll militia officers (apparently contrary to instructions from the War Department) had been met by Brown's promise to arrest any enrolling officers involved. *CR*, 3: 248.

[26]Wayne to Galt, Howell, 1 September 1862, AGLB No. 10, GDAH; Wayne to Dunwody, 5 September 1862, ibid.

[27]Wayne to Galt, Howell, 1 September 1862, AGLB No. 11, GDAH.

There the matter was allowed to drop, but this was not the first or last time that the governor showed himself willing to spark an armed clash between state and Confederate soldiers. His remark that his men were not to be taken by "any other Government" is quite telling.

After the September conscription incident, the bridge guards completed 1862 in relative quiet. As will be shown, the winter of 1862-1863 was committed to raising the two State Line regiments, of which the guards were to comprise two companies. There is no record of the Bridge Guard having been engaged with enemy troops or saboteurs during its tour of duty, May 1862-February 1863. It seems that the Guard's major benefit to the State Road was its deterrent value.

Many of the guards, officers not excepted, seem to have formed bad habits during their time at the bridges. There appears to have been a general laxness, with too much discretion left to the captains. Since his men were seldom engaged in any active pursuit, Galt did not mind making rather unusual requests for them. For instance, he asked the governor to transfer one of his men to a job with the railroad so that he could "see his mother oftener" and "spend the Sabbath at home more often." Captain Howell purred in a letter to Brown that his troops were not "at all dissatisfied for men cannot desire more privaleges [sic] than we have." Unfortunately, it seems that the relative inactivity and easy life of the bridge guards created unrealistic expectations in many men, who later joined the State Line thinking such service would be comparable to that of the bridge guards.[28]

Before the bridge guards were absorbed into the State Line, some of them participated in the organization's only military adventure. During January-February 1863 a number of them left the road and struck into the mountains on an expedition against the Tories (Union loyalists) and deserters infesting many of Georgia's northern counties. This movement foreshadowed Brown's plans to expand the state troops' duties and was also an example of cooperation between state and Confederate authorities in a combined operation.

Northeastern Georgia had from the war's beginning shown a lack of enthusiasm for the Confederacy and the war it was waging. By the winter of 1862-1863, the region harbored a large number of Tories and Confederate deserters who threatened to create civil disturbances. Consequently, Brown was forced to move.[29]

---

[28]Galt to Brown, 22 July 1862, GBIC, GDAH; Howell to Brown, 18 October 1862, Cuyler (Brown).

[29]Georgia Lee Tatum, *Disloyalty in the Confederacy* (Chapel Hill: University of North Carolina Press, 1934) 75-76. In a circular of 26 November 1862—in which he had asked the governors' assistance in enrolling their white male citizens between eighteen and forty-five—President Davis had suggested that state action was necessary to deal with the problems posed by deserters, Tories, and outlaws. He did not suggest to the governors a source of effective troops for such activities. *CR*, 3: 306.

On 13 January 1863 the governor wrote Secretary of War James Seddon that the deserters' numbers were rapidly increasing; immediate action was needed to forestall a calamity. After applying for assistance to Colonel G. W. Lee, commander of the Confederate post at Atlanta, Brown had been informed that Lee did not have enough men to move in and make arrests. Brown, therefore, asked Seddon to send Lee one hundred and fifty cavalrymen. In return, the governor promised to provide a "sufficient infantry force" as well as the assistance of the local sheriffs. Seddon complied, advising Brown on January 16 that the cavalry force was en route.[30]

Meanwhile, Colonel Lee advised Brown that "a large force under a Union flag" was reported marching against Dahlonega, "laying waste the country." Brown responded by ordering Galt to proceed immediately to the area. F.M. Cowen, having already raised a company for the State Line, was ordered to take Galt's place upon the road.[31]

Special Order Number 23, which contained Galt's orders for the expedition, described deserters and disloyalists in Lumpkin and other northeastern Georgia counties as "committing acts of robbery and threatening to burn the dwellings of loyal citizens, and to do other acts of violence. . . , associating themselves together in large numbers with arms in their hands." Upon arrival, Galt was to take charge of Captain Robert Graham's State Line company, recently raised in Lumpkin County. Galt was then empowered to divide his men into squads, scour the mountains, and arrest the insurgents. He was also to distribute and execute a proclamation sent by the governor regarding the rebels. Adjutant General Wayne emphasized that the assignment was "delicate," calling for "sound judgment and discretion." Galt's orders were to be carried out in the "most quiet way" in his power, but he was to "use all the force necessary for the accomplishment of the object." Twice a week Galt was to send reports of his operations to the Milledgeville headquarters.[32]

Apparently elated by the prospect of this exploit, Galt took the train to Atlanta, where he "procured transportation and outfit." Before beginning the five-day march, however, he was much disappointed to learn that Colonel Lee was to have charge of the state companies. Lee had also had Cowen's company ordered to Dahlonega, having been assured that Howell's company alone could protect the road.[33]

------

[30]Brown to James Seddon, 13 January 1863, GLB, GDAH; Seddon to Brown, 16 January 1863, ibid.

[31]G. W. Lee to Brown, 14 January 1863, GLB, GDAH; Brown to Galt, Cowen, 15 January 1863, ibid.

[32]Adjutant General's Special Orders, No. 23, 17 January 1863, Special Orders, 1861-1865 (hereafter referred to as SO), GDAH.

[33]Galt to Wayne, 24 January 1863, AGIC, GDAH; Lee to Brown, two telegrams dated 17 January 1863, Cuyler (Brown).

Resentful at losing his position—and losing it to a Confederate—Galt protested to the governor. Brown pointed out that he had not known Lee was personally taking the field either, but quickly added that "law and army regulations settles the question—Colonel Lee ranks and commands you." The governor, however, stressed that he wanted Galt to cooperate with the colonel "cordially in all things pertaining to the common defense." Brown hoped the alliance would be brief, for he trusted that the mere appearance of the armed force would disperse the insurgents.[34]

Galt's arrival had been anticipated, and there was much excitement when he and his men reached Dahlonega on January 23, several days before the Confederate force. Galt found that part of his job had been done for him: the armed band threatening the town had been turned back by the local authorities and loyal citizens; some of the insurgents' ringleaders were already in jail. Yet there was still disaffection and disorder in the area, and Galt's party captured two deserters and two Tories its first day out.[35]

Galt quickly arranged for the governor's proclamation to be printed as a broadside for wide distribution. Although stressing the gravity of the deserters' offense, the proclamation announced that the Confederate government would pardon absentees who returned to their commands within twenty days; rigorous punishment was promised for those who failed to return. Civilian insurgents were informed that they would be jailed if they did not desist and be "dealt with as the Confederate authorities may direct under the laws of force, and the rules and articles of war."[36]

To this Galt appended a small proclamation of his own directed at the deserters, whom he urged to return to duty, promising them passes back to their commands. "Think of your own fair name," he wrote, "think of your children for whom you live and would die, and suffer not a deserters' doom to be yours."[37]

Colonel Lee's supply train, with fifty convalescent Confederate infantrymen, arrived on January 24, with Lee himself arriving a day later. Not surprisingly, Galt liked the Confederate officer: Lee immediately brevetted Galt major and placed him in charge of the state companies as well as the Confederate infantrymen from Atlanta. The colonel, far from regret-

---

[34]Brown to Galt, 21 January 1863, Hargrett Collection. Although Brown did not tell Galt, Lee was taking command of the expedition by direct order of the Secretary of War. Lee to Brown, 17 January 1863, GLB, GDAH.

[35]Galt to Wayne, 24 January 1863, AGIC, GDAH.

[36]*A Proclamation. By Joseph E. Brown, Governor of Georgia. . .* [Ordering deserters to return to their commands.], Broadside, 17 January 1863, Special Collections, University of Georgia Libraries, Athens GA.

[37]Ibid.

ting his decision, later complimented the governor on Galt's "great energy and sagacity."[38]

The Confederate cavalry—four companies of the 16th Battalion, Geor-

Brown's Proclamation to Deserters and Disloyalists, distributed during the Dahlonega Expedition, January-February 1863. (From a broadside. Courtesy of Special Collections, University of Georgia Libraries, Athens, Georgia.)

[38]Galt to Wayne, 1 February 1863, AGIC, GDAH; *Milledgeville Confederate Union* (quoting the *Dahlonega Signal,* n.d.) 10 February 1863 (hereafter referred to as *Signal*); Lee to Brown, 3 February 1863, GBIC, GDAH.

gia Partisan Rangers, Major Samuel J. Winn, commanding—finally arrived through mud and snow on January 28. By this time Galt and his men had for several days been scouting the frigid, wind-swept mountains of Lumpkin and neighboring counties, rounding up more troublemakers. By February 1, when Colonel Lee returned to Atlanta, about six hundred absentees had been sent back to their regiments. Moreover, fifty-three civilians charged with active resistance to the law had been marched in chains to Atlanta. Among them was "the notorious Jeff Anderson," who recently had broken out of jail with some of Andrews' Raiders. Anderson's capture, wrote Galt, had "given more relief to the public mind than all others besides." Additionally, about five hundred conscription-age men had offered themselves for service.[39]

News of Lee's impending departure had raised fears among the state troops that Major Winn of the Partisan Rangers would be placed over them. Considering him to be a low character with problems in "the drinking line," they were relieved when Lieutenant Colonel F. M. Nix, the Rangers' commander, arrived to take charge of his troopers; Galt was left in charge of the state soldiers and those Confederates not sent back to Atlanta. Before leaving on February 1, Lee ordered state contingents to Ellijay, Blairsville, Clarksville, and Gainesville. The "moral effect of this demonstration," Colonel Lee wrote the governor, "is doing a vast good for the government—while our active performance is doing much to assure to the loyal people the protection the government affords them." He hoped that the state troops could remain until early March so that the Tories could be "totally suppressed."[40]

The expedition, then, was quite successful and was applauded in the press for its timeliness and its example of state-Confederate cooperation. The two forces had worked together to eliminate a dangerous situation; their joint labors had been bountifully rewarded.[41]

---

[39]*Atlanta Southern Confederacy,* 3, 4 February 1863; Jones, *Georgia in the War 1861-1865,* 43; Avery, *The History of the State of Georgia,* 257; Galt to Wayne, 1 February 1863, AGIC, GDAH. Dahlonega was hard put to quarter all these troops. The cavalry lodged in the churches, while most of the other soldiers were taken into citizens' homes. *Signal.*

[40]Cowen to Wayne, 24 January 1863, AGIC, GDAH; Galt to Wayne, 1 February 1863, ibid.; Lee to Brown, 27 January, 3 February 1863, GBIC, GDAH. The Partisan Rangers were "irregular bodies" of cavalry of notoriously bad reputation. Seddon himself said of them later that they "did more harm to the people than the enemy." Wilfred Buck Yearns, *The Confederate Congress* (Athens: The University of Georgia Press, 1960) 75.

[41]*Signal; Atlanta Southern Confederacy,* 11 February 1863. The following month Governor Brown protested when Colonel Lee was demoted to provost marshal at Atlanta. Lee later entered state service, eventually becoming a colonel in the Georgia Militia. Brown to President Davis, 21 March 1863, GLB, GDAH; Wayne to Lee, 15 August 1864, AGLB No. 25, GDAH.

Although such military activities were supposedly Richmond's responsibility, the state's contribution had been much greater than that of the Confederacy. While Confederate authorities apparently helped with supplies, the bulk of the five-hundred-man force was provided by the governor. Moreover, the Confederate cavalry arrived five days later than Galt, when the situation was less urgent; and they left soon after their arrival. All in all, Governor Brown seemed to be upheld in his contention that the Confederacy could not be counted upon to protect Georgia—even from deserters from Confederate armies. The Dahlonega civil disturbance appeared to prove that some sort of state force was indeed necessary. And the need was soon to be filled: in February 1863 the Georgia State Line regiments were mustered.[42]

---

[42]*Signal;* Galt to Wayne, 1 February 1863, AGIC, GDAH. Deserters continued to be a problem in North Georgia throughout the war, and Brown made a great effort to return them to their commands. But seeing that more than military measures were needed, the governor made huge expeditures to aid soldiers' families. (Brown believed that many soldiers deserted because of the indigence of their families.) Tatum, *Disloyalty in the Confederacy,* 76-79; Coulter, *The Confederate States of America, 1861-1865,* 468; Beringer, 233.

CHAPTER III

The Creation
of the Georgia State Line

During November and December 1862, while his bridge guards spent their time in relative idleness, Governor Brown busied himself in Milledgeville at the annual session of the General Assembly. High on the commander-in-chief's agenda was a substantial expansion of the state force, which he had postponed in hope of winning the legislature's approval.[1]

On November 6, as the session opened, the governor's annual message was delivered. Under the heading "Bridge Guards and Home Protection," the governor launched his campaign for another state army. He described the shocking raid of the previous April and the consequent creation of the Bridge Guard, along with the expansion carried out at the suggestion of the House Committee. Citing the military and economic importance of the State Road to both Georgia and the Confederacy, Brown stated that to him the only question was "whether the two companies should not be increased to two Regiments, and thoroughly armed, equipped and trained and kept constantly in the service of the State till the end of the war."[2]

Having said this, he sought to justify the expansion for reasons other than the State Road's protection. He raised the specter of "servile insurrection," asserting that an expanded state force might prevent "scenes of massacre and misery too appalling to contemplate." He also mentioned the threat posed by Tories and deserters in north Georgia; if the legislature would permit it, some of the new state soldiers could be cavalrymen, indispensable to scouring the mountains. Furthermore, the regiments could

---

[1]Albert Howell to Brown, 18 October 1862, Cuyler (Brown); Brown to Colonel John W. Dawson, 20 October 1862, ibid.; H. H. Waters to Howell, 22 October 1862, ESLB, vol. 7, GDAH; *CR*, 2:256.

[2]*CR*, 2:256-58.

be "thrown upon the coast, or into such other parts of the State, as the security of the people might require."[3]

Yet, before the resolutions to create the two state regiments could be introduced in the Senate, the conscription controversy threatened to destroy the governor's hope of retaining any state troops. After the passage of the first conscription act in April 1862, Brown had by executive fiat exempted all state militia officers from enrollment, hoping to win the legislature's sanction in the fall. When the second conscription act of 27 September 1862 had embraced white males from thirty-five to forty-five, the governor refused to allow the new law to be enforced in Georgia until the General Assembly could discuss the matter. These acts by the governor, together with a protracted public correspondence between Brown and President Davis on conscription's constitutionality, had polarized both the public and the legislature.[4]

It was obvious that Brown, in the spirit of John C. Calhoun, sought nothing less than the nullification of the conscription acts within Georgia. Brown felt that the acts were unconstitutional because, among other reasons, their effect was to *"disband and destroy"* Georgia's militia organization, leaving "her people utterly powerless to protect their own families, even against their own slaves." Additionally, in the only conscription case brought before a Superior Court in Georgia, the judge had declared conscription unconstitutional. Now, if Brown could enlist the legislature's support, the hated acts could be set aside in Georgia, and Richmond could be compelled to return to requisition for raising troops in the state—a procedure allowed by the terms of the second conscription act.[5]

But on November 11, only five days after Brown delivered an impassioned attack on conscription to the General Assembly, the Georgia Supreme Court pronounced conscription to be constitutional—a decision which caused much anti-conscription sentiment in the legislature to disappear. At the same time the House began work on a bill which would abrogate the commissions of Brown's militia officers and expose them to enrollment for Confederate service. This bill would also thwart Brown's plan for an increased state force since it proposed a State Guard for local defense drawn mainly from white males above and below conscription age.

---

[3]Ibid., 258-59

[4]*CR*, 3:220, 300; Avery, *The History of Georgia.* 234-38, 248; Hill, *Joseph E. Brown*, 87. The Brown-Davis correspondence on conscription is printed in *CR,* 3:192-291, passim.

[5]*CR*, 3:296; *Milledgeville Confederate Union,* 7 October 1862; *CR,* 3:301; *OR,* series 4, vol. 2:160. A return to raising troops through requisitions of the state governors had been suggested by the Confederate House of Representatives in September 1862. John Brawner Robbins, "Confederate Nationalism: Politics and Government in the Confederate South, 1861-1865 " (Ph.D. dissertation, Rice University, 1964) 102.

It was apparent that there was to be neither nullification, nor, most probably, a new state army.[6]

On November 13 it seemed the governor's luck had turned. He submitted to the assembly an urgent message from the coast, describing destructive raids by black Federal soldiers in Camden County. The local militia colonel asked authority to gather his men to meet this threat. Given that the Confederate government claimed most of these militiamen, Brown asked the legislature's leave to call out the troops in question.[7]

The Senate acquiesced immediately and sent its resolution to the House for concurrence. The House was less helpful. Some members suggested that the Camden County incident was a "got up affair," apparently designed to help the governor flout the conscription acts and retain state troops. Although the Senate's resolution was the subject of lively debate, the House adjourned without taking action on it.[8]

On November 20, resolutions to create two state regiments, with the Bridge Guard as their nucleus, were finally introduced in the Senate and sent to the Committee on Military Affairs. After the committee recommended passage of the legislation on November 24, there was a movement to table it. Several members expressed concern that the regiments would create conflict with Confederate authorities, since they were to include conscription-age men. Apparently more persuasive were arguments that the State Road was inadequately protected and that the central government had no right to deny Georgia's power "to call out her Militia." The movement to table was defeated 22 to 10.[9]

The resolutions were discussed again, amended, and transmitted to the House on November 25. Among the changes were a restriction of volunteers to men not subject to Confederate service, and a requirement that the governor specify the regiments' proposed duty stations. Moreover, the

---

[6]*CR*, 2:283-308 (Brown's anti-conscription address of 6 November 1862); *Milledgeville Confederate Union*, 18 November 1862; Linton Stephens to Alexander H. Stephens, 12 November 1862, Alexander H. Stephens Papers, Special Collections, The Library, Manhattanville College, Purchase NY; *Georgia House Journal*, 1862, 72. The Supreme Court action came on the appeal of a pro-conscription decision that had been handed down by Superior Court Judge Iverson L. Harris on 8 November 1862. *Milledgeville Confederate Union*, 11, 18 November 1862. The House's State Guard bill was also variously called the Home Guard bill and the Reserve Militia bill.

[7]*CR*, 2:317-19.

[8]*Georgia Senate Journal*, 1862, 89-90; *Milledgeville Confederate Union*, 2 December 1862; Avery, *The History of the State of Georgia*, 249-51; Derry, *Georgia*, 107. Federal accounts of this coastal raid are found in *OR*, vol. 14:189-92.

[9]*Georgia Senate Journal*, 1862, 123-24; *Milledgeville Confederate Union*, 2 December 1862.

Senate demanded ratification of the governor's appointments of non-elective offices.[10]

In the House the resolutions were also sent to committee, from which they emerged on the morning of December 10 with a "do not pass." Instead, the committee members advised passage of the House's State Guard bill, with its attack on Brown's militia officers. Temporarily tabled, this bill was passed on December 12 and transmitted to the Senate.[11]

The House bill having passed, the Senate resolutions calling for two state regiments were immediately taken under consideration by the House. Brown partisan James S. Hook of Washington County, however, offered substitute resolutions. An unsuccessful move was made to table both sets of resolutions, and opponents also failed twice to amend Hook's substitute. One amendment provided for the regiments' concentration at Milledgeville, while the other demanded that the State Road's superintendent call out his own bridge guards, paying them from the railway's funds.[12]

When the vote was called to accept the substitute in place of the original, the House narrowly approved with a vote of 61 to 53. The vote on the substitute itself was only marginally better—66 to 50. The next day in the House there was a motion to reconsider, based on what would be a later criticism of the force—that it would be an "unnecessary and ruinous expense on the Treasury." The motion to reconsider failed, however, and the Senate gave overwhelming approval to the House substitute, with only three of the twenty-nine senators present voting against it. The House's State Guard bill was not even brought to a Senate vote before final adjournment.[13]

It was December 13; and though the news from Virginia had not yet reached the capital, Governor Brown's small victory had taken place on the same day as the great Confederate triumph at Fredericksberg. But, while satisfying to Brown and his supporters, the legislative win was not total. The idea of a cavalry contingent had been abandoned, as had a plan—not mentioned in the governor's message—to organize the regiments into a brigade. The governor had hoped to place Henry R. Jackson in charge, making him once again a state general. As Brown wrote Jackson, however, this could not be done "without endangering the whole movement."[14]

---

[10]*Georgia Senate Journal,* 1862, 154.

[11]*Georgia House Journal,* 1862, 309, 327, 345, 353.

[12]Ibid., 354-56.

[13]Ibid., 356-58, 370; *Milledgeville Confederate Union,* 23 December 1862; *Georgia Senate Journal,* 1862, 290, 303.

[14]Brown to W. H. Spier, 4 February 1863, Hargrett Collection; Brown to General Henry R. Jackson, 23 December 1862, Hargrett Collection. Georgia's joy in the Fredericksburg victory was tempered by the death in battle of General T. R. R. Cobb of Athens. Company K, Second State Line, called itself the "Tom Cobb Infantry" in memory of him.

Nonetheless, given the hostility in the House toward Brown's stand on conscription and state troops, the resolutions' passage was a minor miracle, probably based upon skillful behind-the-scenes maneuvering by such Brown allies as Linton Stephens and James Hook in the House and Major George A. Gordon in the Senate. And, although Brown's supporters had been unable to persuade the legislature to uphold the governor's exemption of the militia officers, the War Department had informed Brown in December that these exemptions would not be challenged.[15]

In its finished form the State Line legislation authorized the governor "to organize two Regiments of State troops to be employed in the military service of the State for the protection of her people against invading forces of the enemy, and for internal police duty."[16]

The legislation was divided into four resolutions:

The first restricted the companies' strength to one hundred men rank and file. Of the twenty companies, two would be the Bridge Guard companies, mustered in as organized. The governor could post on the State Road that number of companies he thought necessary; the others could be used when, where, and how the governor deemed advisable.[17]

The second resolution was the most significant since it challenged Confederate conscription legislation. The governor was authorized to call for volunteers "from *all the militia* except the part in *actual service* of the Confederacy. . . . " This use of the word "militia," as well as a description of the force as "two Regiments of Militia," conformed to Brown's definition of the militia as the arms-bearing population of a state. According to the state adjutant general, the italicized words in the second resolution showed clearly that the legislature regarded "constructive enrollment" as unconstitutional; that is, the Confederate government could not merely state that white males between eighteen and forty-five were considered enrolled for service. Each man had to be notified individually and subjected to "actual enrollment." Such men as were not actually enrolled could volunteer for state service. The second resolution also charged the adjutant general with organizing the regiments.[18]

According to the third resolution, the regiments would be subject to and governed by the Articles of War, Confederate military laws, and military

---

[15]*Milledgeville Confederate Union,* 6 January 1863.

[16]*CR,* 3:319.

[17]Ibid.

[18]*Resolutions passed by the General Assembly of Georgia, authorizing the Governor to organize two regiments of state troops to be employed in the military service of the state . . . Approved Dec. 13th, 1863* [n. p., 1863], Broadside, Special Collections, University of Georgia Libraries, Athens GA. (Pertinent italicization does not appear in the copy of the resolutions printed in *CR,* 3:319-320.) *CR,* 3:362; Wayne to General Joseph E. Johnston, 20 April 1864, AGLB no. 23, GDAH.

regulations, "so far as consistent with the Constitution of Georgia." This resolution also most clearly differentiated the Line from the Georgia Militia, which was governed by the state militia code and organized under the Federal Act of 8 May 1792. And since the regiments were "regular" state troops, held in accordance with Article I, Section 10, Paragraph 3 of the Confederate constitution, Wayne argued that the State Line was as distinct from the Georgia Militia and the Confederate Provisional Army "as were the Sardinian, English, and French forces in the Crimea."[19]

Under the provisions of the fourth resolution, officers and men of the state regiments were to receive the same pay and allowances as their Confederate counterparts. This stipulation was in keeping with an act of the 1861 General Assembly, and was to keep step with changes in Confederate policy.[20]

On December 17, following passage of the enabling legislation, the adjutant general issued a proclamation giving further details of the regiments' composition and the process by which their constituent companies were to be raised. The ten companies raised nearest the state's northern border would form the first regiment, the ten closest to the southern border the second.

For fifteen of the companies, entry into the regiments was to be on a "first tendered, first accepted" basis. Aspiring officers who were able to recruit ninety to one hundred men faster than their competitors would have their units automatically accepted; company elections could be held as soon as ninety-four men were "actually associated together."[21]

Of the five remaining companies, three were to be given special treatment. The governor hoped that these three could be raised as a pledge of loyalty within the rebellious northern counties of Gilmer, Fannin, Union, Towns, Rabun, Habersham, White, and Lumpkin. As an incentive, the men in these counties were given extra time—until mid-January 1863—to "take up arms in defense of their own state."[22]

As previously noted, the final two companies were to be the Bridge Guard companies. The governor proposed, however, to reduce their strength somewhat through transfer to other companies. In this fashion, the Guard companies' numbers could be brought nearer the standard while bringing

---

[19]*CR*, 3:320; Wayne to Major General H. W. Mercer, 2 April 1863, AGLB no. 15, GDAH.

[20]*CR*, 3:320; *Acts of the General Assembly,* 1861, 64; James Wilson to Henry C. Wayne (and Wayne's endorsement), 8 March 1864, AGIC, GDAH; Wayne to Elam Johnson, 22 April 1864, AGLB no. 23, GDAH.

[21]*CR*, 3:321.

[22]Ibid. Only three of the counties contributed men to the regiments.

RESOLUTIONS

Passed by the General Assembly of Georgia, authorizing the Governor to organize two Regiments of State troops to be employed in the military service of the State for the protection of her people against the invading forces of the enemy, and for internal police duty.

Resolved by the General Assembly, That the Governor be, and he is hereby authorized to call into the service of the State, two Regiments of Militia, to consist of companies not exceeding one hundred men rank and file, including the two companies now in service on the Western and Atlantic Rail Road; such amount of said force to be employed for guarding and protecting the Rail Road bridges of this State as he may deem necessary; and the remainder of said force to be used for such purposes, and at such points in this State, as to His Excellency shall seem advisable.

Resolved further, That His Excellency the Governor, be, and he is hereby authorized, in raising said Regiments, to advertise and call for volunteers from *all the militia* except the part in *actual service* of the Confederacy, and from such able bodied citizens of this State not subject to military duty as will volunteer; stating where each Regiment will be located or expected to perform service: and the same shall be organized by the Adjutant General of this State, pursuant to the laws of force in said State, and such rules and regulations, consistent therewith, as he may prescribe therefor.

Resolved further, That the Regiments so organized, shall be governed by, and subject to, the rules and articles of war of the Confederate States, the military laws of the Confederate States, and the Confederate regulations for the army, so far as consistent with the Constitution of Georgia.

Resolved further, That the pay and allowances of the officers, non-commissioned officers, musicians and privates, shall be the same as in the Confederate Army; and drawn from the military fund provided for the year, 1863, according to the usage now obtaining.

WARRIN AKIN
Speaker of the House of Rep's.
L. CARINGTON,
Cl'k of House of Rep's.
JOHN BILLUPS,
President of the Senate.
JAMES M. MOBLEY,
Sec'y of the Senate.
Approved Dec. 13th, 1862.
JOSEPH E. BROWN,
Governor.

The resolutions creating the Georgia State Line regiments, December 1862. A Broadside. (From a copy in the Rare Book Collection, UNC Library, Chapel Hill, North Carolina.)

smaller companies up to strength. Since the bridge guards were already organized, their officers would remain in place.[23]

Volunteers for the new army were not enlisted for a specific term, but for an indefinite period to be terminated at the governor's discretion—possibly for the duration of the war. This removed one of the objections to raising state troops: the attractively short enlistment.[24]

All volunteers were to be administered the following oath:

> I, _____ , do solemnly swear . . . that I will bear true allegiance to the State of Georgia, and that I will serve her honestly and faithfully against all her enemies and opposers whatsoever and observe and obey the orders of the Governor of the State of Georgia and the orders of the officers appointed above me, according to the rules and articles for the government of the troops of Georgia.[25]

According to the language of the oath, "enemies or opposers whatsoever" could, of course, be interpreted to include Confederate enrolling officers.

Although the resolutions had given the regiments no particular name, they soon became known as the Georgia State Line. The definite origin of the name—which was not used with much consistency—has not been determined. It may have been suggested by General John B. Floyd's Virginia State Line, state troops raised the previous May. In that case, "line" must have had its military meaning—"the combatant force of an army." But the units' often being called "the Georgia State Line Regiments" raises the probability that a reference was also intended to the railway the new state army was to guard: the Western and Atlantic Railroad, sometimes called the "state line."[26]

For several months, office seekers had been anxiously awaiting the creation of the new state force. After the passage of the resolutions, the governor was bombarded with numerous requests for those staff commissions at his disposal—particularly the potentially lucrative quartermaster and commissary posts.[27] Petitions, most of them political in nature, arrived from a wide variety of individuals. One aspirant's letter, scrawled on a ragged fragment from a ledger pad, asked for a quartermaster's position. "I need it as much as any," wrote the applicant. "By the by turn about is fair play. I have hope you three times."[28] A more literate request arrived written in elegant copperplate on heavy paper:

---

[23]Ibid.; Brown to Second Lieutenant William Tate, 27 December 1862, Hargrett Collection.

[24]*CR*, 3:323.

[25]Ibid.

[26]*OR*, vol. 51, pt. 2:620-22; Wayne to Galt, 4 May 1863, AGLB no. 14, GDAH.

[27]Joseph E. Brown correspondence files for December 1862 and January 1863, passim, Cuyler (Brown).

[28]P. C. Sawyer to Brown, 21 December 1862, Cuyler (Brown).

Can I, coming with suitable recommendation from Honorable A. H. Stephens, Col. Ira Washington, and Judge O. A. Lochrane with each of whom you are personally acquainted, secure the position of quartermaster in one of the regiments? I have been induced by these gentlemen to solicit the appointment.[29]

Neither applicant met with success.

The lure of easy duty drew some. A former Confederate artillery officer, who had resigned his commission because of chronic illness, applied for field officer's rank in the State Line. These troops, he wrote, "will not be in my judgement so much exposed" that he would not be able to carry out his duties.[30]

A major difficulty, now that the governor could again dispense military patronage, was that there was so little to distribute. Brown therefore had a look at an obscure act of 1818 under which he decided he had the power to appoint additional quartermaster and commissary assistants.[31]

The disposition of one of these commissions displays the remarkable scope the governor was allowed in tampering with Confederate troops. Brown wanted Sergeant Major F. E. Waters, who was serving with the 55th Georgia at Cumberland Gap, Tennessee, to fill one of the positions. Therefore he simply wrote to General Edmund Kirby Smith, telling him he wished to promote Waters to a state lieutenancy; he requested and received Waters' discharge. In another instance, Brown wrote directly to Secretary of War James Seddon, requesting that another enlisted man be transferred to Georgia's service. The transfer was ordered as soon as the request was received. This recruitment from Confederate ranks was carried out in other instances.[32]

Brown also utilized the Bridge Guard to expand slightly his appointment powers. Since the guards were already organized, Brown had the power to appoint replacements for several line and staff positions that became open in the Bridge Guard. He made such appointments on several occasions.[33]

---

[29]J. R. Hill to Brown, 22 December 1862, Cuyler (Brown).

[30]H. C. Fryer to Wayne, 26 December 1862, Adjutant General Henry C. Wayne Papers, Box no. 17, Ms. 1170, Telamon Cuyler Collection, Special Collections, University Of Georgia Libraries, Athens GA. Hereafter referred to as Cuyler (Wayne).

[31]Brown to Daniel R. Mitchell, 19 December 1862, ibid.

[32]Brown to General Edmund Kirby Smith, 19 December 1862, Hargrett Collection; Brown to Kirby Smith, 29 December 1862, Hargrett Collection; Brown to Joseph G. Watson, 29 December 1862, ibid.; Brown to James Seddon, 14 April 1863, GLB, GDAH; Brown to Seddon, 28 May 1863, ibid.; Seddon to Brown, 28 May 1863, GLB, GDAH.

[33]Brown to Second Lieutenant William Tate, 27 December 1862, Hargrett Collection; Brown to Joseph G. Watson, 29 December 1862, ibid. Brown to Kirby Smith, 19 December 1862, ibid.

It is safe to say that none of Brown's political enemies received any of the State Line appointments. On the other hand, the governor was able to continue the assistance to his family that had begun after his younger brother George's death. Captain John M. Brown was named commissary for the First Regiment; his thirty-one-year-old brother Aaron, a graduate of Jefferson Medical College in Philadelphia was, given a surgeon's post and a major's rank in the same regiment.[34]

For a time it appeared that the rush for staff appointments would not be remotely matched by volunteers for regular enlistment. On 2 January 1863, Brown admitted to Senator Herschel Johnson that all was not well—the companies needed to form the regiments were not being raised as quickly as anticipated. The sole exception occured in Franklin County, where a company of over ninety men had been formed in less than a week.[35]

Yet within three weeks of Brown's letter to Johnson there was a dramatic turnaround: the eighteen necessary companies had been tendered, others turned away. A pleasantly surprised Brown wrote Johnson that he thought he "could have formed five regiments almost as easily as two."[36]

Since Georgia had met all the manpower requisitions of the Confederacy, and since conscription had been in force for the better part of a year, a question arises: what was the source of these men? Actually, the governor had a huge pool of manpower from which to draw. Although the Confederate armies eventually claimed a total of about 120,000 Georgia soldiers, a significant number of potential soldiers were able to avoid Confederate service. General Braxton Bragg's conscription officer, General Gideon Pillow, claimed in mid-1863 that Georgia was "full of able-bodied men, who have slipped through the hands of the Government, and of refugees." At the end of 1863 there were over 13,000 men aged eighteen to forty-five on the militia rolls out of a total of over 41,000 enrolled during the militia's reorganization. Obviously, Brown's assertion that he could easily have raised five regiments was an understatement.[37]

The two regiments the governor did raise were composed of a variety of men, joining for a diversity of reasons. It would be wrong to assume that most were skulkers who had evaded military service until this ostensibly easy duty had offered itself, though some members doubtless fit this de-

---

[34]Adjutant General's General Orders, no. 10, 1 May 1863, General Orders, 1861-65 (General Orders, 1861-65, hereafter referred to as GO), GDAH; *Atlanta Constitution,* 25 August 1891.

[35]Brown to Johnson, 2 January 1863, Hargrett Collection.

[36]Brown to Johnson, 19 January 1863, Hargrett Collection.

[37]Avery, *History of the State of Georgia,* 331; Bass, "Georgia in the Confederacy," 110; *OR,* ser. 4, vol. 2:681; TABLE No. 1—ENROLLMENT OF THE MILITIA UNDER THE ACT TO REORGANIZE THE MILITIA OF THE STATE OF GEORGIA, *Annual Report of the Adjutant and Inspector General . . . 1864* (Milledgeville GA: Boughton, Nisbet, Barne, & Moore, 1864).

scription. It seems that the primary common denominator among the rank and file was occupation; most of these men appear to have been small farmers, with a sprinkling of professional men—particularly among the officers.[38]

A good number of these men had already seen either state or Confederate service. Some, like Albert Howell, had served with Jackson's state troops at Savannah. Many, according to General Wayne, had fought during the war's first year in the Confederate armies in Virginia and Tennessee; several bore "the scars of honorable wounds received in battle in those States."[39]

The most prominent of these Confederate veterans was Thomas H. Northcutt, who raised a company for the Second Regiment. Formerly a private in the famed 18th Georgia Regiment of Hood's Texas Brigade, Northcutt had heroically captured a stand of colors at Second Manassas, for which act the 1862 Georgia legislature directed that he be presented with a medal for valor.[40]

Some volunteers were legally exempted from service by state or Confederate legislation, but wanted to volunteer nonetheless. As one wrote, "I am not subject to the last conscription act (being a physician of ten years standing and also the owner and superintendent of a fine merchant mill) but I do not desire to stay at home."[41]

Two classes of men who joined had enjoyed the protection of Governor Brown. Some militia officers, whose commissions had shielded them, were allowed the opportunity to serve more actively. Men between thirty-five and forty-five, who had benefited from the governor's temporary ban on enforcement of the second conscription act, could join the state service before the enrolling officer came calling.[42]

---

[38]Wayne to Galt, 24 April 1863, AGLB no. 15, GDAH; Wayne to Richard L. Storey, 26 May 1863, ibid. U. S. Bureau of the Census, Schedule 1, Free Inhabitants, Whitfield, Wilkinson, Washington, Upson, Franklin, Morgan, Forsyth, Lumpkin, Newton, and White Counties, 1860, passim.

[39]Wayne to W. T. Day, 6 February 1862, AGLB no. 6, GDAH; Wayne to D. W. Womble, 6 February 1862, ibid. Thomas O. Heard to Wayne, 20 May 1862, Cuyler (Wayne); Henderson, 1:255; Wayne to General Joseph E. Johnston, 20 April 1864, AGLB no. 23, GDAH.

[40]Derry, *Georgia*, 183; *Report of the Adjutant and Inspector General . . . 1862-1863* (Milledgeville GA: Boughton, Nisbet, Barnes, & Moore, State Printers, 1863) 11-12. Hereafter referred to as Adjutant General's 1863 Report. Brown reminded the legislature that the 18th Georgia had been part of Phillips' state army. *CR*, 2:316.

[41]John J. W. Glenn to Brown, 22 December 1862, Cuyler (Brown).

[42]Beverly D. Evans to Wayne, 14 December 1862, AGIC, GDAH; Seaborn J. Saffold to Wayne, 21 December 1862, Cuyler (Wayne); J. C. C. Blackburn to Wayne, 23 June 1862, Cuyler (Wayne).

As noted by General Pillow, Georgia was a haven where numerous out-of-state men could disappear into anonymity as refugees. This group contributed to the State Line, some hailing from states as distant as Louisiana and Arkansas.[43]

Finally, there was apparently a streak of provincial patriotism and anti-Richmond sentiment that ran through most classes of State Line volunteers. For many the desire to serve their state was coupled with hatred of conscription and the government that had fathered it. One man wrote that he was unwilling to sacrifice himself to "monarchy and despotism. . . . It will afford me pleasure to know that I am . . . in the service of my State, where a freeman's will is at least respected."[44]

Georgia's activities in raising two regiments from a reservoir of men Richmond considered Confederate conscripts did not escape the president's notice. Indeed, Brown informed Davis of what he was doing in a cordial letter of 29 December 1862, which enclosed a copy of the resolution passed by the General Assembly.[45] In defense of what he was doing, Brown quoted from a letter written by Davis himself during their correspondence the previous summer:

> Congress may call forth the militia to execute Confederate laws. The State has not surrendered the power to call them forth to execute State laws. Congress may call them forth to repel invasion; so may the State, for it has expressly reserved the right. Congress may call them forth to suppress insurrection; and so may the State, for the power is impliedly reserved of governing all militia except the part in actual service of the Confederacy.[46]

Therefore, Brown continued, the legislature had authorized him to raise the regiments "in conformity to [Davis's] opinions," which Brown identified as the "doctrine of the concurrent jurisdiction of the State and Confederacy over the Militia." But he would not, he promised, allow to be mustered anyone between eighteen and forty-five "actually enrolled into Confederate service." He sincerely desired "harmony and concord between the State and Confederate authorities in all matters pertaining to the common defense." Yet, by the same token, he respectfully requested that Davis give his Georgia enrolling officers orders that would "cause them to act upon [Davis's] construction of the constitution" and prevent them from interfering with "any part of

---

[43]*Compiled Service Records of Confederate Soldiers Who Served in Organizations From the State of Georgia,* Microcopy no. 266, Rolls 151 and 166, National Archives and Records Service, 1959, passim. Hereafter referred to as Compiled Service Records.

[44]A. D. Nunnally to Brown, 7 December 1862, Cuyler (Brown).

[45]*CR,* 3:317-20.

[46]Ibid., 240, 318.

the militia . . . who have been called forth by the State and actually mustered into her service. . . . "[47]

Davis's response to this bold communication, if he made one, has not been found, but his enrolling officers did their best to interfere with the raising of the companies both before and after Brown's letter was sent. In late December Brown received a letter from Macon informing him that Lieutenant Colonel John B. Weems, Enrolling Officer for Georgia, had ordered enrollment of all State Line volunteers. By that time Weems was in receipt of a letter from Adjutant General Wayne outlining the governor's position: only when a company had been "organized, tendered, and accepted" would Brown investigate any of the enrolling officers' claims on the men. If at that time Weems could prove his claims, the men concerned would be surrendered to him. Otherwise, they would have the protection of the state.[48]

Brown admitted that the enrolling officers had impeded the raising of the regiments,[49] and the pro-Brown *Milledgeville Confederate Union* addressed the matter:

It is said the [regiments'] organization has been somewhat delayed by obstructions attempted to be thrown in the way by Confederate enrolling officers . . . who seem not to labor to promote harmony. While the governor desires perfect harmony with the Confederate authorities . . . he will permit no interference by any enrolling officer with any company or individual when mustered into the service of the State; nor will he permit the State officers to interfere with any one in the actual service of the Confederacy.[50]

However, since Brown had the General Assembly as his unlikely ally, he successfully defied the forces of conscripton. Although the legislators had not acquiesced in Brown's attempt to obstruct the conscription laws— or even passed a resolution of protest condemning conscription, the governor felt their authorization of the State Line regiments had vindicated him.[51] Writing to Senator Johnson, Brown stated that the

action of the legislature in authorizing the organization of this force out of

---

[47]Ibid., 318-19. Brown defined the word "militia" broadly, holding that the militia included "all the arms-bearing people" of the state, whether organized or not. Davis, on the other hand, asserted that "militia" was "a collective term meaning a *body* of men organized." The word could not "be applied to the seperate individuals who compose the organization." *CR*, 3:362, 239.

[48]A. C. Clinkscales to Brown, 28 December 1862, GLB, GDAH; Brown to Clinkscales, 29 December 1862 ibid. Wayne to Colonel John B. Weems, 26 December 1862, AGLB No. 12, GDAH.

[49]Brown to Johnson, 2 January 1863, Hargrett Collection.

[50]*Milledgeville Confederate Union,* 6 January 1863.

[51]Avery, *The History of the State of Georgia,* 251; Brown to Johnson, 2 January 1863, Hargrett Collection.

the men subject to conscription is a practical repudiation of the doctrine [of conscription], of probably greater value than any set of resolutions that may be passed in the nature of a protest. This says, while we will not resist the execution of the law, we will hold our men when the State needs them, notwithstanding the Conscription Act.[52]

As Brown wrote another correspondent, the General Assembly was informing the Davis government that "we only acquiesce in the usurpation as far as we choose to acquiesce but not because we are under any obligation to do so."[53]

Brown further contended that the "people of Ga. ever have been and still are ready to volunteer at any call, but they do now and ever will loathe conscription."[54] Such a Georgian was Sandersville's Beverly D. Evans, soon to become a prominent State Line officer. His experience in organizing a company illustrates the process which went on during the winter of 1862-1863, prior to the regimental organization.

Evans was born in 1826, the son of a wealthy South Carolina merchant. When his father's fortune was wiped out in the Panic of 1841, he was forced to forego the college education he desired, instead educating himself, then teaching school, reading law, and eventually being admitted to the bar in 1847.[55] Five years later, when he moved to Sandersville, he was quickly admitted to the Georgia bar and began a successful law practice. Soon he married a local girl, but she tragically died of typhoid during the couple's honeymoon in Charleston.[56]

Before the war Evans was involved in Democratic politics, serving as a delegate to Georgia's Democratic Convention of 1860. When he ran as an immediate secessionist candidate for the Secession Convention of 1860, however, he was defeated by a cooperationist.[57]

On 18 March 1861, the thirty-five-year-old lawyer joined a local company, the Washington Rifles, for a twelve-month enlistment; the company elected him to a lieutenancy. When his unit became part of the 1st Georgia Regiment (Ramsay's), Evans, accompanied by a black manservant, set out

---

[52]Brown to Johnson, 2 January 1863, Hargrett Collection.

[53]Brown to Dr. O. R. Broyles, 2 January 1863, Hargrett Collection.

[54]Brown to Johnson, 19 January 1863, Hargrett Collection.

[55]"Memorial of the life and services of Colonel Beverly D. Evans," Book of Minutes H, Washington County, Georgia, Superior Court Office; hereafter referred to as Evans Memorial.

[56]Ibid.; Ella Mitchell, *History of Washington County* (Atlanta: Byrd Printing Co., 1924) 124; Louise Evans, interview held in Washington County, Georgia, 6 May 1979. Miss Evans is the granddaughter of Colonel Evans.

[57]Avery, *The History of the State of Georgia,* 120; Michael P. Johnson, "A New Look at the Popular Vote for Delegates to the Georgia Secession Convention," *Georgia Historical Quarterly* 56 (Summer 1972): 262.

for service in Pensacola, Florida. Later transferred to Virginia, his regiment participated in General Robert E. Lee's undistinguished Cheat Mountain campaign of 1861.[58]

During a furlough in October of that year, he married his deceased wife's sister, an influential member of Sandersville's Ladies Volunteer Aid Association. Upon his return to Virginia, Evans, in failing health, still grieving for his recently deceased mother, and wishing to be with his new bride, toyed with the idea of resigning his commission and returning home. But he was greatly troubled by the prospect of being able to walk away while the soldiers who had elected him had to stay in the army.[59] Consequently, Evans re-

Lt. Col. Beverly D. Evans, Second Regiment, Georgia State Line. (From a painting based upon an 1861 photograph. Courtesy of Beverly D. Evans III.)

[58]Henderson, 1:255; Evans to Sallie Smith, 12 May 1861, Evans Collection; Evans to Sallie Smith, 12 September 1861, ibid.

[59]Kenneth Coleman, ed., "Ladies Volunteer Aid Association of Sandersville, Washington County, Georgia, 1861-1862," *Georgia Historical Quarterly* 52 (March 1968): 18, n. 3; Evans to Sallie Evans, 5 December 1861, Evans Collection.

mained in Virginia until he was mustered out at the end of his enlistment on 18 March 1862. Since he was over thirty-five, he was not subject to the conscription act passed the next month.[60]

After resuming his law practice in Sandersville, Evans also acted as agent for a salt manufacturing association in the county. In September 1862, the month before the second conscription act embraced his age group, Evans was elected colonel of the 13th Regiment, Georgia Militia. Determining to raise a company for Confederate service nonetheless, he had gathered thirty men when word of the governor's call for two state regiments reached him. He decided to offer his men for state service and recruited up to the necessary strength, drawing not only from Washington County, but from Warren and Emanuel Counties as well—despite what he termed the "relentless hands of the conscription officers." The company, styled the "Joe Brown Volunteers," was accepted in January 1863. Upon acceptance of the state captaincy to which his men elected him, Evans resigned the militia colonelcy which had until that time protected him from conscription.[61]

As the time approached for regimental organization, Captain Evans had the following notice printed in the *Sandersville Central Georgian* for 11 February 1863:

> Attention Joe Brown Volunteers! You are hereby ordered to parade at Sandersville MONDAY 16th instant at 12 o'clock M. for inspection and pay and to be formally enrolled in the State Service, pursuant to orders from the Adjutant and Inspector General. Every member of the company will be expected to be present and no excuse considered valid that accounts for his absence. Each member will bring with him a Blanket, Quilt, or Counterpane, as the State cannot furnish these articles or a proper substitute for them, and also at least two days' rations to subsist on, preparatory to take the cars for Fort Valley, Houston County, Georgia, the place of rendezvous designated.[62]

The rendezvous for regimental elections was to be on the sixteenth, but not at the place designated. Quartermaster General Foster had not carefully investigated Fort Valley's suitability as a rendezvous point; he discovered only five days before the troops were to assemble there that the village was entirely unsatisfactory: "Timber scarce, no running water in four miles, few wells deep and poorly supplied with water."[63] Foster suggested that one of two stations on the Central of Georgia railroad—Gordon

---

[60]Henderson, 1:255.

[61]*Sandersville Central Georgian,* 16 July 1862; Henderson, 1:255; Evans to Wayne, 14 December 1862, AGIC, GDAH; Wayne to Evans, 21 January 1863, AGLB No. 13, GDAH.

[62]*Sandersville Central Georgian,* 11 February 1863.

[63]Ira Foster to Brown, 11 February 1863, Cuyler (Brown).

or Griswoldville—would serve. The governor chose Griswoldville and telegrams were hastily dispatched to the company commanders involved, notifying them of the change.[64]

So at Griswoldville the Second Regiment met, while the First Regiment assembled above Atlanta at Big Shanty, location of Camp McDonald. The Second Regiment's encampment, called Camp Wayne after the adjutant general, was located west of Sam Griswold's industrial village.[65]

Fifteen counties had contributed troops to the Second Regiment, but Georgia's southern and coastal counties had not responded enthusiastically to Brown's call. No seaboard counties sent companies, and only four companies drew men exclusively from counties south of Milledgeville, the southernmost being Terrell County in southwest Georgia; one company came from as far north as Forsyth county above Atlanta. The other counties were scattered across middle Georgia.[66]

The elections were held on Friday, February 20, and the election commission forwarded the results to Brown the same day:

Colonel:	Richard Storey	474 votes
	James Wilson	379 votes
Lt. Col.:	Beverly D. Evans	461 votes
	Seaborn Saffold	380 votes
Major:	D. W. Womble	425 votes
	T. J. Neal	424 votes[67]

The man elected regimental commander, Richard Lawson Storey, had not seen Confederate service, as had Evans; neither had Major D. W. Womble. Both had, however, been in General Jackson's state army at Savannah. Forty years of age, Storey was a Wilkinson County farmer, and a

---

[64]Brown to Foster, 11 February 1863, GLB, GDAH; Wayne to all company commanders, Second Regiment, Georgia State Line, 11 February 1863, AGLB No. 13, GDAH.

[65]*Milledgeville Confederate Union,* 24 February 1863; *Atlanta Southern Confederacy,* 26 February 1863; A. J. Jackson Diary, A. J. Jackson Diary and Letters, Box 76-7, Microfilm Library, GDAH. Hereafter referred to as Jackson Papers.

[66]Muster Rolls of the Georgia State Line Regiments, passim, Map Cabinet Drawers 1 & 2, 8th Vault Floor, GDAH. Hereafter referred to as Muster Rolls.

[67]N. W. Maddox and Jesse W. Wallace, Election Superintendents, to Brown, 20 February 1863, Georgia Militia/Georgia State Line Miscellaneous File, Box 3337-10, GDAH. Hereafter referred to as State Line Miscellany.

trustee of Irwinton's Talmadge Normal Institute. Womble, thirty-six, was a popular Upson County farmer.[68]

Unlike the companies of the Second Regiment, the First Regiment's companies were drawn from counties restricted to a smaller geographic

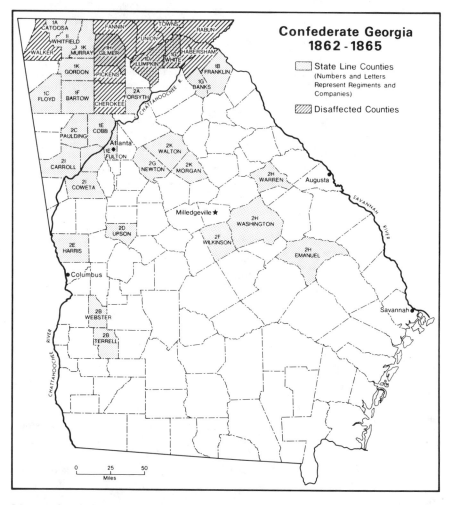

Map 1. Confederate Georgia, 1862-1865, showing home counties of the State Line companies and disaffected counties. (After Johnson's Map of Georgia and Alabama, 1862. Courtesy of Special Collections, University of Georgia Libraries, Athens, Georgia.)

---

[68]Storey to Brown, 25 March 1862, GBIC, GDAH; D. W. Womble to Wayne, 10 April 1862, AGIC, GDAH; U. S. Bureau of the Census, Schedule 1, Free Inhabit-

area. Each county through which the State Road passed sent a company; all but two of the counties sending companies were in north Georgia along or above the Chattahoochee River. In all, thirteen north Georgia counties contributed men to the First Regiment.[69]

At first there seemed to be some question as to whether Galt's, Cowen's, and Graham's companies would be able to return from Dahlonega in time for the rendezvous.[70] Arriving in time for the election was important to the men—they obviously would want to vote—and to Galt, who was favored to win the colonelcy. As the governor wrote an interested observer: "My opinion is that Capt. Galt, on account of his connection with the Bridge Guards and his general acquaintance with the people where most of the counties are located will be rather a formidable opponent."[71]

In the same letter, Brown disclaimed any intentions of interfering with the field officers' elections "as there will be much jealousy about it."[72] This might have been true at the time, but it marked a change from his attitude a month earlier. Then he had written confidentially to his friend Herbert Fielder, recently disappointed in an attempt to procure a judgeship. As consolation, Brown offered Fielder his choice between two positions. One was aide-de-camp to the governor; Brown wrote of the other: "I am of the opinion that it could be so arranged as to put you in command of one of the new State regiments. . . . come and see me immediately, as I must soon make the arrangements with someone."[73]

A further complication to the First Regiment's elections came in the form of threats to burn some of the State Road's bridges. With all bridge guards at Big Shanty and only a "few track hands" on sentry duty, the bridges would be extremely vulnerable. Brown decided that the guards would not assemble early with the others; they would wait until the last minute to come and vote, then return immediately to duty.[74]

The regimental election at Big Shanty was a drawn-out affair, lasting from Friday night, February 20, until nine o'clock the next morning. Galt,

---

ants, Wilkinson and Upson Counties, 1860; Victor Davidson, *History of Wilkinson County*(Macon GA: J. W. Burke Co., 1930) 178; Carolyn Walker Nottingham and Evelyn Hannah, *History of Upson County, Georgia* (Macon GA: J. W. Burke Co., 1930) 640.

[69]Galt to Wayne, 22 February 1863, AGIC, GDAH; Muster Rolls, passim.

[70]W. K. De Graffenried to Galt, 3 February 1863, AGLB No. 13, GDAH.

[71]Brown to John Billups, 5 February 1863, Hargrett Collection.

[72]Ibid.

[73]Brown to Colonel H. Fielder, 23 December 1862, Hargrett Collection.

[74]E. B. Walker to Brown (and Brown's endorsement), 13 February 1863, Cuyler (Brown).

who was voted colonel, wrote "we had a warm time of it electioneering."[75]
James Bryan of Gilmer County won the lieutenant colonelcy, while Captain John M. Brown was elevated to brother Aaron's rank by being elected major.[76]

By February 21, therefore, the Georgia State Line regiments were organized. The companies constituting them were as follows:

First Regiment, Georgia State Line

Company	A	Catoosa County
Company	B	Franklin County ("Joe Brown Defenders")
Company	C	Floyd County ("Fort Infantry")
Company	D	Lumpkin County ("Blue Ridge Rangers")
Company	E	Cobb and Fulton Counties ("State Rights Guards")
Company	F	Bartow County ("Georgia Blues")
Company	G	Banks and White Counties ("Chattahoochee Rangers")
Company	H	Gilmer County ("Gilmer Browns")
Company	I	Whitfield County ("Galt Volunteers")
Company	K	Murray and Gordon Counties ("Railroad Bridge Guards")

Second Regiment, Georgia State Line

Company	A	Forsyth County ("State Guards")
Company	B	Terrell and Webster Counties ("State Rights Volunteers")
Company	C	Paulding County ("Paulding Guards")
Company	D	Upson County ("State Volunteers")
Company	E	Harris County ("Chattahoochee Guards")
Company	F	Wilkinson County ("Georgia Rangers")
Company	G	Newton County ("Newton Guards")
Company	H	Washington, Warren, and Emanuel Counties ("Joe Brown Volunteers")
Company	I	Carroll and Coweta Counties ("Cunningham Guards")
Company	K	Morgan and Walton Counties ("Tom Cobb Infantry")[77]

---

[75]Galt to Wayne, 22 February 1863, AGIC, GDAH.

[76]*Atlanta Southern Confederacy,* 26 February 1863.

[77]*Milledgeville Confederate Union,* 10 March 1863; Muster Rolls, passim. The counties which contributed the majority of the regiments' men had sent co-operationist delegates to the Secession Convention (eighteen of the twenty-eight coun-

Following the elections, these companies ideally would have entered a lengthy period of instruction and drill, but a frantic summons from the coast led to their being sent to Savannah. Events were coming full circle. The city where Brown had lost his second army needed his third one, as yet untrained.

---

ties), while seventeen of the twenty-eight State Line counties had slave populations ranging from zero to twenty-nine percent of the total population. Also, the majority of counties represented in the regiments were in Georgia's least populous congressional districts—the 8th, 9th, and 10th—where the white population averaged eighty percent. Men with such county backgrounds would seem to be more likely to join purely defensive state military organizations than national armies waging war on remote battlefields. Statistics from Michael P. Johnson, *Toward a Patriarchal Republic: The Secession of Georgia* (Baton Rouge: Louisiana State University Press, 1977) 3, 61; Robbins, 252-53.

CHAPTER IV

At Savannah and Charleston

On 16 January 1863, as Governor Brown dispatched Galt's force to Dahlonega, an urgent telegram arrived in Milledgeville. General Hugh W. Mercer, Savannah's Confederate commander, warned Brown of an anticipated enemy thrust against Georgia's major port; the garrison badly needed additional troops—could the governor send at least three of the new State Line companies to Savannah's aid?[1]

His first request meeting with no success, Mercer telegraphed again two weeks later, adding a request for militia. He admitted that he had to request troops from Brown because the Confederate authorities had refused to strengthen his small force, despite the apparent imminence of a heavy Federal attack. "I have now *given up all hope* of the early return . . . of the troops lately sent to North Carolina and my infantry force is exceedingly small . . . ," wrote Mercer. "Even a thousand men would be of great service."[2]

Here again was vindication for Brown—from a general officer of the Confederacy. The situation at Savannah illustrated what was to Brown the major flaw in the Davis administration's hostile attitude toward state-held troops: Georgians in the Confederate service had to serve in Tennessee and North Carolina and Virginia while their threatened state was refused both reinforcements and the right to local defense forces. Because of strategic decisions made at Richmond, decisions whose wisdom Brown and other leaders doubted, portions of Georgia might be lost, and it would probably be Brown—not Davis—who would be held accountable at the polls and elsewhere.[3]

---

[1]General Hugh W. Mercer to Brown, 16 January 1863, GLB, GDAH. On 7 January Brown had been advised by General Beauregard of a probable attack on Charleston. *OR,* vol. 53:274.

[2]Mercer to Brown, 3 February 1863, Hargrett Collection.

[3]For example, as one authority points out, "There seems to be little doubt that Brown's efforts to increase the security of the state were important in his [1861] reëlection." Hill, *Joseph E. Brown,* 165.

Finally responding to Mercer on 6 February, Adjutant General Wayne disclosed that Georgia was ill-prepared to contribute to Savannah's defense; Richmond had stripped the state of "men and munitions of War." In fact, many arms Brown had purchased abroad had been seized by Confederate authorities. The State Line regiments, Wayne continued, would be sent, but they were not to rendezvous for elections until 16 February, and they were to be "but indifferently armed" with "the refuse guns left in the State" and "a few miserable muskets" Richmond had reluctantly sent to replace rifles confiscated.[4]

On 7 February, the governor informed Secretary of War James Seddon that Savannah was threatened and would surely fall if not reinforced. Advising Seddon that he was sending the State Line, he requested that Richmond match his contribution by sending him two Georgia regiments then stationed in Tennessee.[5]

Writing on the 18th to General P. G. T. Beauregard, commander of the military district including Georgia, Brown made more successful demands. He wanted additional guns to replace those seized, plus subsistence for the State Line while it was on loan to the Confederacy.[6]

Beauregard responded immediately, agreeing to Brown's terms. "I have ordered all State troops sent here to be subsisted. The arms you refer to will soon be here. I hope to give the Abolitionists a warm reception." Brown's negotiations had been quite fruitful. The Confederacy would not only feed his troops, but provide them with ammunition and nine hundred stands of arms.[7]

Ironically, the crisis which generated this correspondence seemed to be over by the time all the telegrams had been exchanged. Mercer decided that Charleston, not Savannah, would be the Federals' target. Nonetheless, the State Line, minus three First Regiment companies left to guard the bridges, was on its way.[8]

---

[4]Wayne to Mercer, 5 February 1863, AGLB No. 12, GDAH; *CR*, 2:253-54.

[5]*CR*, 3:325-26. Seddon's response, received 18 February, was that "exigencies of service" prevented the Georgia regiments from being sent to Savannah. He promised to send other reinforcements if possible. Seddon to Brown, 18 February 1863, GLB, GDAH.

[6]Brown to General Beauregard, 18 February 1863, GLB, GDAH.

[7]Beauregard to Brown, 18 February 1863, GLB, GDAH. Brown also sent his militia officers to help protect Savannah. The militia generals became field-grade officers, and company grade officers were temporarily reduced to ranks. By 7 March Mercer had ordered this peculiar army back home. Avery, *The History of the State of Georgia*, 256-57; Mercer to Wayne, 7 March 1863, Cuyler (Wayne).

[8]Mercer to daughter, 18 February 1863, Hugh Washington Mercer Letters, Special Collections Department, Robert W. Woodruff Library, Emory University, Atlanta GA; *Charleston Mercury*, 15 April 1863; Josiah Gorgas to Brown, 17 February 1863, Cuyler (Brown); Wayne to Mercer, 25 February 1863, AGLB No. 13, GDAH.

The regiments' passage through the state prompted complimentary notices in some newspapers. The *Atlanta Commonwealth* judged the First Regiment as "composed of as good and true men as ever shouldered a musket." The Second Regiment, according to the *Milledgeville Confederate Union,* was "as fine a body of men as we ever saw gathered together." By 24 February both regiments were encamped near Savannah.[9]

The welfare, training, and treatment of the men of the State Line was the concern and responsibility of Adjutant General Henry C. Wayne. Any hope the State Line had of becoming an efficient and valuable military force rested in great part with him.

Born in Savannah in 1815, Wayne had graduated from West Point in 1838 with an artillery commission, and served along the Canadian frontier during the Border Disturbances of 1838-1841. One historian who examined his involvement in that episode pronounced him "a splendid soldier and gentleman . . . a model of efficiency at whatever task he essayed." Afterward, Wayne was for five years an instructor at his alma mater, with artillery, infantry, and sword tactics among his subjects. Although a staff officer during the Mexican War, he participated in several battles and was brevetted major for gallantry. Soon after the war, the government published—on General Winfield Scott's recommendation—Wayne's *The Sword Exercise Arranged for Military Instruction* (1850).[10]

In the years between the wars, Wayne spent most of his time with the Quartermaster Department in Washington, D. C. The nation's capital had been his family's home since 1835 when his father, James Moore Wayne, had been appointed an associate justice of the Supreme Court.[11]

Between 1855 and 1858, however, Wayne visited more exotic duty stations as a major figure in the formation of the U. S. Camel Corps. Traveling to Turkey and Egypt at the behest of Secretary of War Jefferson Davis, Wayne gathered camels and brought them to the southwest for experimentation. He disagreed with Davis on the use of the camels. Davis thought of them principally as "gunships of the desert," perfect for fighting Indians. Wayne recommended civilian and commercial as well as military uses for the animals, not only in the west, but on Southern plantations as well.

---

[9]*Atlanta Commonwealth,* 23 February 1863, quoted in the *Rome Tri-Weekly Courier,* 26 February 1863; *Milledgeville Confederate Union,* 24 February 1863; Galt to Wayne, 24 February 1863, AGIC, GDAH.

[10]George W. Cullum, *Biographical Register of the Officers and Graduates of the U. S. Military Academy,* 3 vols. (New York: Houghton, Mifflin, & Co., 1891), 1: 702; Irvin McDowell, "Henry Constantine Wayne," *U. S. Military Academy, the Annual Association of Graduates,* n.d., n.p., 96; Alexander A. Lawrence, *James Moore Wayne, Southern Unionist* (Chapel Hill: University of North Carolina Press, 1943) 227; Henry C. Wayne, *The Sword Exercise, Arranged for Military Instruction* (Washington DC: Gideon & Co., 1850) 4.

[11]Cullum, 1:702; Lawrence, *Wayne,* 83.

Although unable to see the experiment through to its conclusion, Wayne received for his work a gold medal from a French zoological society.[12]

With the election of Abraham Lincoln in 1860 and Georgia's imminent secession from the Union, Wayne faced a dilemma. Should he keep his "comfortable position in the army of the United States" or return to serve his native state? He chose the latter, but it meant separation from his Northern-born wife and his children, as well as from his parents. Justice and Mrs. Wayne remained in Washington throughout the war, where the elder Wayne took "a decisive part . . . in upholding some of the chief measures of Lincoln's administration."[13]

Praised by Governor Brown as "the first man who responded to the call of his State," Henry Wayne was unanimously confirmed by the Senate as Georgia's Adjutant and Inspector General on 13 December 1860. He was

Maj. Gen. Henry C. Wayne, Adjutant and Inspector General of Georgia, 1860-1865. (From a tintype, c. 1860. Courtesy of the Georgia Historical Society.)

[12]Odie B. Faulk, *The U. S. Camel Corps, An Army Experiment* (New York: Oxford University Press, 1976) 185-86; Lawrence, *Wayne,* 136-37.

[13]Lawrence, *Wayne,* 168-69, vii.

to hold this post throughout the war, despite the fact that he held only a colonel's rank at first and was twice offered a brigadier's star by the Confederacy. His motives for staying with Georgia were patriotic in part, but a contributing factor was certainly his rancor toward Richmond's military and political leaders, particularly Jefferson Davis. "The people of the Southern States," Wayne wrote Brown,"elected for their active Commander-in-Chief an inferior, commonplace West Pointer, and they are now suffering for it."[14]

Undoubtedly an extraordinary man in many ways, Wayne was not without a large measure of self-esteem. But he had the self-discipline to serve faithfully a difficult taskmaster like Joe Brown, with whom he had little in common. Realizing and tolerating Brown's military naiveté, he discreetly tried to prevent the governor from foolish meddling in Georgia's military relations with the Confederacy. As religious as Brown, Wayne was a "High Church" Episcopalian who would later convert to Catholicism. Nonetheless, he and his Baptist commander-in-chief coexisted cordially, both personally and politically.[15]

Converting the raw regiments into an efficient force was a daunting task for the adjutant general, but he met the challenge with characteristic common sense, realizing that with the citizen-soldiers of the regiment—particularly the officers—acting the martinet would be counterproductive. He was, therefore, patient but firm with those who soon bombarded him with correspondence. Ever ready with advice and never loath to offer explanations—but insistent that the men of the Line strive for military effectiveness—Wayne gave his charges the opportunity to become real soldiers.

Shortly after the State Line's arrival in Savannah, Wayne was presented with a major problem: a petition addressed to the governor by the field officers of the Second Regiment. Both regiments had been placed in Confederate brigades at Savannah. Resenting this, the officers of the Second requested their unit be reunited with its sister regiment and placed

---

[14]*CR*, 2:275; *Georgia Senate Journal*, 1860, 338; Lawrence, *Wayne*, 194-96; Wayne to Colonel William R. Boggs, 9 January 1862, AGLB No. 5, GDAH; *Milledgeville Southern Federal Union*, 14 January 1862; Wayne to Brown, 13 June 1862, a note written on the reverse of A. P. Burr to Brown, 9 June 1862, GBIC, GDAH. Wayne served at colonel's rank until promoted to major general (a state commission) on 14 December 1863. He was bitter over what he seems to have considered Richmond's lack of appreciation for his military worth. *Acts and Resolutions of the General Assembly of the State of Georgia*, 1863, 58; Lawrence, *Wayne*, 194-95.

[15]Lawrence, *Wayne*, 194; Robert Manson Myers, ed., *The Children of Pride* (New Haven: Yale University Press, 1972) 1718; Avery, *The History of the State of Georgia*, 260. Wayne advised Brown during his "conscription correspondence" with Davis in the summer of 1862, and championed Brown's stand in the press, writing under the pseudonym "Georgia." Wayne to Brown, 17 July 1862, AGLB No. 9, GDAH; Adjutant General's Book of Commissions, B-49, 688-95, GDAH; *Macon Daily Telegraph*, 16 May 1862.

under a "State commander subject to Confederate authority *only* during an engagement."[16]

Referring to dissension and jealousy between the state and Confederate troops, they stated that it was their desire "to convince the whole State that Georgia volunteers are as capable of defending Georgia soil as any command now in Confederate service."

> We know the opposition you have had in defending State rights and the contempt with which "Joe Brown's army" has been treated by those who oppose the present organizations, and we beg leave to assure you that so long as we have minds to think, arms to strike, or hearts to feel that you will find us . . . hearty coadjutors in your defense of the principles which induced our separation from our enemies.[17]

This resentment of the Confederates was understandable. Clearly Confederates would be inclined to taunt the state troops as cowards and shirkers. Former members of the Bridge Guard, as well as those who had seen other state military service, had already experienced slights at the hands of Confederate troops. Galt probably spoke for many in the Line when he wrote before his departure for Savannah: "I think there exists with most of the Confederate officers but little love for State Troops."[18] Galt, of course, had personally had a good experience with Confederate Colonel Lee: "If all were like [him] I could get on with them well. He acted the perfect gentleman and showed some common sense."[19]

The state troops, for their part, seem to have been ultrasensitive (not to mention chagrined at finding themselves forced suddenly into Confederate units); they also seem to have subscribed to the view occasionally suggested by the governor that Confederate soldiers were troops of a foreign power. This created a regrettable adversary relationship between state and Confederate forces.

Despite the governor's views on this matter, which probably coincided with those of the petitioners to some degree, there was no attempt by either Brown or General Wayne to foster or promote anti-Confederate attitudes among the state troops. Wayne's endorsement on the petition shows that he considered the best action to be no action: "No answer necessary. No rights have been invaded nor wrongs done and General Mercer is the best judge of the proper disposition of the troops."[20]

Wayne had, however, corresponded with General Mercer, advising tactful handling of the green troops. "The regiments are new from head to

---

[16]Storey et al. to Brown, 25 February 1863, State Line Miscellany.

[17]Ibid.

[18]Galt to Wayne, 22 February 1863, AGIC, GDAH.

[19]Ibid.

[20]Wayne's endorsement on R. L. Storey et al. to Brown, 25 February 1863, State Line Miscellany, GDAH.

foot," he wrote, "but are zealous to do their duty. I must ask from you . . . as much consideration for their mistakes and shortcomings as can reasonably be allowed." Having written this, Wayne hoped for events to take their course in a reasonable fashion,[21]

Writing to Wayne on the same subject as the petitioners, Galt revealed that such jealousies had been rife among his own command, but that he had worked to alleviate matters. Wayne applauded his actions, noting that "soldiers have much idle time and the devil is always ready to take advantage of idleness to sow discord and confusion. The governor is much pleased with your discreet conduct."[22]

Yet Wayne apparently received more complaints, and he put enough credence in them to write to General Mercer also on the subject of the devil and his works:

> As that ArchEnemy, the Devil, has always at hand busy bodies and meddlers ready to do his promptings in creating dissatisfaction and confusion . . . permit me to invite your attention respectfully . . . to the necessity of urging upon you and your subordinates . . . great tenderness in dealing with the Officers and men in the two State Regiments under your command. Coming from the mountains and unaccustomed to Coast Life, manners, and climate, and to the privations of a soldier's life, belonging to movements or organizations different from that of the masses around them, discontent and jealousy are easily excited on slight grounds, and unless disarmed may ripen into serious differences. No reasonable grounds have yet been presented to me for finding fault with Confederate authorities but murmurs have come to me which induce me to call attention to the matter.[23]

It was in the governor's interest, as well as that of the State Line, that "serious differences" be avoided. As General Wayne commented to Galt, "With officers and men suddenly thrown into active service, you will learn much more quickly & be better off, by being thrown together with a regiment that has seen service."[24] Thus the Confederacy would be providing not only subsistence but also training, which the Line had missed by being sent directly to Savannah after the elections.

After their original vexation at being placed under Confederate officers had passed, the men of the Second Regiment settled down to soldiering. Major J. C. C. Blackburn, the regiment's surgeon (and a signatory to the petition), wrote to the *Milledgeville Confederate Union* that from

> the imposing appearance of the regiment . . . at Battalion Drill and Dress Parade, I think that we will give a good account of ourselves whenever our enemy "lets slip the dogs of war." . . . Our regiment is fast improving in drill,

---

[21]Wayne to Mercer, 25 February 1863, AGLB No. 14, GDAH.

[22]Wayne to Galt, 16 March 1863, AGLB No. 14, GDAH.

[23]Wayne to Mercer, 20 March 1863, AGLB No. 14, GDAH.

[24]Wayne to Galt, 27 February 1863, AGLB No. 14, GDAH.

and from the energy of the field and company officers, I predict that it will soon be able to do honor to our noble old commonwealth.[25]

The First Regiment was also in fairly good shape for a new unit. Galt's men were inspected by a Confederate officer four days after their arrival and were given a generally favorable assessment. Major H. Bryan wrote:

I visited informally the 1st Georgia State Troops and found them quite raw, but able bodied and willing and progressing favorably in drill. One company has been organized eight months as bridge guards and is better—The Regiment . . . is well armed but short of ammunition; they were deficient in haversacks, canteens, knapsacks, and blankets. The Colonel and Lt. Colonel were inexperienced but intelligent and attentive.[26]

Obviously the state quartermaster general had not supplied the troops well. While the required tentage had been delivered, there were deficiencies in forage, clothing, and stationery. The matter of clothing was not, however, the quartermaster general's responsibility; the governor instead offered a monetary commutation as he had for the bridge guards. As Brown pointed out, the funds could be sent home, where thrifty relatives could cheaply make the necessary clothes and keep the extra money for the family's use. In any event, State Line mustering officers, who inspected the men on their pay days, frequently described the troops' clothing as "country jeans," "country made and worn," or "country made, not supplied." Only the officers, it appears, normally had uniforms.[27]

As to stationery, more than pens, ink, and paper were needed. The numerous records that had to be kept required a large number of blank forms: muster rolls, monthly reports, discharges, and surgeon's certificates. Colonel Storey had much difficulty getting his original stationery requisition filled. In a testy letter of 21 April, Storey told Wayne that he had never gotten any forms—"to all appearances General Foster has forgotten that there was ever a design to have a 'State Line' or at least a Second Regiment."[28]

---

[25]*Milledgeville Confederate Union,* 10 March 1863. Blackburn, a physician and politician from Stewart County, was editor of the pro-Brown *Lumpkin Palladium.* Avery, *The History of the State of Georgia,* 79, 86, 89-90.

[26]Report on Inspection of Brigade No. 2, commanded by Colonel G. P. Harrison, Jr., 28 February 1863, Record Group 109, Departmental Records, Department of South Carolina, Georgia, and Florida, Box 47, Document No. 86, National Archives, Washington, D.C.

[27]Wayne to Storey, 27 February 1863, AGLB No. 14, GDAH; Wayne to Galt, 16 March 1863, ibid. Later in the war, when the commutation money was apparently going to feed families instead of to purchase cloth, the governor had clothing and shoes distributed to those who needed them. Officers of the Second Regiment to Wayne, 19 January 1864, Adjutant General—Courts-Martial, Box 1, 3336-17, GDAH. Hereafter referred to as Courts-Martial.

[28]Storey to Wayne, 24 February 1863, AGIC, GDAH; Storey to Wayne, 21 April 1863, ibid.

Supplied more speedily were numerous copies of William Gilham's *Manual of Instruction for the Volunteers and Militia of the Confederate States,* which were sent with orders for wide distribution. Study and instruction of these manuals were mandatory, wrote General Wayne, to instruct the men "in their duties and reflect credit upon [the] State as well as upon the Regiment and themselves."[29]

In Savannah, the quartermaster's department paid the officers and men of the Line for the first time. By the governor's order they were to be paid six times a year (at the end of January, March, May, July, September, and November), with arrears in pay never exceeding two months "unless unavoidable." Officers' pay ranged from $80 (second lieutenant) to $195 (colonel) per month. Non-commissioned officers made from $13 (corporal) to $21 (sergeant major), while privates were paid $11 per month.[30]

The state ordnance department was unable to supply some needs: the State Line's field and staff officers had no swords or side arms for a time. The state had little more than flintlock pistols to offer at first, along with cavalry and artillery sabers for officers' swords.[31]

A source of persistent trouble in Savannah was the medical department. Illness among the men was inevitable. Unaccustomed to camp life or the coastal climate, they were also camped unhealthily near swampy areas.

Surgeon Blackburn felt that illness could best be dealt with by means of a *"discreet* furlough system." He wrote,

> It is the sheerest folly to keep sick men in camp where diseases are aggravated by the want of proper hospital facilities, when such men, if suffered to return to their homes, where they can be properly and kindly nursed by their loved ones around their hearthstones, would soon recover and make available troops.[32]

Blackburn felt hampered by the Confederate regulations under which he had to operate; they required a surgeon to state that it was an absolute necessity to the patient's recovery that he be sent home. The Confederate surgeons, moreover, "claimed the right to direct these matters," and Blackburn was yielding them "reluctant obedience."[33] In early March, however, Blackburn reported that his regiment's health was good; there

---

[29]Wayne to Storey and Galt, 26 February 1863, AGLB No. 14, GDAH.

[30]General Orders, No. 8, 9 April 1863, GO, GDAH; Adjutant General's 1863 Report, 14.

[31]Wayne to Storey, 31 March 1863, AGLB No. 15, GDAH.

[32]*Milledgeville Confederate Union,* 27 February 1863.

[33]Ibid.

had only been one death since organization and a mere fifteen of his thousand charges were on the sick list.[34]

The First Regiment, on the other hand, reported over fifty men sick by 7 March, and had fewer than 700 men present in Savannah. Further complicating the situation, the regimental surgeon (the governor's brother Aaron) was providing medical discharges on what the governor termed a "wholesale scale." Many of the recipients of such discharges were probably in for a surprise, for the enrollment officers did not honor state medical discharges.[35]

Surgeon Brown was also giving too many certificates of sick leave with transportation. The governor put a stop to the situation by advising his brother that he himself would henceforth make all determinations relative to medical discharges and sick leave on a case by case basis. He ended his letter with a piece of advice: "You should remember that your position is a responsible one and that no favoritism can be allowed."[36]

To stress discretion to both regimental surgeons, General Wayne issued General Order No. 3, dated 13 March 1863, directing that "the Rules, Laws, and Regulations of the Confederate Army . . . especially those relating to the care and management of the sick . . . be strictly observed and conformed to, and that nothing contrary to them be *ordered or permitted*."[37]

Less than a month later Blackburn discharged himself through resignation, stating that he had had neuralgia for sixty days and would probably lose one of his eyes. So home he went, although he became one of Brown's aides-de-camp before the year's end, apparently having recovered his health.[38]

In early March the governor acted to provide hospital space for his sick troops. He authorized Colonel Galt to contract with Dr. B. W. Hardee of Savannah's Georgia Hospital for the treatment of members of the State Line. But the arrangement with Hardee was unaccountably delayed and,

---

[34]Ibid., 10 March 1863. Blackburn was, however, low on supplies. He had the following "card," dated 19 March 1863, placed in the *Macon Daily Telegraph,* 21 March 1863; "I respectfully, in behalf of my regiment, call upon the ladies of Middle Georgia, for a supply of sage, red pepper, and bandages for the sick of the command. An engagement seems imminent here, and we are greatly in need of bandages, having none on hand."

[35]Dr. Aaron Brown to Brown, 8 March 1863, GLB, GDAH; Brown to Dr. Brown, 11 March 1863, ibid.; Wayne to Galt, 25 February 1863, AGLB No. 14, GDAH.

[36]Brown to Dr. Brown, 11 March 1863, GLB, GDAH.

[37]General Orders, No. 3, 13 March 1863, GO, GDAH.

[38]Dr. J. C. C. Blackburn to Brown, 8 April 1863, GLB, GDAH; Wayne to Blackburn, 30 December 1863, AGLB No. 20, GDAH; Blackburn to Brown, 3 May 1864, GBIC, GDAH.

once entered into, was the source of much confusion. When Dr. Hardee took charge of the sick state troops, he too began granting sick leave liberally.[39]

It was also difficult to deal with Dr. Hardee. He wanted everything from a stove to a captain's commission, and he did not wish to use the stock of medicine the state had on hand for his use. Refused the commission, he got the stove—but neglected to use state medicinal stores as directed. Wayne was soon inquiring suspiciously about the large amount of drugs Hardee was purchasing.[40] The entire issue was deeply complicated, and the contractual and other difficulties with Hardee were not settled until some weeks after the State Line's departure from Savannah.[41]

In terms of excitement, March 1863—the Line's first full month of service—was disappointing; a futile bombardment of Fort McAllister by Federal gunboats on 2 March was the closest Savannah came to a Federal attack while the State Line was part of its garrison. But, as expected, the conscription officers claimed numerous men. The matter was disposed of as the governor had promised—valid claims were honored, but if the conscription officers could not provide convincing evidence, the alleged conscripts were protected by the state. "We wish to do justice to all parties," wrote Wayne. Thus, some were given up, some retained.[42]

Along with the regiment's first court-martial, March also brought another attempt by Albert Howell to transfer to Confederate service; this time he wished to take forty of his men with him. His action would present no difficulty to recruitment, he assured the governor, since so many men wanted to enter the State Line.[43] Predictably, Howell met with refusal, as did those men who wished to hire substitutes; the governor, an ardent opponent of substitution, ordered that it not be allowed in his volunteer organization.[44]

A practice consistent with the Confederacy's commitment to democracy was also initiated in March. With a special session of the General As-

---

[39]Brown to Galt and Dr. Brown, 9 March 1863, GLB, GDAH; Wayne to Galt 16 March 1863, AGLB No. 14, GDAH; Wayne to Galt, 21 March 1863, AGLB No. 15, GDAH; Dr. B. F. Hardee to Wayne, 18 April 1863, Cuyler (Wayne).

[40]Wayne to Hardee, undated, March 1863, AGLB No. 15, GDAH; Wayne to Galt, 9 April 1863, ibid.; Wayne to Hardee, 15 April 1863, ibid.; Wayne to Storey, 29 April 1863, ibid.

[41]Wayne to Storey, 20 May 1863, AGLB No. 15, GDAH.

[42]*Milledgeville Confederate Union,* 10 March 1863; John B. Weems to Wayne, 23 March 1863, AGIC, GDAH; Wayne to Captain R. N. Norris, 28 March 1863, AGLB No. 15, GDAH; Wayne to Galt, 25 May 1863, ibid.

[43]Wayne to Galt, 16 March 1863, AGLB No. 14, GDAH; Howell to Brown, 20 March 1863, GBIC, GDAH.

[44]H. H. Waters to Howell, 23 March 1863, ESLB vol. 9, GDAH; Wayne to James D. Clements, 20 March 1863, AGLB No. 14, GDAH. Opposition to substitution was one of the few policies on which Brown and President Davis agreed. Hill, *Joseph E. Brown,* 99 n. 103.

sembly imminent, Governor Brown instructed General Mercer to grant leaves to the officers and men who were legislators so that they could return to Milledgeville for the session.[45]

Unlike March, April proved to be full of incident. First, Tories and deserters fomented a civil disturbance in Walker County. Colonel Galt was told to choose a company acquainted with the area and hasten them there to assist some Confederate cavalrymen in putting down the insurgents. Galt accomplished this efficiently, sending Captain William Howe of Rome and his Company C to perform the "delicate service of quieting the disturbances."[46]

At approximately the same time, both regiments, much to their surprise, were sent out of state to Charleston, South Carolina, which was threatened by the Federal fleet and in need of reinforcement. Permission was asked of and granted by Governor Brown for his state troops to leave Georgia. The State Line made up part of an expeditionary force commanded by General W. H. T. Walker, a former state brigadier at Savannah who had returned to Confederate service.[47]

Not surprisingly, men in both regiments were upset by the governor's action. A soldier of the First Regiment wrote a friend that "the regiment generally was opposed to going but most went." An officer of the Second Regiment, apparently assuming that the movement had been made without the governor's permission, complained bitterly to General Wayne. Informing the officer that the movement had been made "with the consent of the Governor, previously obtained," Wayne added that there was no danger of the Confederate authorities sending the State Line anywhere without the governor's consent. According to one State Line officer, a major worry of some men was that they would be "turned over to the Confederate service."[48]

Despite evident reluctance to aid South Carolina, the Line received good notices after the Yankees' wildly unsuccessful naval attack. The *Charleston Mercury* spoke of the First Regiment as "those brave troops of our sister Georgia," who served in South Carolina despite having been raised for state defense only. According to the article, which noted the enthusiasm pervading the regiment's ranks, the officers expressed themselves "alone

---

[45]Wayne to Lieutenant N. N. Beall, 19 March 1863, AGLB No. 14, GDAH. President Davis, moreover, also allowed officers and men of the Confederate armies who were members of the General Assembly to attend the session. General Robert E. Lee put a stop to this practice the following year. *CR*, 3:330-31; R. E. Lee to Brown, 3 March 1864, GLB, GDAH.

[46]Wayne to Galt, 2 April 1863, AGLB No. 15, GDAH; Wayne to Galt, 8 April 1863, ibid.; Wayne to Captain William Howe, 8 April 1863, ibid.; *OR*, vol. 23, pt. 2:737-38.

[47]Wayne to Mercer, 31 March 1863, Cuyler (Wayne); *Charleston Mercury*, 15 April 1863; Wayne to Captain James Wilson, 24 April 1863, AGLB No. 15, GDAH.

[48]Benjamin Martin to T. Fowler, 22 April 1863, Fowler Papers, Civil War Miscellany—Personal Papers, GDAH; F. M. Cowen to George Fowler, 19 April 1863, ibid.

apprehensive that they would be retained at Savannah, under the plea that the regiment was too recently organized to be effective on the field."[49]

In a letter from General Wayne, Colonel Galt was congratulated "upon the good impression the State troops made abroad." He added that General Mercer had also paid a handsome compliment to the State Line, which was gratifying both to the governor and to Galt's friends in the legislature. Mercer had written, as the state troops were leaving for Charleston, that they "appeared willing and anxious to aid our sister city, and were not disposed to weaken our common cause by standing upon nice points of law. These Regiments are now efficient and valuable bodies of men; large, well armed and equipped, and greatly improved in discipline and drill; they will render noble service if called upon to meet the enemy."[50]

The Second Regiment also received praise:

> Among the troops who have rallied to the defense of the city, none deserve higher praise than the Second Georgia State Troops . . . raised in Georgia to serve for the limits of the war *within the* limits of the State of Georgia. . . . They recognize a common cause and are willing to oppose strong arms and dauntless breasts to resist the . . . invader. . . . We predict for this regiment if ever engaged with the enemy they will give a good account of themselves.[51]

By the end of April the State Line was again bivouacked near Savannah, the First Regiment forming part of Walker's Brigade, and the Second performing detached service on the river batteries. There Brown had intended they should stay until June, but enemy movements along the state's northwestern border changed his mind. Word of Union Colonel Abel D. Streight's raid brought about the complete withdrawal of the State Line, already substantially weakened by transfers for duty along the State Road near Chattanooga.[52]

However, the State Line was not destined to tangle with Streight's Raiders. That task fell to General Nathan Bedford Forrest's Confederate troopers, who decisively defeated the Federal force near Rome on 3 May while the State Line was still preparing to leave Savannah.[53] Yet rumors of enemy designs against the State Road and the towns of northwest Georgia persisted. Consequently, Wayne determined that a large portion of the State Line should be stationed in the threatened area. He felt that the Fed-

---

[49]E. Milby Burton, *The Siege of Charleston, 1861-1865* (Columbia: University of South Carolina Press, 1970) 141-42; *Charleston Mercury,* 15 April 1863.

[50]Wayne to Galt, 24 April 1863, AGLB No. 15, GDAH; Mercer to Wayne, 11 April 1863, Cuyler (Wayne).

[51]*Charleston Daily Courier,* 10 April 1863.

[52]*OR,* vol. 14:930; Wayne to Mercer, 30 April 1863, AGLB No. 15, GDAH; Wayne to Mercer, 4 May 1863, ibid.; Wayne to Mercer, 29 April 1863, ibid.

[53]Bryan, *Confederate Georgia,* 77; Wayne to Mercer, 4 May 1863, AGLB No. 15, GDAH.

erals' failure at Charleston had "taken all the starch" out of them, leaving the coast safe for the time being. Therefore Wayne ordered both regiments to Atlanta. From there they were sent to Rome to aid in the "mopping up" operations following Forrest's victory.[54]

While at Rome, Colonel Storey stated in the local press that a gap west of Rome would be the best post for his regiment. He received orders, however, to move to Kingston, where the Rome railroad joined the State Road. Galt and his men were sent further southeast to Etowah.[55]

The transfer of these troops provoked an attack on the governor and General Wayne by the *Rome Tri-Weekly Courier,* which claimed that the State Road could best be protected in Rome. Acceptance of the governor's plan meant that the "old men, women, and children of Rome" would be protecting the Western and Atlantic: "Place yourselves as a bulwark between the enemy and the State troops. Unless our Heavenly Father . . . should again send us a *Forrest,* you are on your own hook."[56] Despite this criticism, Brown and Wayne adhered to their original plan,and the State Line finally began duty on the State Road.

Although the regiments had never staved off a Federal attack, they had, during their short life, been the object of spirited assaults by legislators in Georgia's capital. In late April Representative Z. B. Hargrove of Floyd County urged passage of a bill that would effectively destroy the State Line. This legislation proposed to repeal the resolutions that had created the regiments. In Hargrove's opinion it would be best for the men, seventy-five per cent of whom he classed as being of conscription age, either to be turned over to the Confederacy or disbanded to raise provisions for the state. Hargrove's major argument against the Line was fiscal: the annual maintenance expences, estimated to be from nearly $1.5 to $1.7 million, were too high—"more than the whole taxes in Georgia in one year." Nonetheless, the votes were not there; the bill was tabled on 20 April by a vote of fifty to thirty-five.[57]

The anti-Brown forces did not concede defeat, however. Only a week later they resurrected the State Guard bill, with its abrogation of the militia officers' commissions. The governor vetoed the bill immediately. In explaining his reasons, he specifically cited the value of the State Line:

The State has two fine regiments of troops in her service . . . , who hold themselves in readiness to obey the Governor's orders, and march at a mo-

[54]Wayne to Galt, 4 May 1863, AGLB No. 15, GDAH; Brown to Elizabeth G. Brown, 7 May 1863, Joseph E. Brown Papers (microfilm), Special Collections Department, Robert W. Woodruff Library, Emory University, Atlanta GA.

[55]*Rome Tri-Weekly Courier,* 23 May 1863; General Orders, No. 11, 20 May 1863, GO, GDAH.

[56]*Rome Tri-Weekly Courier,* 23 May 1863.

[57]*Milledgeville Southern Recorder,* 21 April 1863.

ment's warning to any part of the State, should an emergency arise to require their services. . . . This is an effective *organized* force of brave men, always ready, and is as many as the State can arm, or is likely to need as a State Guard.[58]

Twice more during the course of the war the legislature attacked the Georgia State Line. In the spring of 1864 another attempt was made to disband, or tender to the Confederacy, both regiments, described as being composed of "hale and vigorous young men living at ease and luxury, secure from the dangers of the battlefield." The House defeated the bill by a lopsided vote of 101 to 8.[59] Finally, in November 1864, another House resolution was offered to give the State Line to the Confederacy. Referred to the Committee on Military Affairs, the bill received a "do not pass."[60] It was not in the cards for the Line to be destroyed by the body that created it.

---

[58]As Brown noted, there was "little over a bare quorum" present in either chamber when the State Guard bill was passed. The House vote was 53 to 46; the Senate's vote was 14 to 10. *Milledgeville Confederate Union*, 28 April 1863; *Georgia House Journal*, Extra Session, 1863, 230; *Georgia Senate Journal*, Extra Session, 1863, 189.

[59]*Georgia House Journal*, Extra Session, 1864, 88-89. One officer, however, wrote to General Wayne, "I entertain in common with many others, the opinion on account of the universal disfavor our service is getting into, that we will be disbanded by the next Legislature." P. W. Douglas to Wayne, 29 May 1864, Cuyler (Wayne).

[60]*Georgia House Journal*, 1864, 46, 56, 82. Not all of the State Line's legislative attention was hostile. In the House, there was an unsuccessful attempt to pay $50 bounties to the State Line's enlisted men. Toward war's end there was an attempt, also unsuccessful, to increase the Line's forces. *Georgia House Journal*, 1864, 79; *Georgia House Journal*, Extra Session, 1864, 70; *Georgia House Journal*, 1865, 103-104.

CHAPTER V

On the Western
and Atlantic Railroad

As May 1863 ended and summer began—the summer of Gettysburg and Vicksburg—the two regiments of the State Line, finally free of Confederate control, were settling into their new headquarters and duties. Galt's unit was stationed forty-six miles above Atlanta at Etowah, with several of his companies detached to guard the major bridges; just above Etowah at Cartersville the State Line's hospital was located. Storey's regiment was posted north of Etowah at Kingston, from which a spur of the State Road led west to Rome.[1]

With both regiments now withdrawn from Confederate service, state Commissary General Jared I. Whitaker began to supply the troops with food and other articles. Supplies of meat included fresh and salt beef and pork, as well as bacon and mutton. Rice, peas, and corn were generously supplied, while grain products issued included flour, corn meal, hard bread, and loaf bread. Molasses, lard, salt, sugar, vinegar, and coffee were also provided, along with articles like candles and soap. Records indicate that the State Line's commissary stores were adequate throughout the war.[2]

---

[1]General Orders, No. 11, 20 May 1863, GO, GDAH; Brown to Dr. Brown 30 May 1863, Hargrett Collection; Wayne to Storey, 19 May 1863, AGLB No. 15, GDAH. The First and Second Regiment's camps, Camp Foster and Whitaker respectively, were named for two state officers: Quartermaster General Ira R. Foster and Commissary General Jared I. Whitaker. Although Camp Foster was near Etowah Station on the Etowah River, its telegraph and post office were at Cartersville. General Orders, No. 13, 23 May 1863, GO, GDAH.

[2]Commissary General. Purchases and Issues for Subsistence to Troops of State Line, 1863-1865, GDAH, passim. This volume also indicates that issues were made to the militia, laborers, and "exiles" (refugees). Destruction by Stoneman's Raiders at the state supply depot in Madison during August 1864 is documented in this source, along with supplies captured by Wilson's Raiders in Macon and elsewhere at war's end.

On 20 May General Wayne issued General Order No. 11 directing the regimental commanders to put their men into the "highest condition of military efficiency." To this end, the officers were to provide daily, hour-long instruction in tactics and army regulations; squad drill and other martial exercises were to occupy at least three and one half hours per day. Those companies of the First Regiment detached as bridge guards would be relieved monthly by other companies, so that all of Galt's men could alternate guarding the bridges with drilling in camp. "As the two Regiments are now each under its own Colonel," Wayne wrote Galt, the governor "wished to see which will make the most improvement when he shall inspect them."[3]

If Wayne thought this remark would induce Galt to whip his men into fighting fettle, he would be disappointed. He must have received Galt's response with something less than pleasure. Pleading overwork, Galt admitted that he had "but little opportunity for study and mind slow to retain what I read—It will have to be *mauled into me* if I ever make much proficiency in my new position."[4] Only a month earlier, Galt, already on leave, had requested a thirty-to-sixty-day extension.[5]

Increasing the governor's desire to have Galt and Storey bring their men into fighting shape were the recent troubles in northwest Georgia. Streight's Raiders had come "within an ace" of breaking the State Road, shaking the governor into realizing that his two infantry regiments might be of little use when raiders struck so swiftly. Supporting cavalry units seemed to be the answer, but the legislature was not disposed to grant him any. Furthermore, Brown admitted to Herschel Johnson a reluctance to risk conflict with the conscription officers over raising state troopers.[6]

On 25 May Brown therefore dispatched a cordial and conciliatory letter to President Davis, applying for military aid in the form of the cavalry he sought. If Davis would provide a regiment whose men could be posted along Georgia's western and northwestern borders, these troopers could "concentrate rapidly" at threatened points. The state regiments, he added, could provide timely reinforcement, stationed as they were along the area's rail line; they could be "held in readiness to move either up or down the Road . . . and to support Rome and other points on the flank of the Road." He hoped for a "judicious arrangement and understanding" between the Confederate and state troops.[7]

---

[3]General Orders, No. 11, 20 May 1863, GO, GDAH; Wayne to Galt, 29 May 1863, AGLB No. 15, GDAH.

[4]Galt to Wayne, 29 May 1863, AGIC, GDAH.

[5]Wayne to Galt, 25 April 1863, AGLB No. 15, GDAH.

[6]Robert C. Black III, *The Railroads of the Confederacy* (Chapel Hill: University of North Carolina Press, 1952) 223; Brown to Herschel V. Johnson, 15 May 1863, GLB, GDAH.

[7]Brown to Davis, 25 May 1863, GLB, GDAH.

Confessing that he had no power to raise cavalry himself, Brown also reminded Davis that his request, if granted, would benefit not only Georgia, but the Confederacy as well. Destruction by raiders of any of the bridges along the 138-mile-long railway that Georgia was protecting "would seriously affect, if not disastrously act upon the operations of our Army in Tennessee and Virginia." Furthermore, coal and iron supplies for Georgia foundries, many with important Confederate contracts, would be cut off.[8]

> I would not trouble you with this request but for the impression derived from several sources, and from the bold and insolent threats of the captured "raiders," that the destruction of Rome, Atlanta, and the Bridges on the State Road, are prominent objects in the mind of the enemy, and that other and persistent attempts will be made again to destroy them.[9]

The president responded that, while he concurred with Brown as to the importance of the State Road and other Yankee targets, "exigencies of the service" prevented his sending the cavalry regiment. He suggested instead that a mounted regiment of the soon-to-be organized Georgia State Guard be assigned to cooperate with the State Line "for the purposes and in the manner" that Brown suggested. Additionally, Davis seems to have ordered duplicate bridge frames constructed for the most important State Road bridges.[10]

Two days after his aid request to Richmond, Brown was telling a critic that Davis had acquiesced in the creation of the State Line:

> Upon the Conscript act, I have conscientiously differed from the President, and I have not acted the insincere part, but have boldly contended for my principles. . . . There is no misunderstanding between me and the President about the two State Regiments. They are now rendering important service in protecting the State Road bridges and the Georgia frontier against raids of the enemy. The only regret among the people at present seems to be that we have not four regiments in place of two.[11]

Although the people may have had a single regret, the two regiments had an overabundance: their year-long tour on the state Road would be a time of great dissatisfaction, frequent disputes, and constant backbiting. Much time would be spent in what were described as "passive" duties, and General Wayne's "Devil" would find much work among the idle minds of the officers and men of the State Line.

Their behavior had been relatively good during their stay in Savannah, when they were preoccupied with imminent combat and hatred of Confederates. But with increased leisure, they became more troublesome

---

[8]Ibid.

[9]Ibid.

[10]*CR*, 3:347; Brown to Captain L. P. Grant, 31 July 1863, GL, GDAH.

[11]Brown to P. W. Douglas, 27 May 1863, Hargrett Collection.

to General Wayne and the governor, while animosity grew unhindered in their ranks.

The first major controversy arose over requests from both regiments for agricultural leave. Arriving at the capital just before the units' departure from the coast, the requests came initially from the regimental command- ers; later the rank and file joined in persistent demands.[12] There were ap- parently two major reasons for this persistence. First, there was the precedent set the previous year in the Bridge Guard; agricultural leave had been left to Galt's discretion, and there is no evidence that he was conser- vative in granting such furloughs. Second, Representative Hargrove's ar- guments in favor of dissolving the regiments had contained a suggestion that "the troops return home and assist in raising provisions." Rumor and wishful thinking turned proposal into fact, apparently, for Galt based his request on reports from the General Assembly. He was informed that since no such legislation had passed, the matter was back where it properly be- longed—in the governor's discretion.[13]

At the same time Wayne unwisely left Colonel Storey some hope, writ- ing that the governor might permit the officers and men to "go make their crops" if the state of affairs permitted it. Regrettably for those wishing to return to their fields, the state of affairs within the next few days included Streight's Raid, which effectively ended any consideration of agricultural furloughs.[14]

There were those who would not accept this fact. On 19 May, Wayne wrote to Galt at the governor's direction to "disabuse your mind and that of your officers and men of an erroneous impression you all appear to have fallen into, that the State regiments are to be farmers as well as sol- diers."[15] Therefore the aforementioned General Order No. 11, issued the next day, endeavored to make things plain: "No officers or men will be per- mitted to be absent from their camp for a longer time than twenty-four hours, except by the authority of the commander-in-chief obtained through [the adjutant general]."[16] As Wayne wrote to one of Storey's soldiers, the colonels needed to be drilling their men so that when "called into the field . . . they may be able to harvest Yankees in the most effective manner."[17]

-----

[12]Wayne to Storey, Galt, 24 April 1863, AGLB No. 15, GDAH; Wayne to Joshua Baget, 20 May 1863, ibid.; Wayne to Galt, 19 May 1863, ibid.

[13]One of the State Line's supporters had also called for "furloughs in the dis- cretion of the governor, so as to have the wheat crops harvested." *Milledgeville Southern Recorder,* 21 April 1863; Wayne to Galt, 24 April 1863, AGLB No. 15, GDAH.

[14]Wayne to Storey, 24 April 1863, AGLB, No. 15, GDAH.

[15]Wayne to Galt, 19 May 1863, AGLB, No. 15, GDAH.

[16]General Orders, No. 11, 20 May 1863, GO, GDAH.

[17]Wayne to Joshua Baget, 20 May 1863, AGLB No. 15, GDAH.

Storey continued his requests, sending a petition from his regiment's officers asking for furloughs to cut wheat. Responding on 26 May, Wayne simply referred him to the applicable general order, adding that the governor had no more to say on the subject.[18] A little over a week later, however, the adjutant general was again writing Storey on the matter: "In not being able to go home the State regiments are in no worse state than our other gallant State regiments in Confederate service, and it would be as reasonable to disband one of them to go home to harvest."[19]

One reason for the governor's reluctance to allow furloughs should have become obvious on 10 June 1863. Responding to reports of a Federal raid in Elbert County, Brown ordered both regiments to be ready to entrain at a moment's notice to meet the threat. Yet Galt continued to send his men's numerous leave requests, bringing a very direct response from General Wayne: "In the regular army you would be arrested," wrote Wayne, "for after the Commander-in-Chief has given orders, it is expected that every officer will cheerfully carry them out."[20]

Obviously, the belief had been widespread among the State Line volunteers that enlisting would keep them out of Confederate service and inside the state, while also allowing them to tend their crops. In less than three months they had found all three notions illusory.

But the relentless leave requests ultimately led to a partial concession by the governor. Under General Order No. 17, company commanders could grant their men ten-day furloughs, given that no more than three men be furloughed at a time. Officers, however, had to submit their leave requests to the governor, and were to be allowed only twenty-four-hour furloughs—not more often than once in ten days.[21]

Over time Colonel Galt proved troublesome over more than furloughs. When in the field conducting active military operations (during the Dahlonega expedition, for instance, and later, during the Atlanta Campaign), Galt did well, but in what was essentially garrison service, the colonel was not at his best. His frequent failure to enforce military discipline; his temperament, simultaneously sensitive and assertive; his preference for tending to personal and business affairs—all these factors undercut his usefulness as a regimental commander. Realizing that the citizen was dominant in this citizen-soldier, General Wayne warned Galt against too much indulgence in dealing with his men. "As the Colonel of a Regiment," Wayne wrote, "you must frequently close up your heart, when as plain Mr.

---

[18]Wayne to Storey, 26 May 1863, AGLB, No. 15, GDAH.

[19]Wayne to Storey, 4 June 1863, ibid.

[20]Brown to Galt and Storey, 10 June 1863, GLB, GDAH; Wayne to Galt, 30 June 1863, AGL No. 16, GDAH.

[21]General Orders, No. 17, 2 July 1863, GO, GDAH.

Galt you might have opened all its avenues." Permissiveness continued, however, infrequently alternating with uncharacteristic stringency.[22]

Galt's combative personality, much like the governor's, also created problems. The colonel was ever ready with advice for both superiors and subordinates, and he seldom overlooked perceived slights. Although not quite as prolix and prolific a correspondent as Brown, Galt did share the governor's propensity for frequent and long-winded letters. Once, having offered Wayne his unsolicited opinions, Galt received a brusque note in response: "Get to work and learn to be a finely drilled regiment, and leave other matters to the Governor's care, whose appropriate business it is, and who will not neglect it."[23]

Unfortunately, Galt's understandable preoccupation with his personal financial concerns seems to have displaced much of the interest he should have shown in military matters. Until the winter of 1863-1864, when he moved his large family to Cuthbert in southwest Georgia, numerous personal and business distractions were just up the track from his headquarters. His extravagant requests for personal leave apparently sprang from his desire to keep watch over both his family and his upcountry business dealings, a wish more easily fulfilled when he commanded the Bridge Guard from his home town.[24]

Galt would be a chronic problem, but Wayne was to have no further trouble from Colonel Storey. In early June, shortly after receiving the adjutant general's last letter forbidding leave, Storey tendered his resignation; he had been a colonel of the Line for less than six months. Unmilitary to the last, he attempted to leave the service before completing his duties as officer of a sitting court-martial. Wayne ordered that he not be released until he had finished his work.[25]

Storey's resignation came at a time when morale was low among his men and conspiracy rife among his officers. One of his soldiers wrote home, "Colonel Dick has resined [sic] and gone home to collect Confederate taxes . . . and our regiment is going to the dogs as fast as it can go and we are doing no good hear in any way only fooling about."[26]

Among the officers, Captain James Wilson, a thirty-four-year-old lawyer from Terrell County who had served fifteen months in the 5th Georgia Regiment, most clearly coveted the colonelcy. Calculating that Lieuten-

---

[22]Galt to Wayne, 1 February 1863, AGIC, GDAH; Wayne to Galt, 30 June 1863, AGLB No. 16, GDAH.

[23]Wayne to Galt, 23 May 1863, AGLB No. 15, GDAH.

[24]Galt to Joel Galt, 10 January [1864], Galt collection, in private possession.

[25]Storey to Wayne, 9 June 1863, AGIC, GDAH; Wayne to Storey, 15 June 1863, AGLB No. 16l, GDAH.

[26]O. H. P. Chambers to "Dear Companion," 2 July 1863, Civil War Miscellany—Personal Papers, GDAH.

ant Colonel Evans would probably be his most dangerous rival for the office, Wilson attempted to undercut him by writing confidentially to General Wayne, charging Evans with "tactical incompetency."[27] As Wayne informed Wilson:

> there can be between the Commander-in-Chief and his Officers no confidential detraction of another officer's professional reputation. . . . If Colonel Evans is incompetent and so reported is it not our duty to the State to bring to test and if found guilty remove him?[28]

Wayne concluded by stating that Wilson's charge would be laid before the governor for action.

Unknown to Wilson, Evans had already taken himself out of the running. During the same week Wilson made his charge, Evans wrote his wife:

> The election for colonel will come off next Wednesday the'8th[of July]. Captain Wilson, who opposed Colonel Storey [in the February election], will likely be elected. I shall be much gratified at it. He is by far the most competent man for the position.
> This Regt is composed of very ignorant officers and men, very little intelligence among them. I am perfectly satisfied that I have made the resolution not to run for Colonel—it relieves me of much responsibility and must ultimately save my reputation. I had all to lose and nothing to gain by being Col.[29]

The election was duly held and Wilson won the colonelcy. He seems to have made a belated attempt to withdraw the charges against Evans when he saw that Evans would not challenge him; Evans's confidential dismissal, which Wilson had desired, was no longer necessary. At any rate, Wayne left the matter in Wilson's hands, noting that as colonel it was his *duty* to remove incompetent officers. He added that he had told Evans nothing of the charges and that Evans had expressed satisfaction at Wilson's election. " . . . it is desirable that the perfect harmony that now exists should continue between you," Wayne wrote.[30] Wilson brought no charges, instead soon traveling from Kingston to Rome to be fitted for his colonel's uniform. Despite the fact that Wilson was to hold his colonelcy for the remainder of the war, his regiment was always to be "Storey's State Line" to its veterans.[31]

---

[27]U.S. Bureau of the Census, Schedule 1, Free Inhabitants, Terrell County, Georgia; James Wilson to Brown 13 November 1862, GBIC, GDAH; Wayne to Wilson 4 July 1863, AGLB No. 16, GDAH. Wilson was a 2d lieutenant in the 5th Georgia when he resigned in June 1862 because of liver disease and general debility. Henderson, 1:682.

[28]Wayne to Wilson, 4 July 1863, AGLB No. 16, GDAH.

[29]Evans to Sallie Evans, 6 July 1863, Evans Collection, in private possession.

[30]Wayne to Wilson, 14 July 1863, AGLB No. 16, GDAH.

[31]Wilson to Wayne, 8 August 1863, AGIC, GDAH; Confederate Pension Applications, passim, GDAH.

During the late spring and early summer, a major concern of both regiments was arms and ammunition. In 1862 the Confederacy had seized forty-three hundred rifles imported by Georgia, and Brown frequently demanded restitution. Yet among the nine hundred guns promised by Richmond during the Savannah scare, only three hundred had been Enfields, the major type seized; the rest were "refuse guns." Galt reported in late May that many of his guns were "not to be relied upon in an engagement. Many of these will not burst a cap only occasionally."[32] He was especially dissatisfied with the Mississippi and Belgian rifles with which his men were armed. These rifles were of different calibers, and it was difficult and confusing to supply them with ammunition. Half of his companies had Enfields, the weapon of his choice, but substandard state ammunition soon "leaded up" the guns so that they would not shoot. He requested Enfields and better ammunition for all his men.[33]

Wayne would have gladly accommodated him, but while the Richmond government promised to replace the confiscated rifles, it offered in their place only notoriously inferior Belgian rifles. Wayne held out for 1500 Enfields—his usual request. Writing Confederate ordnance chief Josiah Gorgas in July 1863, Wayne noted that a good measure of the need for a well-armed State Line was the value to the Army of Tennessee of the State Road, which the regiments guarded.[34]

While no Enfields were forthcoming, Wayne accepted fifteen hundred Austrian rifled muskets from Richmond in August. Consequently, the Second Regiment received standard issue arms: one thousand rifles with bayonets and scabbards, along with twenty thousand cartridges and caps. Galt's most poorly armed company received one hundred of the rifles; the others were sent to the state arsenal. Although considered only slightly better than the Belgian model, the Austrian rifle had "proved itself a good gun," Wayne later noted, "both as to range and precision. The officers and men of the 2d Regiment speak well of and are pleased with it."[35]

In any case, it became increasingly clear that there would soon be need for arms. Chattanooga, northern terminus of the State Road, had become headquarters for the army of General Braxton Bragg, who would soon be contending with massive Union armies. Georgia now was threatened not with

---

[32]*CR*, 2:253; Brown to Seddon, 11 April 1863, GLB, GDAH; Galt to Wayne, 29 May 1863, AGIC, GDAH.

[33]Ibid. Five companies had Enfields, two had Mississippi rifles, one had Belgian rifles, and two had old muskets. Galt to Colonel Joseph Claghorn, 5 August 1863, AGIC, GDAH.

[34]Wayne to Galt, 1 June 1863, AGLB No. 15, GDAH; Bell Irvin Wiley, *The Life of Johnny Reb* (Baton Rouge: Louisiana State University Press, 1978) 291; Wayne to Josiah Gorgas, 11 July 1863, AGLB No. 16, GDAH.

[35]Colonel James Wilson's Receipt for Ordnance Stores, 5 September 1863, State Line Miscellany; Wiley, 290; Adjutant General's 1863 Report, 9-10.

isolated raids but with a formidable invasion from the north. Circumstances dictated that the State Line's training period had passed; the time for active duty had arrived. The Western and Atlantic Railroad, now the major supply and communication line of the Army of Tennessee, was certain to be the target of determined attacks.[36]

Consequently, Governor Brown ordered General Wayne to inspect the road to determine the most judicious disposition of the state regiments. He provided a special train for Wayne, who proceeded up the line accompanied by several officers of both regiments, as well as a civil engineer. During the second week of July the party traveled to Dalton and thence to Chattanooga for an interview with General Bragg. The general told Wayne he was gratified to have fifteen hundred state troops to his rear, glad that the governor "had given attention to the security of his line of communication."[37] (This was a marked improvement from Bragg's recent relations with Brown—he had a few months earlier attempted to seize the State Road. His action had come near to creating an armed conflict before he reconsidered.)[38]

Now all was harmony. In response to Wayne's request for artillery, Bragg gave Wayne "fifteen or twenty field pieces." He also informed Wayne that Confederate troops would take charge of the road's three uppermost bridges, since all were within Bragg's camp. The State Line would remain responsible for the rest of the bridges.[39]

Following the interview, Wayne and his party returned to Atlanta, reexamining the road as they went. Soon afterward, Wayne composed his "Memoir of the Examination of the State Road and Plans, in General, for the Defence of the Bridges." These plans, later slightly modified, were contained in General Order No. 19 of 20 July 1863.[40]

The First Regiment would take charge of the road from Atlanta to Resaca:

(1) The Chattahoochee Bridge, seven miles from Atlanta, would be defended by one strong company, which would also furnish the guard for the state property at Atlanta.

(2) The Etowah Bridge, forty-six miles above Atlanta, would be protected by four companies and four guns. Wayne considered this bridge, "a large and expensive structure resting on high stone piers. . . . exposed on both sides," to be extremely important. If necessary three hundred men

[36]Bryan, *Confederate Georgia,* 77.

[37]Wayne to Brown, 13 July 1863, AGLB No. 16, GDAH.

[38]Black, *Railroads,* 195.

[39]Wayne to Brown, 13 July 1863, AGLB No. 16, GDAH.

[40]"Memoir of the Examination of the State Road and Plans, in General, for the Defence of the Bridges," 11 July 1863, Cuyler (Wayne)—hereafter referred to as "Memoir"; General Orders, No. 19, 20 July 1863, GO, GDAH.

from the nearby Etowah Iron Works and six hundred from Rome were expected to help in this structure's defense. A detachment from the force would guard the trestle bridge over the Allatoona, six miles south.[41]

(3) The Pettis Creek Bridge, fifty miles from Atlanta, would be protected by a small company and one gun.

(4) The bridge at Resaca, which crossed the Oostanaula River eighty-five miles from Atlanta, Wayne considered the most exposed on the line. The bridge, itself over four hundred feet long, was approached by six hundred feet of trestle. Wayne ordered four companies and five pieces of artillery for its protection.

Wayne also posted the First Regiment's officers to specific posts along the road. The lieutenant colonel would be stationed at Etowah Bridge; he would command the troops there and at the nearby Allatoona and Pettis Creek Bridges. Both the colonel and the major were posted to Resaca, where the major would be in immediate command; the colonel was relieved of post duties so he could travel up and down his segment of the railroad, "examining critically the guards and posts." If any point along the line was threatened, the colonel was to hasten there "to take command of the troops and of the defense."[42]

The Second Regiment would defend that portion of the road "from one mile north of the village of Resaca to within two miles of General Bragg's Guard" near Chattanooga.

(1) The trestle at Dalton, about one hundred miles from Atlanta, would be guarded by one company.

(2) Tunnel Hill, 107 miles from Atlanta, would be guarded by two companies, which could also provide protection for several nearby points. Wayne was not particularly anxious about the tunnel since any attempt to damage it extensively would be so time-consuming that numerous reinforcements could be summoned to prevent large-scale destruction.[43]

(3) Catoosa Platform, 115 miles from Atlanta, was the "jumping-off point" for Catoosa Springs, self-styled "Saratoga of the Confederate States," until its closure and conversion into Confederate hospital space.[44] Four companies and four guns were to guard the nearby bridges, which spanned winding Chickamauga Creek, at four points within only two miles.

(4) Just below the Tennessee line at Graysville, 120 miles from Atlanta, two other bridges crossed the creek. There, three companies and as many guns would be stationed, also guarding two Tennessee bridges.

---

[41]"Memoir."

[42]Ibid.

[43]Ibid.

[44]"The Saratoga of the Confederate States: Catoosa Springs, Catoosa County, Georgia," pamphlet, 1861; Carroll Proctor Scruggs, ed., *Georgia Historical Markers* (Helen GA: Bay Tree Grove, 1973) 66.

The assignment of regimental officers was similar to the First Regiment's. The lieutenant colonel would be posted at Graysville, and the major was to have immediate command at Catoosa Platform, the regimental headquarters. Colonel Wilson, like Galt, would be responsible for his entire section of the road.

Ordering these dispositions was just the start for Wayne. He advised also that all bridges be floored to facilitate the crossing of soldiers and artillery and that duplicate timbers be stored near all bridges to accelerate any necessary reconstruction.

Furthermore, he wrote, stockades and earthworks should be constructed to protect the bridges and their guards. Stock gaps should be installed to prevent cavalry from rushing into the works; movable barriers should be on hand to block the roadway if necessary. Pikes should be stored at all locations; the fort's defenders could use them to prevent raiders from climbing over the walls.[45]

Having reported on the situation in north Georgia, Wayne informed the governor of another request for military aid from General Mercer in Savannah. Wayne suggested that the time for hard choices was fast approaching: "Georgia is now hard pressed and there is much to be done for both ends of our State. The greatest importance though attaches to Atlanta and the State Road, for they gone Tennessee is irrevocably lost to us, and the heart of the Confederacy will have been reached. If *compelled* to choose between the Seaboard and Atlanta, we must give our whole energies for Atlanta. The loss of Savannah as sinful and mortifying as it would be yet in its consequences to the State and the Confederacy would not be as disastrous as the loss of Atlanta." Nonetheless, Brown said he would send Mercer one of the State Line regiments if the emergency was extreme.[46]

Wayne suggested that he himself be stationed on the road, where he felt he could provide "the most important service to be rendered to the State."[47] The governor concurred. "So great is my confidence in your ability, discretion, and valor," wrote Brown, "that I trammel you with no definite instructions." On 28 July Wayne arrived at Cartersville, where he set up headquarters and assumed command of the State Line.[48]

Not surprisingly, the adjutant general directed that the first fortifications be constructed at the most vulnerable points: Etowah and Resaca. Etowah's defenses were based upon plans by G. W. Smith, former Confed-

[45]"Memoir."

[46]Wayne to Mercer, 10 July 1863, Cuyler (Wayne); Wayne to Brown, 13 July 1863, AGLB No. 16, GDAH; Brown to Wayne, [July 13, 1863], Cuyler (Wayne).

[47]"Memoir."

[48]Brown to Wayne, 20 July 1863, Hargrett Collection; Adjutant General's 1863 Report, 4.

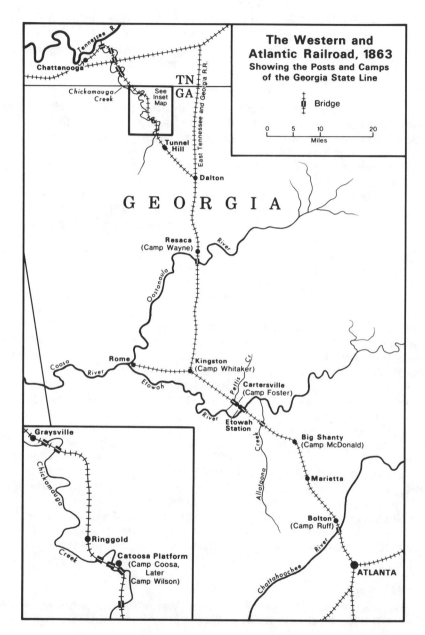

Map 2. The Western and Atlantic Railroad, 1863, showing the posts and camps of the Georgia State Line. (After "Map of the Atlanta Campaign," Century Illustrated Magazine 34 [July 1887]: 446.)

erate general and noted military engineer, then supervising the Etowah Iron Works. General F. W. Capers, Superintendent of the Georgia Military Institute, planned the works for Resaca. In both cases, construction would be completed entirely by men of the State Line, mostly from Galt's regiment.[49]

Volunteering his services—as had Smith and Capers—was a young Englishman, Captain T. G. Raven, who served on Wayne's staff as Engineer and Inspector of Fortifications. Also assisting with the earthworks were Captain Calvin Fay, engineer and architect at Etowah Iron Works,

The railroad bridge over the Etowah River, showing earthworks constructed by the First State Line. (From an 1864 photograph by George N. Barnard. Courtesy of the Library of Congress.)

---

[49]Adjutant General's 1863 Report, 4.

and Captain B. F. Roberts, a Confederate engineer detailed to assist with the works at Resaca.[50]

Artillery for the Etowah and Resaca works, as well as for the State Line's other posts, was the responsibility of Colonel Joseph S. Claghorn, formerly captain of Savannah's famed Chatham Artillery and also a member of Wayne's volunteer brigade staff. By the end of August he had secured from General Bragg and elsewhere five six-pounder guns and one twelve-pounder howitzer for both Etowah and Resaca. By early October there were seven batteries at Resaca and four at Etowah; the number of artillery pieces had nearly doubled at both places.[51]

The men to serve these guns were almost all drawn from the State Line. In July Wayne ordered nine of "the most intelligent Officers from the classes of subalterns "—representing all the State Line duty stations—to report to General Capers at G.M.I. in Marietta. After receiving ten days' training in the artillery manual, each was to return to his post to school its batterymen. Wayne also added an instructor of artillery to his staff. In October, when Colonel Claghorn went on a round of inspections, the State Line artillerists' proficiency in drill was rated as fair to good.[52]

Just after taking command, Wayne began to receive complaints about the men of the Second Regiment. Upon hearing of the charges, Colonel Wilson responded that the citizens must have confused his men with Confederate infantry and cavalry who were "straggling all through the country." By the end of the month the Confederates had left. "All quiet in *Our Army*," Wilson reported.[53]

Soon, stirrings to the north indicated that the great armies there would clash presently. In a telegram sent 1 September, General Bragg warned

---

[50]T. G. Raven to Wayne, 27 July 1863, AGIC, GDAH; Adjutant General's 1863 Report, 7; Wayne to Galt, 16 November 1863, AGLB B-44, Part 1, GDAH; G. W. Smith to Wayne, 25 July 1863, Cuyler (Wayne); Wayne to Galt, 13 August 1863, AGLB No. 18, GDAH. An eight-year veteran of the Chatham Artillery, Captain Fay was put in charge of the artillery at Etowah. Later he was placed in charge of constructing the fortifications at Milledgeville. *OR*, vol. 52, pt. 2:820; Claghorn to Fay, October 11, 1863, Georgia Ordnance—Incoming Correspondence, Box 3337-05, GDAH. Hereafter cited as Georgia Ordnance.

[51]Adjutant General's 1863 Report, 7; Ordnance Receipts, 5, 21, and 24 August 1863, Georgia Ordnance; Claghorn to Wayne, Inspection Reports (Resaca: 3 October 1863; Etowah: 8 October 1863), AGIC, GDAH.

[52]Wayne to Galt, 29 July 1863, AGLB No. 17, GDAH; Wayne to Charles C. Jones, Jr., 3 September 1870, Charles C. Jones, Jr., Papers, Manuscript Department, Perkins Library, Duke University, Durham, NC.

[53]Wilson to Wayne, 26 August 1863, AGIC,GDAH. Criticism of Confederates came to Wayne from Line posts at the Chattahoochee Bridge and at Kingston, where Galt said that State Line troops were necessary to protect the public from Confederate depredations. Cowen to Wayne, 2 August 1863, Cuyler (Wayne); Galt to Wayne, 10 August 1863, ibid.

Wayne to "look out for trouble along the line of the road."[54] Later reports suggested increased danger, and by the tenth Wayne was in Resaca, where some Confederate batteries had been added to his command, as had a portion of the newly raised Georgia State Guard—the large force of non-conscripts that the governor had brought out to serve the Confederacy as local defense troops.[55]

By this time Bragg had abandoned Chattanooga and withdrawn to LaFayette, Georgia, twenty-two miles south. From there he hoped to protect the State Road, which would bring him reinforcements from the Army of Northern Virginia—General James Longstreet's Corps. All points north of Resaca were rapidly evacuated, including the Second Regiment's posts. Wilson's men had just received their new Austrian rifles and risked losing them—along with their ordnance, commissary supplies, tents, and other materiel—if they were overrun by a Federal advance or swept up in a retreat of Bragg's army. Lieutenant Colonel Evans had been forced to withdraw from Graysville on the ninth as General Bragg moved west of the road toward LaFayette. As the Confederate army moved, an enemy force pressed down upon the railroad. The country above Dalton, Evans reported, was "in the wildest excitement. Everybody that can move is bringing their personal effects and Negroes by every conceivable kind of conveyance."[56]

On the evening of the ninth, as Evans fell back with his supplies to Catoosa Platform, Wilson was told by the railroad authorities that "no more trains would pass above Dalton"—that they had been unable to bring off

---

[54]Adjutant General's 1863 Report, 5. The governor was meanwhile clashing with the conscription officers. He had Captain Cowen arrest one of the officers for enrolling a militia officer. Brown ordered Wayne to protect Cowen from retaliation "with all the force necessary." Brown to Wayne, 1 September 1863, GLB, GDAH.

[55]Adjutant General's 1863 Report, 5. One Georgia State Guard unit was created specifically for the defense of the Western and Atlantic Railroad: the Independent State Road Guards, commanded by Captain William A. Fuller, hero of the Great Locomotive Chase. After disbandment of the State Guard in February 1864, Brown continued the unit as a state company of detailed men. By May 1864 rank and file had increased to almost three hundred; soon after the unit became the three-company State Road Battalion, commanded by Major George Hillyer. With the State Road by that time under enemy control, some of the men guarded the road's stock at Griswoldville and elsewhere, while others were apparently transferred to the Second State Line. William A. Fuller to Wayne, 31 August 1863, AGIC, GDAH; Wayne to Fuller, 12 February 1864, AGLB No. 22, GDAH; Wayne to Fuller, 17 May 1864, AGLB No. 24, GDAH; Fuller to Wayne, 28 May 1864, AGIC, GDAH; James M. Mobley to James R. Wylie, 18 August 1864, AGLB No. 25, GDAH; Wayne to George Hillyer, 15 November 1864, AGLB No. 27, GDAH.

[56]Adjutant General's 1863 Report, 5; Thomas Lawrence Connelly, *Autumn of Glory: The Army of Tennessee, 1862-1865* (Baton Rouge: Louisiana State University Press, 1971) 173; Wilson to Wayne, 9 September 1863, AGIC, GDAH; Adjutant General's 1863 Report, 5; Evans to Wayne, 10 September 1863, Cuyler (Wayne).

all the Confederate stores at Chickamauga "because of the close proximity of the enemy." Indeed, Federal cavalry was reported within nine miles of Wilson's headquarters at Catoosa Platform.[57]

At 4:00 A.M. on 10 September Wilson called in his pickets and moved back to Dalton, gathering his troops as he retired. His move was timely: his camp was occupied by the enemy two hours after his departure and General Nathan Bedford Forrest's cavalry skirmished with the enemy at Tunnel Hill the following day. By 5:00 P.M. on the eleventh, Wilson's men and all their supplies were safely in Resaca, where General Wayne awaited them. Wilson reported that they had fallen back leisurely with no straggling; the closeness of Federal troopers must have had a salutary effect on any potential laggards. Having had to abandon its section of the road, the Second Regiment was to remain for the next three months at Resaca, now the northernmost post of the Georgia State Line.[58]

During the Second Regiment's retreat, many of the men of the First Regiment continued to strengthen Resaca's fortifications, though hampered by guard and picket duties. When Galt requested reinforcements, Wayne told him to "Rally the reserve Home Guards. . . . " Galt replied that, unarmed as they were, he "had about as well summon the Jay Birds." Wayne himself received orders concerning Resaca from the Commander-in-Chief in Milledgeville: unless Bragg decided to give up the country as far down as Kingston, Wayne was to "fight for Resaca Bridge and never surrender it while . . . possible to hold it."[59]

Soon, to the north, battle was joined as Bragg's men attacked the Union army of General William S. Rosecrans. The "longest Confederate troop movement by rail" of the war had not yet been completed; ramshackle trains rattling up from Atlanta had brought Bragg only three brigades of Longstreet's Corps when the first phase of the Battle of Chickamauga began on 19 September near LaFayette. That afternoon, as the fighting wound down into bloody stalemate, Longstreet himself arrived at Catoosa Platform and struck out with his aides to locate General Bragg. Two more

[57]Wilson to Wayne, 12 September 1863, Cuyler (Wayne); Adjutant General's 1863 Report, 5.

[58]Wilson to Wayne, 12 September 1863, Cuyler (Wayne); Adjutant General's 1863 Report, 5; Nathan Bedford Forrest to Brown, 12 September 1863, GLB, GDAH; Morning Report Book, First Regiment, Georgia State Troops, passim, Special Collections, University of Georgia Libraries, Athens GA: (hereafter referred to as Morning Report Book). Colonel William H. Dabney's First Regiment, Georgia State Guard, is listed in the Morning Report Book as serving with the Second Regiment and a battalion of the First Regiment, Georgia State Line, during October and November 1863.

[59]Wayne to Galt, 6 September 1863, Cuyler (Wayne); Galt to Wayne, 6 September 1863, AGIC, GDAH; Brown to Wayne, 12 September 1863, GLB, GDAH.

brigades followed him. When fighting was renewed on the twentieth, the Army of Tennessee "won its greatest victory," although at great cost.[60]

After the scare was past and the battle won, General Wayne received favorable notice from the press. A special correspondent of the *Atlanta Intelligencer* wrote of the "skill and expedition with which General Henry C. Wayne has organized and put into the field the state troops. . . . General Wayne has no superior for administrative talent as a field officer."[61]

But the abandonment of Chattanooga during the Chickamauga Campaign and its permanent loss during the disastrous campaign of the following October and November left "twenty-five miles of the state road . . . in enemy hands. The Western & Atlantic had become two railroads, each a supply artery for an army."[62]

When he made his annual report to the governor, General Wayne was very complimentary of the two regiments. Dated 26 October 1863, his report began with a glowing history of the State Line and a call for its continued service:

> In addition to their appropriate duties, the State Line has done much effective service in arresting deserters, suppressing disloyalty, preventing straggling from the army, and protecting the inhabitants from oppression; and the 1st Regiment has contributed materially to the efficient running and condition of the State Road, by furnishing details for laying track, cutting wood and cross ties, rebuilding bridges, guarding depots and workshops and performing other details in connection with the Road, for which labor could not otherwise have been obtained.[63]

In defense of the State Line's continued existence, Wayne invoked the specter of slave rebellion. Some men, Wayne noted, suggested that a home guard would be cheaper, but such critics exhibited an unmilitary cast of mind; there was simply no comparison. On the one hand was "the superior efficiency and moral force of a regularly organized, permanent military body, devoted to military duties exclusively"; on the other hand, a "*quasi* military organization scattered throughout the country, in pursuit of civil

---

♥ [60]Joseph B. Mitchell, *Decisive Battles of the Civil War* (Greenwich CT: Fawcett Publications, Inc., 1955) 163, 165; G. Moxley Sorrel, *Recollections of a Confederate Staff Officer* (New York: The Neal Publishing Co., 1905) 185; James Longstreet, *From Manassas to Appomattox* (Philadelphia: J. P. Lippincott Co., 1896)437-38; Connelly, *Autumn of Glory,* 208, 226.

[61]*Atlanta Intelligencer,* 22 September 1863. The reference probably embraces Wayne's work with the Georgia State Guard as well as the State Line.

[62]Black, *Railroads,* 248.

[63]Adjutant General's 1863 Report, 5-6. Later both Bragg and his successor Johnston expressed dissatisfaction with the service provided by the road, but there were numerous reasons for the increasing inefficiency, few of them the fault of Brown. Black, *Railroads,* 195-96. It can be assumed that the service would have been even worse without the labors of the State Line.

occupations, and who on a sudden surprise are to be brought together, without discipline, or proficiency in military exercises. . . ." These "few scattered white men," Wayne asserted, would be "like separate sticks, easily broken," while the State Line was "like a bundle of rods securely tied, strong, firm, and powerful in use."[64]

Strangely enough, late November found this "bundle of rods" in the possession of none other than Major General Howell Cobb, Governor Brown's archenemy, then commander of the Georgia State Guard. General Wayne had had to return to the capital to help the governor deal with the legislature and to carry out a number of duties—foremost among them the reorganization of the Georgia Militia. Consequently, Brown persuaded General Cobb to assume temporary command of the State Line, whose services had been tendered to General Bragg for duties of any nature anywhere within the state.[65]

The Line's tour under Cobb was brief and fairly uneventful, despite another controversial episode involving Colonel Galt. Cobb found Galt uncooperative, even to the extent of not forwarding his troop strengths in a timely fashion. More seriously, Cobb received charges from a Confederate officer at Resaca that there was a "want of vigilance" on Galt's part at the garrison there; artillery and ammunition were said to have been left unguarded. This report brought a sharp rebuke of Galt by Wayne: Galt's customary excuses followed.[66]

In late December the Line, still commanded by Cobb, was pulled back from Resaca and the companies redistributed. The First Regiment's headquarters was at Camp Foster, Etowah. The Second Regiment had headquarters at Camp Ruff, near Bolton—a Cobb County railway station just north of the Chattahoochee and some seven miles from Atlanta. There Wilson's men were employed in constructing fortifications and guarding the bridge.[67]

---

[64]Adjutant General's 1863 Report, 6.

[65]Wayne to General Joseph E. Johnston, 28 December 1863, AGLB No. 20, GDAH; Wayne to General Howell Cobb, 16 November 1863, ibid.; Wayne to General Braxton Bragg, 25 November 1863, ibid.

[66]Cobb abandoned an early plan to shift the First Regiment to Rome. R. J. Hallet to Galt, 25 November 1863, Howell Cobb Letter and Telegram Book, 1863-1864, Cobb-Erwin-Lamar Collection, Special Collections, University of Georgia Libraries, Athens, GA; Hallet to Galt, 16 November 1863, ibid.; Wayne to Galt, 24 November 1863, AGLB No. 20, GDAH; Wayne to Galt, 1 December 1863, ibid.

[67]Wayne to Johnston, 28 December 1863, AGLB No. 20, GDAH; Wayne to Johnston, 20 April 1864, AGLB No. 23, GDAH; Wayne to Johnston, 28 December 1863, AGLB No. 20, GDAH. Camp Ruff was apparently named for Colonel S. Z. Ruff of the 18th Georgia. Formerly an instructor at G.M.I., he had been killed at Knoxville on 29 November 1863. Lynwood M. Holland, "Georgia Military Institute, The West Point of Georgia: 1851-1864," *Georgia Historical Quarterly* 43 (September 1959): 235.

By December's end, Bragg had been replaced by General Joseph E. Johnston, who took command of the Confederate army at Dalton; there began that "long period of inactivity" from December until May which preceded General William T. Sherman's Atlanta Campaign. Brown informed Johnston, as he had Bragg, that the state regiments were at his service for any function within Georgia, including field duty.[68]

Johnston took Brown up on his offer. Soon a request for State Line men was forwarded by Colonel Leon von Zinken, Confederate commander at Marietta; he wanted two companies for guard duty at his post. This re-

The railroad bridge over the Chattahoochee River, showing earthworks constructed by the Second State Line. (From an 1864 photograph by George N. Barnard. Courtesy of the Library of Congress.)

---

[68]Wayne to Johnston, 28 December 1863, AGLB No. 20, GDAH; Connelly, *Autumn of Glory,* 281.

quest came to Colonel Wilson in mid-December, just before his relocation to Bolton. He was at Resaca with his regiment and four companies belonging to Galt, who was on leave. Wilson reasoned that it would be better to leave the Second Regiment intact and send two of Galt's companies to Marietta. As might be expected, several months of controversy were generated by this decision. The attitude of Galt and his men to Von Zinken—not only a Confederate officer but also a Prussian martinet with a heavy accent—can be readily imagined.[69]

The new year brought more problems with both regiments. Galt complained about trouble with Confederates: those at Cartersville had been cursing and terrorizing the State Line troops stationed there, he wrote Wayne. But an increasing number of problems were related to Galt personally; he had become progressively bothersome, and Wayne had had to chastise him a number of times. Accompanying his lack of vigilance at Resaca had been such misdeeds as the "trivial arrest" of one of his men, interference with a court-martial, and tampering with the Line companies at Marietta, where Colonel von Zinken complained that Galt continuously sought to impede his lawful orders.[70]

Also involved in this last-mentioned controversy was Major John M. Brown. He had written a letter containing "improper and insulting language" that fomented disobedience in the command at Marietta. Major Brown received a reprimand from Wayne, who informed him that the governor's first reaction to the letter was to have his brother tried for "insubordination and conduct subversive of military discipline." Fortunately he had decided on reflection that John's actions were more thoughtless than deliberate; the reprimand was deemed sufficient punishment.[71]

Since Galt and young Brown had claimed their actions had been provoked by the Confederates, Wayne went on to point out that any "injuries" done to members of the Line by the Confederates were not to be settled by the men involved but by General Johnston and the governor. Wayne concluded:

> His Excellency trusts that this is the last he shall hear of jealousies and disagreements between the State Line and Confederate troops, and he directs me to say that while he is ever ready to maintain the just rights of Georgia troops, he will not countenance or uphold them in conduct subversive to order

---

[69]Wilson to Wayne, 13 December 1863, AGIC, GDAH; Ella Lonn, *Foreigners in the Confederacy* (Gloucester MA: Peter Smith, 1965) 142-43.

[70]Galt to Wayne, 19 January 1864, AGIC, GDAH; Wayne to Galt, 4 February 1864, AGLB No. 22, GDAH; Wayne to Galt, 5 November 1863, AGLB No. 20, GDAH; Colonel Leon von Zinken to Colonel George W. Brent, 20 January 1864, Civil War Miscellany—Personal Papers, GDAH.

[71]Wayne to Major John M. Brown, 3 February 1864, AGLB No. 22, GDAH.

and discipline, without which our Armies can never hope to be successful or our country independent.[72]

In March, however, the governor's other State Line brother became involved in the Marietta controversy. At Galt's instigation, Dr. Aaron Brown traveled from the State Line hospital in Jonesboro to investigate charges of "maltreatment and neglect" of State Line soldiers in the Confederate hospital at the Marietta post. In Colonel von Zinken's absence, Captain Albert Howell properly resisted Brown's interference, further fueling the controversy in some eyes. It was later found that the charges were baseless, having been made by a soldier who wanted a transfer to the Jonesboro hospital because he had heard there were few patients and an abundance of "good things to eat" there. This episode led the governor to forestall further interference from Galt by detaching the State Line companies and putting them directly under von Zinken's orders. Captain Howell also clashed with Galt personally over the colonel's refusal to return Howell's company's Enfield rifles, loaned to Galt's original company while Howell's men were on artillery duty. Major Brown had sided with Howell in the controversy, which ended with Galt's being ordered to surrender the arms.[73]

The Second Regiment was also bothersome, when, during January 1864, Colonel Wilson engaged in an unseemly squabble with Seaborn Saffold, one of his company commanders. A graduate of Virginia Military Institute, Saffold, twenty-six, was an attorney from Morgan County, namesake of his noted physician father and brother of influential politician Thomas P. Saffold. In a letter to General Wayne, dated 17 January 1864, Saffold outlined a number of charges and specifications against Colonel Wilson, requesting that his commanding officer be court-martialed. The charges against the regimental commander were drunkenness while on duty, conduct unbecoming an officer (including "coarse, vulgar, and obscene language regarding ladies known to the officers and men present"), and conduct prejudicial to good order (allowing officers and men to bring liquor to camp). According to Saffold, eleven other officers had witnessed various of Wilson's offenses.[74]

Wayne then received a letter dated the nineteenth charging that Saffold had made his charges in a "malicious and vindictive spirit" inspired

---

[72]Ibid.

[73]Wayne to Dr. Brown, 22 March 1864, AGLB No. 22, GDAH; Wayne to Dr. Brown, 6 April 1864, AGLB No. 23, GDAH; Wayne to Galt, 17 May 1864, AGLB No. 24, GDAH.

[74]*Selma (AL) Times-Journal,* 7 November 1927; U.S. Bureau of the Census, Schedule 1, Free Inhabitants, Morgan County, Georgia; Mattie Saffold, interview held in Morgan County, Georgia, 27 August 1980; Captain Seaborn Saffold to Wayne, 17 January 1864, Courts-Martial.

by "some sharp words drawn from the Colonel" by Saffold's unofficerlike conduct regarding a clothing requisition. This letter was signed by twenty-two officers including, interestingly enough, several who had supposedly witnessed instances of the colonel's misconduct.[75]

On the twentieth, Wayne returned Saffold's charges, which had not been sent properly through the chain of command. In an attempt to prevent Saffold from getting into deeper trouble, Wayne—showing more knowledge of the affair than Saffold might have expected—called his attention to five of the Articles of War, all of which Saffold had violated. Undeterred, Saffold had Colonel Galt reforward the charges on 26 January.[76]

By that time, Wilson, informed of Saffold's action, had placed the captain under arrest and forwarded seven charges against him to General Wayne. Among the charges were that Saffold had submitted false musters and received pay and allowances for discharged men, that he had disobeyed the orders of a superior officer, and that he had twice been absent without leave from his post—once after having been left in command of the camp. Furthermore Wilson stated that Saffold had violated the twenty-fifth Article of War by twice sending him a letter demanding an apology and that he had said he would shoot Wilson if the colonel entered his tent.[77]

After his arrest, a chastened Saffold informed Wayne in an "unofficial and confidential" letter that Wilson was indeed guilty on all counts, but the captain proclaimed his own innocence of the false muster charge and desired vindication. In regard to the other charges, he professed unconcern—they did not reflect upon his honor. He added that he wished Wilson no harm, that he had been his friend and had helped make him colonel. Saffold ended by asking Wayne to have him freed and sent home until his court-martial convened since "confinement with nothing to divert my mind is unpleasant in the extreme."[78]

Wayne did not officially submit either set of charges to the governor, discussing both with him instead. Brown's opinion was that the officers' differences should be accommodated without an official investigation, since

---

[75]Officers of the Second Regiment, Georgia State Line, to Wayne, 19 January 1864, Courts-Martial. On New Year's Day 1864 Saffold had entered Wilson's quarters in a "boistrous and disrespectful" manner. He had ranted about a clothing requisition and had declared that the clothing commutation "did not amount to a damned pinch of [dung]." Wilson, in turn, had "remarked in passionate terms"—and with some profanity—that he "did not care to have any more of [Saffold's] _____ - _____ slack Jaw." This incident sparked the entire controversy. Saffold to Wayne, 17 January 1864, Courts-Martial; Wilson to Wayne, 23 January 1864, ibid.

[76]Wayne's and Galt's endorsements on Saffold's letter of 17 January 1864, Courts-Martial.

[77]Wilson to Wayne, 22 January 1864, Cuyler (Wayne); Wilson to Wayne, 23 January 1864, Courts-Martial.

[78]Saffold to Wayne, 24 January 1864, Courts-Martial.

it was obvious that the charges, some of which dated back several months, were produced "by a personal animosity, and not by public good." Any charges should have been brought forward when the offenses occurred, "not . . . when personal rancor [gave] them vent."[79]

In Wayne's response to Saffold, which he ordered shown to Wilson, the adjutant general advised that all charges be dropped and that the two "come to a courteous if not a friendly understanding." Otherwise, Wayne, said, he would arraign them both for neglect of duty.[80]

Even before Wayne suggested the matter be dropped, several officers of the regiment had attempted to reconcile Saffold and Wilson. Prominent among them was Lieutenant Colonel Evans, himself previously the subject of confidential charges. According to Wilson, these officers talked him into the compromise. In his letter to Wayne, however, he continued to defend all his actions and avowed himself "as good a friend as [Saffold] had in the regiment."[81] He explained, in an admission that suggests one cause for the lack of discipline in his command, "it has been my object to secure the friendship and good will of the officers of the Regt. that our labors . . . might be more effective." Wilson concluded, "I shall treat Capt. Saffold as a Gentleman & officer, but he must obey my orders."[82] Wayne wrote Evans that the governor was "gratified with the Settlement of the Matter without recourse to judicial proceedings. . . . " The matter would be considered closed when both officers wrote officially that they withdrew their charges. This was done, finally bringing the affair to a close.[83]

In early February, men of the First Regiment again had to deal with insurgents. Wayne had Galt send an officer with "fifteen to twenty men" to Cherokee County where a "mob of women," apparently incited by two Confederate deserters, had broken into a tannery and stolen a quantity of leather. The rioters had escaped punishment when they were upheld at their trial by two renegade constables. The state troops were to return the deserters to the authorities at Atlanta, recover the leather, and see that the trial be reheld. The constables would be investigated with a view toward having them removed for malpractice. In March increased problems with Tories and deserters in north Georgia led to the creation of a State Line cavalry company drawn from Galt's regiment.[84]

There continued to be a deterioration in the conduct of the First Regiment and its commander. In mid-April 1864 Colonel Galt finally exhausted his su-

---

[79]Wayne to "My dear Saffold," 4 February 1864, AGLB No. 21, GDAH.

[80]Ibid.

[81]Wilson to Wayne, 9 February 1864, Courts-Martial.

[82]Ibid.

[83]Wayne to Evans, 12 February 1864, AGLB No. 22, GDAH.

[84]Wayne to Galt, 1 February 1864, AGLB No. 21, GDAH; Cowen to Wayne, 29 March 1864, AGIC, GDAH. See Appendix I.

periors' patience by neglecting to see that a scheduled court-martial proceed
as ordered. Wayne informed Galt that the governor wished him to know that
he had long been aware of a lack of discipline in Galt's force, but that the matter of the court-martial marked a "greater deficiency than he had supposed
to exist. . . . " The governor wished to see Galt "bring the regiment into proper
training and discipline."[85]

Galt's intemperate, excuse-ridden response[86] drew a remarkably
scathing letter from the usually tolerant adjutant general. After assuring
Galt that the governor's order for the court-martial to proceed was not an
unwarrantable interference in Galt's affairs, Wayne wrote:

> Discipline does not consist, as your letter seems to convey the idea of it, only
> in "drilling"—but embraces the higher and more important duties of knowl-
> edge of regulations and military law; prompt, hearty obedience to them, which
> is called subordination; and a strict fulfillment of all the requirements of the
> profession—A knowledge of the "drill" is essential, but by no means all of a
> soldier's duty. . . . It was to the absence of a proper sense of the higher duties
> of which the Governor spoke and directed a reproof; and in which your letter
> . . . justly sustains them.
>
> Neither he nor I take any pleasure in "raking a fellow down" as you express
> it. But where a due regard to duty requires censure, it must be given though
> the giving it be unpleasant to both parties. The difficulties you mention present
> no difficulties in reality to one conversant with military duty.[87]

Galt's unfitness as an officer had also been brought to General Johnston's attention, for the governor had determined that both regiments
should join the Confederate army for the spring campaign. In advising
Johnston how to employ the regiments, Wayne informed the general of the
difficulties with Galt's command:

> The First Regiment has been drawn upon heavily for details . . . and having
> field officers by no means of a military aptitude or ambition, is not in a good
> state of military instruction or discipline, and cannot be unless after long
> service in the field. Under these circumstances it would be well not to sep-
> arate the companies of that Regiment, weakened as it is, by assigning them
> to garrison duty with other troops, but to keep them as far as can be done at
> their headquarters, Camp Foster, or if necessary to detach them, to do so on
> duty by themselves.[88]

Wayne continued by saying that it would be best in the governor's view
to put both units in the field. Brown hoped to be able to brigade them to-

---

[85]Wayne to Galt, 14 April 1864, AGLB No. 23, GDAH.

[86]Galt to Wayne, 19 April 1864, AGIC, GDAH.

[87]Wayne to Galt, 26 April 1864, AGLB No. 23, GDAH.

[88]Wayne to Johnston, 3 February 1864, AGLB No. 22, GDAH.

gether with Wayne in command, but until that time the regiments should be separate units. Otherwise, Galt, the senior colonel, would be in command, and, as Wayne noted, he was "not competent for the position."[89]

Serious business was obviously at hand. The officers and men of the Georgia State Line were leaving their relatively secure posts to enter war's crucible.

---

[89]Ibid.

CHAPTER VI

With the Army of Tennessee

By May 1864 the State Line had spent fourteen months on duty along the Western and Atlantic Railroad. They had successfully protected the bridges and helped keep the trains moving; they had done much in fortifying strategic points along the rail line; and they had several times moved away from the road to quell insurrections and capture deserters. Also, two companies had helped to garrison the Confederate post at Marietta.

Despite all these constructive labors, much about the State Line's tenure on the road had been less than praiseworthy. There had been debilitating dissension among both officers and men, as well as conflict with Confederate troops and authorities. And there had been insubordinate acts directed toward both the governor and the adjutant general. Some of these problems were engendered by the personalities of the Line's officers; some doubtless were spawned by the monotonous and burdensome nature of the men's duties.

In May all this ended. As the Confederate and Union armies once again began to stir, and the Army of Tennessee began to fall back under General William T. Sherman's advance, General Joseph E. Johnston finally accepted Governor Brown's offer to send the State Line to the front. His acceptance made sense. Since Johnston's bloody retrograde movement from Dalton to Resaca to Cassville had finally brought the Confederate army to the Etowah River, much of the railroad that the Line had helped defend was now in enemy hands, supplying enemy soldiers. And the First Regiment's long-held posts[1] at Cartersville and Etowah station had to be abandoned to the enemy.[1]

---

[1]Bryan, *Confederate Georgia,* 156-157. Galt and Wilson had been warned by Special Orders, No. 1, 21 January 1864, to prepare their men for service with the Army of Tennessee. The Confederacy was to provide everything but pay and clothing while the troops were attached to the army. Seddon, however, wrote Brown, "The troops must be turned over as militia to Confederate service; in that event the enemy are bound and have always respected the captives as prisoners of war. They have refused so to recognize troops merely in State Service." John O. Ferrill to P. W. Douglas, 1 November 1864, AGLB No. 27, GDAH; Seddon to Brown, 7 June 1864, GLB, GDAH.

On 20 May 1864, the First Regiment received orders to report to General Johnston near Etowah, where the Army of Tennessee had just that day crossed the Etowah River. Galt's men, heretofore relatively fortunate in their military duties, were about to be initiated into the horrors of war, and they would have to undergo their initiation at half strength. About sixty men were hospitalized, and another one hundred—withdrawn to form Cowen's cavalry—were never to rejoin the regiment. Moreover, a substantial number of men had deserted, while other men carried on the rolls had actually been detailed to various factories and had never seen a State Line camp. This left the First Regiment with only 550 men present for duty.[2]

The First Regiment, and particularly its commander, must have been greatly chagrined by Johnston's first order. The command was to report to Galt's nemesis, Lieutenant Colonel Leon von Zinken, for duty with the Marietta garrison. Upon arrival some men were made provost guards while others were assigned to move Confederate supplies from Marietta to Atlanta.

As might have been foreseen, some of the regiment's officers petitioned Johnston to move them to a "post of duty and honor" with the Confederate army. And on the twenty-eighth, as the fighting along Johnston's Dallas-New Hope Church line was degenerating into skirmishing, the First Regiment was sent to the front. There it joined five other Georgia regiments in Brigadier General Marcellus A. Stovall's Brigade, Stewart's Division, Hood's Corps. There they began to take part in Johnston's attempt to withstand Sherman's advances and block his flanking movements, a process accurately described as a "slow retreat southward along the Western and Atlantic Railroad."[3]

Writing to Wayne from near New Hope Church on 31 May, Galt described the area as a "broken wilderness country"; the army, which was in a strong position, Galt described as "in fine spirits & confident." Galt's small portion of that army, however, had apparently overindulged in spirits, probably due to the stresses produced by the "skirmish fighting" in which they had been engaged since they reported for duty: "Had whiskey ration issued us yesterday & I think much the worse for it today—I would be glad to have no more for my regiment. My Lieut Col was drunk . . . when . . . an engagement was most probable."[4] Galt wished that he had put him in arrest and left him behind; in any case, the officer was to resign within two

---

[2]Report of the Operations of the First Georgia State Line from 20 May 1864 to 24 October 1864, State Line Miscellany, GDAH (hereafter referred to as Report of Operations); Report of Sick in General Hospital at Jonesboro, 15-31 May 1864, Map Cabinet Drawer 1, Folder 16, GDAH; Special Orders, No. 65, 19 April 1864, Special Orders, GDAH (hereafter referred to as SO); Wayne to Galt, 3, 5 May 1864, AGIC, GDAH; Cowen to Wayne, 31 March 1864, ibid.

[3]Report of Operations; Bryan, *Confederate Georgia*, 157; *OR*, vol. 38, pt. 3:649

[4]Galt to Wayne, 31 May 1864, AGIC, GDAH.

weeks. Galt's letter continued in a positive vein that must have surprised and pleased General Wayne. Combat duty seemed to be the prescription that the recalcitrant colonel had needed.[5]

On 2 June half the regiment was "placed out on picket duty in a very dangerous and much exposed position." Although this was their first time out, the men held up well—so well that they received the compliments of General Stovall.

During the next few days, as Johnston shifted his line eastward, the Line's brigade evacuated the trenches near New Hope Church and fell back to Lost Mountain. There the troops remained for several days, putting up works before withdrawing again eastward.[6] Galt reported some of his men sick and a number barefoot. "Cloth shoes are a great humbug," he wrote.[7]

By this time, the Second Regiment, which had remained at Bolton, had received its marching orders. Delayed at first because there was no one to relieve them of duty, the men of the regiment also had to await the return of three companies that were cutting a road to Marietta. In mid-June, near Kennesaw Mountain, Wilson's command, approximately seven hundred strong, joined the four Georgia regiments of Brigadier General Alfred Cumming in Stevenson's Division of Hood's Corps. They arrived just in time for the struggles that centered around Kennesaw from 10 June to 3 July.[8]

The First Regiment's division continued moving to the right, crossing the State Road just below Big Shanty; it then crossed the Marietta Road and moved back to within half a mile of the railway, throwing up works and remaining there until 15 June. During these movements the men continued to do their part as pickets and skirmishers.[9]

By the twentieth, Stevenson's Division had recrossed the rail line and was encamped close to Kennesaw Mountain. From there they marched through Marietta and down the Powder Springs Road some three miles. The First Regiment helped hold the foward line while works were con-

---

[5]Ibid.; James Bryan to Wayne, 11 June 1864, AGIC, GDAH.

[6]Report of Operations.

[7]Galt to Wayne, 6 June 1864, AGIC, GDAH.

[8]Wilson to Wayne, 6 June 1864, AGIC, GDAH; Monthly Report, Second Regiment, Georgia State Line, May 1864, State Line Miscellany, GDAH; OR, vol. 38, pt. 3:649; Bryan, Confederate Georgia, 157. The assignments of the State Line regiments during the Atlanta Campaign are found in the OR volume previously cited, on pages 649, 657, 663, 664, and 672. The regiments are invariably styled 1st and 2nd Georgia State Troops in these citations. Colonel John B. Willcoxson, commander of the Second Calvary Regiment, Georgia State Guard, is erroneously listed as the Second State Line's commander on 663.

[9]Report of Operations.

structed in the rear; then they withdrew to those works and participated in heavy skirmishing until the next withdrawal the first week in July.[10]

During this time Galt's men suffered few casualties—a skirmish on 18 June provided the major exception. Describing the action of that day, the *Atlanta Intelligencer* stated that "for two hours a galling fire was poured into [the First Regiment's] ranks, sixteen of them being wounded."

> Among the wounded was Major Jno. M. Brown . . . whom we had the pleasure of seeing yesterday and who has been assigned to one of the hospitals in this city. This gallant young soldier was wounded on the occasion referred to in the right shoulder. The wound is a painful one but will not long, we learn, keep him from his regiment.[11]

The article added that the Second Regiment was serving with like gallantry, having recently skirmished with the enemy, and lost eleven men out of one company alone. The "active and gallant service of these regiments," said the paper, "should vindicate them in the eyes of those who had considered them 'Brown's Pets.' "[12]

By this time Johnston's new line stretched from Kennesaw Mountain eastward across the State Road.[13] On 22 June Lieutenant Colonel Evans described the Second Regiment's portion of that line, his men's earlier movements, and his opinions on the Confederate situation in a letter to his brother, Confederate brigadier N. G. Evans:

> We are bivouaced in the woods with no covering or conveniences whatever & the rain for the last 15 days has been incessant—I have not been dry in a week and everything I have is in like condition. Roads are intolerably muddy & retard movements very much—perhaps this is to our advantage. Since I have been with Gen Johnston's Army we have done nothing but retreat, yet these retreats have been so far successful if we except the country given up. The fact is Johnston is sagacious enough but has not the force to resist the enemy in his line of policy—Here "Spades are trumps" & both armies do but form line of battle & entrench for miles. The Yankees tho' outnumbering us greatly, will not meet us in open field or accept battle when we tender it; having large numbers, [they] continue to flank on the left & then on the right. Sherman's Army it is estimated number 120,000 men which is much disproportioned to ours. Our lines three days ago were three miles in advance of Kennesaw Mt. and Marietta. Now they run along the base & this side making an obtuse angle with Kennesaw for the right. It is most probable that [there will be] a further falling back to the Chattahoochie River before

---

[10]*OR*, vol. 38, pt. 3:814; Evans to N. G. Evans, 22 June 1864, Evans Collection, in private possession; Report of Operations.

[11]*Atlanta Intelligencer*, 23 June 1864, quoted in the *Daily Columbus Enquirer*, 25 June 1864.

[12]Ibid.

[13]Connelly, *Autumn of Glory*, 357-59.

Private S. J. Baldwin, Company E, First Regiment, Georgia State Line. Aged fifteen years, he was a casualty of the fighting around Kennesaw Mountain. (From a wartime ambrotype. Courtesy of Kennesaw Mountain National Battlefield Park, Marietta, Georgia.)

anything like a decisive conflict will take place. We can and do whip the enemy whenever they come out and fight us like men in open field—but both armies seem distrustful of charging the other's breastworks. What the end will be none of us can foretell—And even all my speculations may be very much at fault, as men of my grade know very little & have few opportunities of observation. Gen Hardee repulsed the enemy yesterday very handsomely with heavy loss in their side & captured 500 prisoners. Our Corps—Hood— have not been engaged, as yet—except in heavy skirmishing.[14]

The first engagement came that afternoon. The Second Regiment was in the first line as Stevenson's Division charged over "unfavorable ground" and struck the enemy's works at Kolb Farm near Kennesaw Mountain. As General Stevenson reported, "The fire . . . was exceedingly heavy, and the artillery of the enemy, which was massed in large force and admirably posted, was served with a rapidity and fatal precision which could not be surpassed."[15] The Second Regiment suffered eighty casualties, representing ten percent of Stevenson's heavy loss.[16]

In early July, as the Second Regiment's division withdrew toward Atlanta, its sister regiment's division held the line. Then on 5 July the First Regiment took over guard duty from the Georgia Militia at the Chattahoochee Bridge fortifications, where there was again intense skirmishing. General Johnston, alarmed by reports that the enemy was crossing the Chattahoochee to his right, ordered his army to move to the river's south bank. When the army completed the crossing on the ninth, it struck out to the southeast. Before long the Confederates were again throwing up works, skirmishing, and retreating again.[17]

Having lost Richmond's confidence, General Johnston was replaced by General John Bell Hood on 17 July. Three days later came "Hood's First Sortie," the Battle of Peachtree Creek. Although the First Regiment's brigade was not involved in the battle proper, Colonel Galt somehow received a serious wound in the left forearm during the day's fighting. He was never to resume field command. John M. Brown, lately elected to replace Galt's drunken second-in-command, became commander of the First Regiment.[18]

Two days after the repulse of the twentieth, Hood launched his second sortie, later known as the Battle of Atlanta. During this battle east of the city, the brigade including Brown's command attacked the enemy's works near the Troup Hurt house. During the first charge the governor's brother sustained what proved to be a mortal wound in the thigh. Since the major's

---

[14]Evans to N. G. Evans, 22 June 1864, Evans Collection.

[15]*OR,* vol. 38,: pt. 3:815.

[16]Ibid.; *Macon Daily Telegraph,* 29 June 1864.

[17]Report of Operations.

[18]Ibid.; Connelly, *Autumn of Glory,* 241.

position, vacated by Brown, had not been filled, command devolved on Albert Howell, senior captain of the regiment.[19]

According to a later account, perhaps somewhat embellished, Howell and his men were at that point

> lying on the ground under withering fire from an entrenched battery of the enemy, but . . . Howell sprang to the command and yelled: "Follow me, boys, and let's take the works!" Waving his sword he ran down the line through a hail of bullets calling on his men to follow. Following their gallant young leader they stormed the Federal breastworks and captured DeGress' battery, which had been playing havoc in the Confederate lines.[20]

Lt. Col. John M. Brown, First Regiment, Georgia State Line. (From a photograph, date unknown. Courtesy of the Atlanta Historical Society.)

---

[19]Report of Operations.

[20]*Atlanta Constitution,* 25 August 1927.

Having taken eighty-seven prisoners, Howell's men and the other Confederate troops retained possession of the battery for the better part of an hour before being forced to fall back. The regiment had suffered ninety-two casualties.[21]

In his report of the battle, Major General Henry D. Clayton, division commander, wrote, "In this engagement I lost many brave men and officers. Conspicuous among the latter [was] Lieutenant-Colonel Brown, of First Georgia State Line, Stovall's Brigade."[22] Transported to Milledgeville, Brown died there on 25 July. Funeral services were held in the Executive Mansion, after which Brown was buried in the nearby city cemetery. Years later the governor had a large monument placed over his brother's grave.[23]

During the siege that followed the Battle of Atlanta, both regiments did duty in the "ditches" around the city. As one State Line private recalled,

> I have watched the burning fuses of shells as they passed over our heads for many nights, and while we were doing picket duty between our lines and the enemy, the shot and shell were continually passing over our heads, crashing into houses and mowing down trees and playing havoc with everything they came in contact with.[24]

On 7 August a Federal assault on some of the entrenchments near Utoy Creek west of the city resulted in the capture of about three hundred and fifty Confederates, among them thirty-nine members of the First Regiment.[25] Three days later Howell reported to Wayne that he had less than one hundred men reporting for duty.[26]

On 30 August Hood sent Generals S. D. Lee and William J. Hardee from Atlanta to defend the railroad at Jonesboro; both State Line regiments saw action in the ensuing battle of 31 August. Stovall's Brigade suffered twenty-five percent casualties, sixteen of them Howell's men, while the Second Regiment met catastrophe. Out of the two hundred men sent into battle, one hundred and five were killed or wounded. "Many of our bravest and

---

[21]Report of Operations.

[22]*OR,* vol. 38, pt. 3:819.

[23]*Milledgeville Southern Recorder,* 3 August 1864; Brown's monument, Memory Hill Cemetery, Milledgeville, Baldwin County, Georgia, on-site inspection by author, 16 April 1979. The monument, sixteen feet tall, was purchased by Brown for $700 in 1879. William Gray to Brown, 2 December 1879, Brown Scrapbook, Box 8, Brown/Connally/Spalding Collection, GDAH.

[24]Jackson Diary, Jackson Papers.

[25]*OR,* vol. 38, pt. 1:510.

[26]Howell to Wayne, 10 August 1864, AGIC, GDAH.

best men fell in the engagement," wrote the regimental surgeon. One company commander was killed. Captain Northcutt, hero of Second Manassas, had to have an arm amputated; two lieutenants were also consigned to the bone saw, while a third lost both eyes. There were also great losses among the non-commissioned officers, as well as a heavy toll in the ranks.[27]

The Confederate capture of the De Gress Battery during the Battle of Atlanta, in which State Line troops participated. (From an engraving by Alfred R. Waud. Courtesy of the Atlanta Historical Society.)

---

[27]Report of Operations; Jackson Diary, Jackson Papers; *OR,* vol. 38, pt. 3:822, 824-25; *Milledgeville Confederate Union,* 20 September 1864. Written inside the front cover of the First Regiment's Morning Report Book, now held by Special Collections, University of Georgia Libraries, is "This Book was Captured at the Battle of Jonesboro Ga. Augt. 31st 1864. We made the Rebels Dust."

By 1 September the Federals held all railroads leading from Atlanta. Hood abandoned the city, and Sherman's men began to occupy it on 3 September. With Atlanta's fall, it might have seemed certain that Governor Brown would withdraw the State Line. He did withdraw his militia from Hood's force in early September, and the Line's regimental officers wanted their units withdrawn for recruitment. The State Line, however, continued to serve with Hood. After encamping for some time at Lovejoy's Station south of Atlanta, the Line joined the Army of Tennessee on 19 September for its northward march—Hood's attempt to lure Sherman from Atlanta by attacking the Federal supply line.[28]

Lt. Col. Albert Howell, First Regiment, Georgia State Line. (From a postwar photograph. Courtesy of the *Atlanta Constitution.)*

[28]Connelly, *Autumn of Glory,* 466; Bryan, *Confederate Georgia,* 163, 165-66; Hill, *Joseph E. Brown,* 224; Jackson Diary, Jackson Papers; Evans to Wayne, 22 September 1864. AGIC, GDAH. (Although recuperating from his wound far behind the lines in Cuthbert, Georgia, Galt continued to keep in touch with his regiment. In his absence, Albert Howell, newly elected lieutenant colonel, commanded the unit.) A few State Line companies had apparently been withdrawn to Milledgeville in early September because of lack of officers. Special Orders, No. 117, 3 September 1864, SO, GDAH.

The army reached its first destination, a spot between East Point and Palmetto, on the twenty-first; after erecting fortifications they remained there for about a week. Soon afterward Colonel Wilson wrote to General Wayne, saying that both regiments then mustered only two hundred muskets for duty. He requested that the Line be garrisoned at some exposed point in the state so that it could be of service while its members were recruiting and recuperating. Justly concerned that General Hood was about to move from the state, Wilson wrote that the "State Line is not desirous to take one of General Bragg's Kentucky foot races." However, Wilson described his troops as "willing to serve wherever duty requires & I think their Record will show that they are not afraid of the racket."[29]

From 30 September to 3 October, Hood's army moved from Palmetto to the vicinity of Big Shanty. Twenty-year-old Private A. J. Jackson of the Second State Line described the last night of the movement as the "terriblest" he had ever experienced. "We was called into line at dark. We had then too miles to march that night before camping. It had been raining very hard all evening . . . in fact, it had been raining over a week off and on & the army wagons had been passing all day. It was powerful muddy. The mud varied from ankle to knee deep, and it was so very dark that we could not see how to shun the mud at all, so we just plunged in as we came to it. Some lost their shoes; others fell coslap into the mud. I never saw men confused any more in a battle. I herd some as hard swearing that night . . . as I ever herd in my life."[30]

By the twelfth of October the army had reached Resaca. As Jackson recalled, "Just twelve months before . . . we were quietly camping at Resaca, guarding bridges and fortifying the place, little thinking that we would attack the enemy 12 months from that time, in our own works." The enemy defied them, and the Confederates moved toward Dalton. During the day the Second Regiment helped tear up part of the road it had been created to protect.[31]

Having destroyed a considerable amount of track, and having captured several enemy garrisons, Hood's army moved west as Sherman's force arrived at Resaca. Private Jackson did not have pleasant memories of the army's brief encampment in Snake Creek Gap the night of the thirteenth. "We camped on the steepest hillside that night that ever I saw men live on before. A man had to lie right up or down the hill. If he got anyways crossways of the hill, he would have rolled plumb to the bottom before he would stop, without he could catch to a bush . . . , and it was so rocky that it would

---

[29]Jackson Diary, Jackson Papers; Wilson to Wayne, 2 October 1864, Cuyler (Wayne).

[30]A. J. Jackson to "Mr. Editor," 10 November 1864, Jackson Papers (hereafter cited as Jackson Letter). Capitalization and punctuation have been added; the spelling is Jackson's.

[31]Jackson Diary, Jackson Papers.

have bruised him nearly to death by the time he would have gotten to the bottom. Then there was a creek ready to receive him."[32]

The next day, Hood had his men blockade the gap with large trees. Passing through Villanow and Summerville, the Confederate army crossed over into Alabama on 18 October. As Jackson recounted, " . . . we were Georgia State Troops, therefore we did not like to go out of State. But we went on, grumbling as usual. . . . "[33] This grumbling became so consider-able that the officers, fearing that the men would desert, promised them pay and clothing when they reached Blue Pond, Alabama. They drew nothing, and the march and the grumbling resumed. On 21 October the army reached Gadsden, from which Hood was to strike toward Nashville; there all troops but the State Line drew clothing. There also the Confed-erate officers tried to get the Georgia state troops to accompany them on their campaign into Tennessee. Jackson wrote,

> When General Lee heard that we was a going to leave him, he seemed to hate it very much. He asked us to remain with him. Yes, he begged us. Said that he remembered our gallantry at Mount Zion [Kolb Farm] and at At-lanta and also at Jonesborough. He said that we was brave and gallant Georgians. . . . that he felt like he was losing a strong arm when he lost us. . . . We was bound for Georgia, so we left Cumming's old brigade. They also asked us to remain with them. Said that their brigade would be ruined when we left for they often laughed and said that our Regt. was not detached to their Brigade, that their Brigade was detached to us.[34]

Nonetheless, on the twenty-second the State Line departed. As Hood's army marched toward disaster at Franklin and Nashville, the Georgia troops struck off for Blue Mountain, where they took the train to Selma and then a steamboat to Montgomery. There they were given crackers and bacon before departing for Columbus in passenger cars, having been treated "very kindly by the Alabamans." In Columbus, however, they found Geor-gia hospitality somewhat wanting: they had to switch to open boxcars. They left the morning of the twenty-seventh for Macon and arrived there that afternoon, having gotten a good soaking from rains along the way.[35]

---

[32]Richard M. McMurry, *John Bell Hood and the War for Southern Independence* (Lexington: The University Press of Kentucky, 1982) 161; Stanley F. Horn, *The Army of Tennessee: A Military History* (New York: The Bobbs-Merrill Co., 1941) 376; Jackson Diary, Jackson Papers.

[33]Jackson Diary, Jackson Papers. The march of the Army of Tennessee from Palmetto, Georgia, to Gadsden, Alabama, is described in Horn (375-79), McMurry (158-64), and Connelly, *Autumn of Glory* (477-84).

[34]Jackson Diary, Jackson Papers.

[35]Ibid. General Hood, according to Governor Brown, was "prompted by his high sense of propriety" to order the State Line back to Georgia. Brown to General R. C. Tyler, *Athens Southern Watchman,* 18 January 1865.

Meanwhile, Governor Brown had received a telegram sent from Gadsden on 24 October by General Beauregard: "Two regiments Georgia State Line Troops have just been returned to their State. Please send them forthwith to Genl. Smith, if their organization is still to be maintained." Brown replied that he would send them, although his regiments were "nearly destroyed."[36]

Although the troops were allowed several weeks in Macon to recover from their four-hundred-mile odyssey, they found themselves by 14 November back at Lovejoy's Station, the starting point for the "memorable march" so recently concluded. There they joined General G. W. Smith's State army near Atlanta. Soon Sherman's columns would emerge to reintroduce the State Line to the rigors of campaigning.[37]

---

[36]Beauregard to Brown, 24 October 1864, GLB, GDAH; Brown to Beauregard, 25 October 1864, ibid.

[37]Jackson Letter, Jackson Papers.

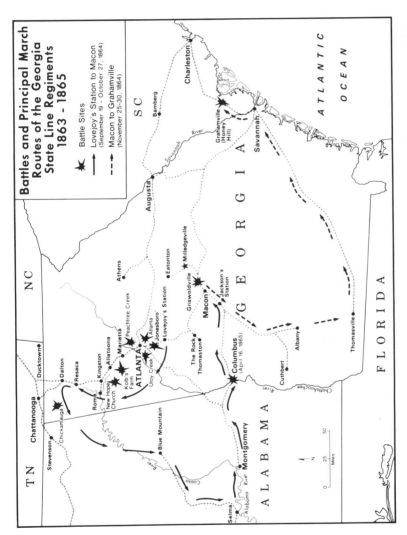

Map 3. Battles and principal march routes of the Georgia State Line regiments, 1863-1865. (After Plates 76, 1; 88, 1; and 135-A, Atlas to Accompany the Official Records of the Union and Confederate Armies [Washington DC: Government Printing Office, 1881-1895]).

CHAPTER VII

"Their Shattered Ranks"

During the spring and summer of 1864, while the State Line was fighting alongside the Army of Tennessee, Governor Brown was once again doing battle with the Richmond government and its agents. This new round of verbal skirmishing had been sparked by the passage of the third and last conscription act on 17 February 1864. This piece of legislation effectively wrecked Brown's militia reorganization, which he claimed could have produced nearly 30,000 local defense troops to confront Sherman.[1]

General Howell Cobb, tasked by Richmond with organizing the latest conscripts into the Georgia Reserve Force, attempted to persuade the governor to give up some of his thousands of exempted civil and militia officers to serve as Confederate reserves for local defense. This futile undertaking led to over six weeks of amazingly rancorous correspondence.[2]

Having routed Cobb, the governor was faced with the general's good friend, the Anglo-Irish Colonel William M. Browne, Georgia's Commandant of Conscripts, who sought to gather State Line detailed men into Richmond's armies. These men—released from military duty to perform labors considered indispensable to the war effort—had sometimes been detached from their companies and assigned to other tasks: for example, chopping wood for the State Road, working in the State Shoe Shop at Acworth, and serving as teamsters to transport provisions to soldiers' families. But in many cases the men in question would already be employed in factories with state contracts. To keep them safe from the enrolling officers, Governor Brown would have their names added to the State Line muster rolls with the notation that they were detailed to the Milledgeville Manufacturing Company or some other establishment; the men would also be given certificates to prove that they were State Line details. By March

---

[1]*OR*, ser. 4, vol. 3: 178-81; *CR*, 2: 601; *CR*, 3: 659.

[2]Montgomery, *Cobb*, 118-20; *CR*, 3: 504-73, passim.

1864 there were two hundred and thirty-nine detailed men in Galt's regiment alone.[3]

The Confederacy also detailed men from the army in similar fashion under the laws of Congress. But what, Colonel Browne inquired, was the governor's authority for detailing State Line soldiers that he had found employed in a textile factory?[4]

Brown responded on 6 June 1864 that the resolutions which created the organization authorized him to post a sufficient force for the protection of the State Road and use the remainder for "such purposes, and at such points in this State" as the governor deemed advisable. Brown asserted that he could not have been given broader discretion, provided that he was using the men for military purposes. And he was; the men were employed, he said, in making clothes for the soldiers and sacks for hauling corn to soldiers' families.[5]

Colonel Browne was not satisfied that the governor had the right to grant such details, but decided not to press the issue. The governor, however, raised the subject again when, in a proclamation of 9 July he ordered Georgia's Confederate details—except those employed in such war-related industries as munitions factories—to report to the battle front at Atlanta; non-compliance would lead to arrest.[6]

In protesting this decree, Colonel Browne declared that Brown had no more power over the Confederate details than he had over Confederate soldiers "fighting in the ranks." Moreover, he noted that the governor's most recently claimed State Line details had been enrolled in state service after the passage of the third conscription act; therefore, Brown had no claim on those between seventeen and fifty—they were *ipso facto* in Confederate military service under the terms of the act. Consequently, the colonel demanded, with Richmond's concurrence, that the Confederate details be left undisturbed and that state details be enrolled.[7]

---

[3]Wayne to Galt, 30 November 1863, AGLB No. 20, GDAH; Wayne to Evans, 10 November 1863, ibid.; Wayne to Jared I. Whitaker, 12 December 1863, ibid.; Wayne to Galt, 12 February 1864, AGLB No. 22, GDAH; Wayne to Galt, 9 February 1864, ibid.; Wayne to Galt, 11, 17 March 1864, ibid.; Muster Rolls, passim—particularly Company A, First State Line. Brown's sometime agent Leopold Waitzfelder of the Milledgeville Manufacturing Company was among those given State Line details, as was W. J. Kubitshek of the same firm. Wayne to Galt, 9 February 1864 and 25 March 1864, AGLB No. 22, GDAH. Brown's dealings with the Waitzfelders led to scandalous but unsubstantiated charges of private profit at public cost. Fielder, 419.

[4]Moore, *Conscription and Conflict in the Confederacy,* 76-77; Brown to Colonel William M. Browne, 6 June 1864 (citing Browne's query of 1 June 1864), GLB, GDAH.

[5]Brown to Browne, 6 June 1864, GLB, GDAH.

[6]*CR,* 2: 712-13.

[7]Browne to Brown, 20 July 1864, Hargrett Collection.

The gubernatorial salvo this provoked was similar to most of Brown's responses in such cases—a strongly worded rehash of previous arguments. Brown assailed the weaknesses of Confederate strategy, particularly noting Davis's refusal to reinforce Georgia adequately. This refusal, Brown wrote, had forced him to send many state-exempted men and reserve militia to the front. The Confederate details also belonged on the firing line, Brown argued, and would be sent there; their exemptions were no better than those of the state officeholders who were presently serving with the Georgia Militia at Atlanta.[8]

Colonel Browne's contention that the last conscription act had automatically placed certain Georgians in Confederate military service was an absurdity, the governor contended. The Confederacy was entitled only to those men taken by actual enrollment—men who "were served with orders in person to report to Camps of instruction." "Constructive enrollment," such as Colonel Browne described, would not be countenanced in Georgia. Moreover, the State Line details were not to be touched by the Confederacy; their employment, as previously insisted, was vital to the state's war effort. Besides, Brown added, the Confederate government still had details in Georgia cotton factories; when they were all sent to the front, the State Line details would be ordered to go also.[9]

Apparently tiring of merely verbal clashes, Brown concluded, "As you are now fully advised of my position . . . , and as I shall maintain it if necessary with all the force at my command, which is now nearly ten thousand armed men, no further discussion is necessary. . . ."[10]

In his response, Colonel Browne chided the governor and forcefully restated his own arguments, but appeared to capitulate:

I assure your Excellency that there is not the least cause to apprehend any encroachment upon the sovereignty and dignity of the State of Georgia by any officer acting under the authority of the Confederate government, and that therefore the ten thousand men who now constitute the force at your command need not be directed to combat any power but that with which they are now contending with so much credit to themselves and advantage to their country.[11]

This seemed to end the conflict; the State Line details were not disturbed, and many Confederate details marched to the front. But there was soon a serious sequel to the "detail controversy." On 30 August 1864 Secretary of War Seddon made requisition on the governor for the ten thousand troops with which he had threatened Colonel Browne. In fairness to Brown, these men were already under Confederate command and likely to

[8]Brown to Browne, 9 August 1864, ibid.

[9]Ibid.; John B. Weems to Wayne, 23 March 1863, AGIC, GDAH.

[10]Brown to Browne, 9 August 1864, Hargrett Collection.

[11]Browne to Brown, 20 August 1864, ibid.

remain so—as long as the Atlanta Campaign continued. Also, Richmond had no legal claim over the majority of the men involved. Most were either exempted state civil and military officers or reserve militia. The latter, most aged sixteen to seventeen and fifty to sixty, were neither subject to conscription nor—according to statute—subject to a call for militia.[12]

In any case, after Atlanta's fall (and two days before he received Seddon's requisition order), the governor withdrew the Georgia Militia from the Army of Tennessee—with General Hood's concurrence—and granted the men a thirty-day agricultural furlough. When they reassembled, Brown told Seddon, they would probably be loaned once again to the Confederate general defending Georgia. But the requisition would not be honored; Georgia would retain control of her troops.[13]

In the five-month correspondence that Brown's refusal generated, Seddon brought up the battle with Colonel Browne over the State Line details as one reason the president had felt compelled to call for the ten thousand troops. Some state troops, Seddon wrote, "had been detailed for objects not admitted by the enrolling officers in the State to be authorized by Confederate law, and others were claimed as primarily liable, or previously subjected to Confederate service. This had engendered controversy, and endangered collision between the local, Confederate, and State authorities which it was most desirable to anticipate and preclude."[14]

Brown responded sarcastically that this tactic displayed "magnanimity and statesmanship" on Davis's part. Since the governor had contended for the rights of the state in protecting these men, the president had determined to "relieve the State of her *whole* militia." That done, "the State, having no militia left, need have no further controversy about her right to any particular individuals as part of it." And thus the controversy dragged on.[15]

In late October, with the militia back on duty and the State Line preparing to join them at Lovejoy's Station, General Wayne made what was to prove his last annual report to the governor. Again, he led off with a report on the State Line: "While Georgia may with mournful pride point to

---

[12]*OR*, vol. 52, pt. 2:765-66; *CR*, 3: 607, 644; *OR*, series 4, vol. 3: 178; Peters, *The Public Statutes at Large of the United States of America*, 271.

[13]*CR*, 3: 609; *OR*, vol. 38: part 3, 971; *CR*, 3: 620. "With his militia he abandoned the starry cross to its fate," said one of Brown's postwar critics. A more recent commentator on this episode drew a different conclusion: "If the governor's withdrawal of Georgia militia from Confederate forces in September, 1864, was of major significance, then another presumption must follow: the march of Sherman's army . . . could have been arrested by the use of the Georgians. It seems manifest that neither presumption is tenable." Curtis Arthur Amlund, *Federalism in the Southern Confederacy* (Washington: Public Affairs Press, 1966) 105.

[14]*CR*, 3: 607-701, passim; ibid., 630.

[15]Ibid., 661.

the bloody fields of other states and of her own, for the record of her sons in the Confederate armies, she can with no less gratification regard the history of the two Regiments peculiarly her own, known as the State Line."[16]

Continuing, he described the regiments' exploits with the Army of Tennessee and their return to Georgia to recruit "their shattered ranks." He cited their casualties, 214 and 277 respectively, which were fairly heavy considering their reduced numbers at the beginning of the campaign. Detailed lists—giving the names of the killed, wounded, and captured—were appended, and the general urged the governor to consider support for those among the wounded and disabled.[17]

Unmentioned in Wayne's report were those who had left the regiments without leave during and after the Atlanta Campaign. Their number, while considerable, was more than matched by Confederate desertions, which became "epidemic" during the months following Atlanta's fall.[18] As of 7 September, deserters from the First Regiment approached two hundred and fifty men, and those of the Second Regiment seem to have come near that number.[19] A general order of 12 October 1864 had, however, offered pardons to all those who would return to their regiments within forty days. This amnesty was being offered, according to the order, because it was believed that many of the men, those north Georgians of the First Regiment particularly, had

left their colors under the pressure of the enemy sweeping over their homes, and for the care of their families, with no intention of deserting; and are only now kept from rejoining their Regiments by a conciousness of their fault, and a consequent sense of shame and apprehension of the fearful punishment that awaits desertion.[20]

Any returnees would indeed be welcome, for the State Line, as it existed at this time, numbered only four hundred men. On 14 November they joined General G. W. Smith's militiamen at Lovejoy's Station; the com-

---

[16]*Annual Report of the Adjutant and Inspector General for 1864* (Milledgeville GA: Boughton, Nisbet, Barnes & Moore, 1864) 3.

[17]Ibid., 3-4 and accompanying casualty lists. In his own annual message to the legislature, Brown praised the State Line's "cool courage and intrepid valor on the battlefield." Remarking on their casualties, he noted that many of the fallen "were as gallant as any who have bled in freedom's cause." *CR*, 2: 774.

[18]James M. McPherson, *Ordeal by Fire: The Civil War and Reconstruction* (New York: Alfred A. Knopf, 1982) 468; Beringer et al., 327.

[19]Deserters, First Regiment, Georgia State Line, 7 September 1864, State Line Miscellany, GDAH; Monthly Report, Second Regiment, Georgia State Line, May 1864, ibid.; Evans to Wayne, 22 September 1864, AGIC, GDAH.

[20]General Orders, No. 29, 12 October 1864, GO, GDAH.

bined regiments were under the command of Lieutenant Colonel Evans during Colonel Wilson's absence.[21]

Smith's men were preparing to demonstrate against Atlanta when Sherman's juggernaut, an army of two wings and several columns, left smoldering Atlanta and began to move seaward. Consequently, the state forces fell back on the nineteenth to Macon, where the State Line was placed in a fort north of the city.[22]

On the morning of 22 November, as Sherman's columns moved into Milledgeville and the country to the southwest, the State Line accompanied three of the militia brigades on a movement toward Augusta, then thought by Lieutenant General William J. Hardee to be one of Sherman's major objectives. Since the Central Railroad had been broken by Federal cavalry, Hardee was sending the men past the break to be met by a train from Savannah and carried to their destination.[23]

They were not fated to make the connection. General Smith stayed behind temporarily in Macon, sending his forces under senior brigadier P. J. Philips. General Philips was ordered to avoid battle with a superior force and halt his command at Griswoldville until Smith could join it.[24]

As they neared the village where the Second Regiment had been organized, the state troops met a handful of Confederate troopers and two battalions of Confederate reserves. They reported a recent skirmish between Federal and Confederate cavalry. Sending out the state regiments as a heavy skirmish line, Philips led his men and the reserves into the village's ruins. Their advance was not contested.[25]

Regrettably, Philips, who had been drinking, determined to move past the village, contrary to orders. Throwing out the State Line a second time, he again advanced his men.[26] The State Line soon struck Union pickets, who fell back to a nearby wooded ridge. Examining its crest, Philips discovered a Union force lightly entrenched there. Having received intelligence that the force was inferior to his, the general ordered an attack.[27]

---

[21]*Reports of the Operations of the Militia* . . . . (Macon GA: Boughton, Nisbet, Barnes & Moore, [1865]) 9. Hereafter referred to as Militia Operations. This pamphlet is the source for the reports of the militia and State Line operations found in *OR* vol. 53.

[22]Militia Operations, 4; Jackson Diary, Jackson Papers.

[23]Gustavus W. Smith, "The Georgia Militia during Sherman's March to the Sea," R. U. Johnson and C. C. Buel, eds., *Battles and Leaders of the Civil War,* 4 vols. (New York: Century Co., 1907) 4:667; *OR,* vol. 44 667; *OR,* vol. 44:877.

[24]Militia Operations, 4-5.

[25]Ibid., 13.

[26]Ibid., 14; Burke Davis, *Sherman's March* (New York: Random House, 1980) 53.

[27]Militia Operations, 12-13.

What followed was disastrous, for the blue line was composed of battle-hardened veterans with reinforcements handy. The State Line was in the forefront of the fighting, charging up the slope along with the militiamen only to be blown back to the heavily thicketed branch that wound along the ridge's base. In this imperfect refuge they found that their position was extremely precarious; it was impossible to retreat and suicidal to advance. Yet during the afternoon's fighting they did charge up the ridge several more times, always with calamitous results. Allowed to limp back to Griswoldville at dusk, the state troops found that they had sustained almost seven hundred casualties. But the State Line had been comparatively lucky, especially considering its full participation. They had lost only three killed, with forty wounded—including Lieutenant Colonel Evans—and nine missing.[28]

Drawn back to Macon, where Colonel Wilson resumed command of the Line, the troops were soon sent to Savannah via Albany and Thomasville. The night of 29 November, the State Line, one militia brigade, and some Confederate reserves reached the city. There word had reached General Hardee that a strong Union force was advancing to break the Charleston and Savannah Railroad at Grahamville, South Carolina, forty miles up the coast. General Smith, who had rejoined his force, immediately was asked to take his troops to meet the threat. After some discussion of state rights and much complaining from the troops, this was done.[29]

Fortunately, the situation at Grahamville was the reverse of that at Griswoldville. This time the Georgia troops were to be on a ridge, known as Honey Hill, in heavy earthworks blocking the road to the railway. When the Federals, many of them black troops, charged up the slope, they were punished severely by the Confederate batteries and supporting riflemen. Although the State Line was in the center of the Confederate line, its losses were negligible; the men fired and fired until their rifles overheated, then enjoyed the rare opportunity of advancing victorious upon the field and scavenging among the well-equipped Union dead.[30]

Soon after returning to Savannah, the State Line once again boarded the cars. This time, again accompanied by a militia contingent, the Line moved to augment General Wayne's foward line at the Little Ogeechee railroad bridge, northwest of Savannah. There they stayed 3 and 4 December, pulling back to an intermediate position on the fifth, and finally with-

---

[28]Ibid., 9-10, 14-15; *Macon Daily Telegraph,* 25 November 1864; Evans Memorial.

[29]Smith, 667-68.

[30]Militia Operations, 6-7; Jackson Diary, Jackson Papers.

For detailed accounts of these engagements, see the author's "A Little Battle at Griswoldville" and "The Fight at Honey Hill," *Civil War Times Illustrated* 19 (November 1980): 44-49 and 22 (January 1984): 12-19, respectively.

drawing soon after to General Smith's line near the city. Both regiments combined at this time mustered about 470 men total.[31]

Smith's division, of which the Line continued to form a part, was stationed on the right some three miles northwest of the city; Smith's line extended from the Savannah River to the Central Railroad, with the State Line toward the left near the Louisville Road. Before the enemy appeared on the ninth, Smith's men were able to construct strong earthworks. Although the Federals later pressed upon them, they made "no direct or determined attempt to carry them."[32]

When it became obvious that he could not hold Savannah much longer, Hardee had a pontoon bridge constructed for the withdrawal into South Carolina. The movement began on the night of 20 December, with Smith's command acting as the rear guard. After a march to Bamberg, South Carolina, Smith's men boarded a train for Augusta, leaving Hardee's troops to deal with Sherman's advance.[33]

The State Line remained in Augusta through February 1865. While Sherman was marching through South Carolina, the state organization helped protect the town and its mammoth powder works. During its stay "Joe Brown's Army" was praised by a local paper:

> The record of the State Line from Resaca to [Grahamville] is a brilliant one. They fought side by side with the veteran troops of the Army of Tennessee, and have fallen with them in the same hot conflicts, but in all emergencies they have fought with the unwavering determination which is characteristic of the blood that is in them. Georgia will never blush at the record of her State Line.[34]

The General Assembly was also laudatory, passing in joint session a resolution of thanks to Smith's militia and the State Line "for their conspicuous gallantry at Griswoldville . . . and especially for their unselfish patriotism, in leaving their State, and meeting the enemy on the memorable and well fought battlefield at Honey Hill in South Carolina."[35]

By March the State Line was encamped near Milledgeville, forming part of the capital's garrison. The *Confederate Union* stated that the regiment's

---

[31]Militia Operations, 20-21; Charles C. Jones, Jr., *The Siege of Savannah—Confederate Operations in Georgia* (Albany NY: Joel Munsell, 1874) 90.

[32]Militia Operations, 27-28.

[33]Ibid., 29; Jackson Diary, Jackson Papers. Returns dated 20 January 1865 list the Georgia State Line regiments, both commanded by Colonel Wilson, as still part of Smith's First Division, Georgia Militia. *OR,* vol. 47, pt. 2:1071.

[34]*Augusta Chronicle and Sentinel,* 21 February 1865.

[35]*Georgia Senate Journal,* 1865, 36.

commander was Lieutenant Colonel Evans; Colonel Wilson's name does not appear in any subsequent records of the regiments.[36]

In late March the governor received a request from General Robert E. Lee through General Cobb: "Thomas and Stoneman are reported to be concentrating rapidly at Knoxville, to advance on the Virginia and Tennessee Railroad. Cannot a force be organized in Georgia, to cut his communication with Chattanooga and Nashville? Please consult with Governor Brown."[37]

The governor reported to Cobb that all the state forces but two hundred men of the State Line at Milledgeville were on leave; he was, however, agreeable to sending them out of the state with any force Cobb raised. The troops were to be organized by General W. T. Wofford, Confederate commander of the Department of Northern Georgia.[38]

But before the State Line could embark on this adventure, Brown and Cobb came to the conclusion that enemy movements in Alabama represented too great a threat to Georgia. Federal cavalry commander James H. Wilson had begun a raid across Alabama, directed at Georgia, that threatened to split and destroy the Confederacy's final stronghold. Troops could not safely be detached for the Tennessee expedition.[39]

By 8 April, Jefferson Davis, having fled from Richmond to Danville, Virginia, was ordering Cobb and Wofford to "aid in the defense of Alabama."[40] Before leaving Macon for Montgomery on the ninth—the day of Lee's surrender—Cobb wrote to Brown concerning the situation in Alabama. The general hoped that by advancing to Montgomery with all available troops he would be able to save Georgia. He concluded,

> I write more particularly, however, to know whether you will consent to the removal of the regiments of the State Line to Montgomery, if I should determine after reaching Montgomery to order troops to that point. I do not feel authorized to carry these regiments beyond the State without your approval, and I have made the foregoing statements that you might have all the facts before you as I am at present informed.[41]

---

[36]*Milledgeville Confederate Union,* 14 March 1865. By this time, their "ranks almost depleted" by service and disease, the men were in charge of Major J. N. Scott (First Regiment) and Captain T. J. Neal (Second Regiment)—both under the command of Lieutenant Colonel Evans.

[37]Lee to Cobb, 21 March 1865, transmitted in Cobb to Brown, 22 March 1865, GLB, GDAH.

[38]Brown to Cobb, 22 March 1865, GLB, GDAH.

[39]Brown to Wofford, 5 April 1865, GLB, GDAH; Montgomery, *Cobb,* 131.

[40]*OR,* vol. 47, pt. 3:767.

[41]Cobb to Brown, 9 April 1865, Howell Cobb Papers, Manuscript Department, Perkins Library, Duke University, Durham, NC.

All of Cobb's care and diplomacy went for naught. Brown responded that he wished Cobb to take the troops no farther than Columbus until it could be seen whether or not it would be necessary to keep the troops in the state.[42]

By 11 April the State Line was encamped below Macon at Jackson's Station, a handy point from which to take the cars to Columbus. The regiments' final court-martial was underway when word came that the Line should move to meet the enemy threat to west Georgia. On reaching Columbus—where the Confederate commander happened to be Colonel Leon von Zinken—the state troops found that they were to be part of an extremely diverse two-to-three-thousand-man defending force. The Georgia Militia's Chief of Staff, Robert Toombs, telegraphed the governor that there had been a slight skirmish the evening of the sixteenth; there would be a "decided fight" the next day. Toombs did not realize that even then General James Wilson, using only about three hundred of his numerous troopers, was preparing to launch the "gallant night attack" that would result in Columbus's speedy fall.[43]

Along with most of the other troops, the State Line had been sent across the Chattahoochee to fortifications near Girard, Alabama. Private Jackson recalled the fight that followed:

> Just about sunset . . . the pickets opened fire. Our pickets came in and the firing became general about dark. We being in breastworks held our ground; finally firing ceased for a while, and some one suggested we cross fire and see if we could locate the enemy. And sure enough we did, for they had broken the lines on our left, and were just coming along up the lines undisturbed, but when we began to cross fire, they returned the fire right up to the trenches. We then realized our situation. We, of course, leaped out of our ditches and made for the bridges and while running down a steep slant, I remember running against Lieut. Col. Evans and knocking off his hat. I never stopped to pick it up for him, for every fellow was for self now, and while running through a field in the darkness, I ran into a gully over my head and had to go down it until I found a gully leading out from it before I could get out. We finally came to fence. I remember that I climbed to the top of it and being almost out of breath, just fell off. Then up the railroad bankment and crossed the river on the railroad bridge. Once across, I felt safe. Some soldiers had piled up bales of cotton there for breastworks and begged us to rally, but we were so demoralized and scattered that we didn't.[44]

---

[42]Brown to Cobb, 10 April 1865, GLB, GDAH.

[43]R. J. Hallett to Commanding Officer, Georgia State Line, 11 April 1865, Howell Cobb Order and Letter Book, 1865, Cobb-Erwin-Lamar Collection, Special Collections, University of Georgia Libraries, Athens GA; General Orders, No. 5, 13 April 1865, GO, GDAH; James Pickett Jones, *Yankee Blitzkrieg; Wilson's Raid through Alabama and Georgia* (Athens: University of Georgia Press, 1976) 132-33, 139; Toombs to Brown, 16 April 1865, GLB, GDAH; *OR*, vol. 49, pt. 1:364.

[44]Jackson Diary, Jackson Papers.

Some of the men, like Jackson and two of his comrades, continued on toward Macon—or home. Others, among them Lieutenant Colonel Howell, were rounded up by the victorious Federals. Cobb's remaining force, including Lieutenant Colonel Evans and a State Line contingent, hastened to Macon's fortifications to prepare for the inevitable Union attack. Yet, although there were skirmishes near the city on 20 April, Macon fell almost bloodlessly the same day. Men of the State Line, along with other soldiers of the captured garrison, were then confined for a time in the stockade at Macon's Camp Oglethorpe, formerly a Federal officers' prison.[45]

When General Cobb wired Governor Brown of Macon's fall and of the armistice that had been declared, the State Line's commander-in-chief fell

Pvt. A. J. Jackson, Company G, Second Regiment, Georgia State Line, State Line Memoirist (From a postwar photograph. Courtesy of Mrs. Natalie Redfern.)

---

[45]Ibid.; Henderson, 1267; James Pickett Jones, 139; *OR,* vol. 49, pt. 1:366; James Harrison Wilson, *Under the Old Flag,* 2 vols. (New York: D. Appleton & Co., 1912) 2: 278.

back to Augusta. He apparently considered gathering a militia force in Augusta for a last stand; but the city was in turmoil, and it was increasingly obvious that the war was over. After conferring with Toombs and Stephens at their homes, the governor returned to Milledgeville. Hoping to maintain his position as governor, Brown called upon the legislature to convene later in the month.[46]

This hope was futile. When Brown finally met with Wilson on the morning of Saturday, 6 May, he found the general determined to strip him of his political and military powers. Having forbidden the meeting of the General Assembly, however, Wilson did send to Washington Brown's appeal to have this decision set aside.[47]

Wilson then demanded the surrender of the state troops, along with that of the commander-in-chief and all state military officers. The governor, Wilson confided to his diary, was "much exercised for fear of compromising his official position." The general, however, instructed the governor to "reconcile himself" since the only official position he held was "by sufferance." Brown then "tarried awhile" in conversation with Wilson, making it obvious that he and General Cobb were "not on good terms." Brown told Wilson that he had "seen Cobb and other leading men the night before repeating more than once . . . in a tone of ridicule the words that Cobb used in describing the recent battle: 'My God! How the Georgia line did fight in defense of Columbus.' " Apparently, the last word on the Georgia State Line was a gibe.[48]

The following day Wilson received "the surrender of the Georgia State Line and Militia, including the commander-in-chief and General Wayne," and the day afterward all were paroled. According to Wilson's parole certification, the officers and men of the State Line were finally to be allowed

---

[46]Three telegrams: Cobb to Brown, Brown to Cobb, Cobb to Brown, all dated 20 April 1865, GLB, GDAH; Florence Fleming Corley, *Confederate City: Augusta, Georgia, 1860-1865* (Columbia: University of South Carolina Press, 1960) 93-94; Brown to "My dear daughter," 2 May 1865, Hargrett Collection; Brown to Gabriel Toombs, 7 October 1865, ibid.; *CR*, 2: 878-79. General R. W. Carswell's First Brigade, Georgia Militia, was stationed in Augusta at this time, along with the G. M. I. Cadet Battalion and a Confederate force under Major General Lafayette McLaws. Apparently, McLaws also considered resistance to the Federals. Hill, *Joseph E. Brown*, 250; *OR*, vol. 53: 420; *OR*, vol. 49, pt. 2:586.

[47]6 May 1865, Wilson Diary, James H. Wilson Manuscripts, Historical Society of Delaware, Wilmington, Delaware; Wilson, 2: 353. General Wilson also recorded in his diary that General Wayne "said he had been using Brown in the Davis quarrel to advance the Union interests. Wayne furnished the Conscript articles and others." 7 May 1865, Wilson Diary.

[48]6 May 1865, Wilson Diary; Wilson, 2:353.

to return home "not to be molested by the military authorities" as long as they observed the terms of their paroles.[49]

Nonetheless, their former commander-in-chief was arrested in Milledgeville the following night and soon occupied a cell in Washington's Carroll Prison. Unfailingly resourceful and resilient, he was quickly released and returned to Georgia to resume the political career many had

Governor Joseph E. Brown, 1865. Taken only days before Brown's arrest, this photograph shows clearly the strains of war. (Courtesy of the Atlanta Historical Society.)

[49]*OR,* 49, pt. 2:663; Parole and Certification, 8 May 1863, Hargrett Collection. Other than those paroled at Macon, State Line troops received paroles at Milledgeville, Albany, Hartwell, Kingston, and other towns—places where they had been hospitalized or captured. Others traveled to these points from their homes to be paroled. Several received their paroles when released from such Northern prisons as Johnson's Island and Fort Delaware. Compiled Service Records, passim.

thought destroyed. Despite bitter controversies, Brown's power, wealth, and prominence increased through the decades up to his death in 1894. Although the subject of much debate, his place in the history of Georgia and the Confederacy is conspicuous and secure.[50]

As for the Georgia State Line, its fate was an almost instant obscurity.

[50]9 May 1865, Wilson Diary; Brown to Andrew Johnson, 20 May 1865, Hargrett Collection; *Milledgeville Southern Recorder,* 4 July 1865. Brown's parole was considered by Wilson and Secretary of War Edwin M. Stanton to cover only his activities as commander-in-chief of the state forces, not his actions as governor—specifically his action in calling the legislature to convene. 8 May 1865, Wilson Diary; *CR,* 3: 728. Characteristically, Brown informed President Johnson (in the letter cited above) that when the soldiers sent to take him demanded his parole papers, "I could have commanded force enough to capture the squad sent to arrest me."

EPILOGUE

The State Line's significance was twofold: it was a major extension of Governor Brown's state rights policy, and it was unique among Georgia state military organizations.

In terms of Brown's policy, the State Line was an important expression of state sovereignty, a successful repudiation of the conscription acts, and the governor's sole sustained attempt to keep a body of state troops.

The Line was also important as a vindication of Brown's assertion that such a permanent state force was necessary. Aside from its services under Generals Bragg, Johnston, Hood, and Hardee, the State Line performed valuable service in dealing with the problem of deserters and insurgents in north Georgia. The regiments were also able, when needed, to go to the defense of Savannah and Charleston in the spring of 1863, when the Confederate coastal authorities, denied assistance from Richmond, were forced to ask Governor Brown for troops. Before the Confederate army's inevitable abandonment of the State Road, the Line served the Confederacy well by contributing to the efficiency of the railroad's operation through chopping wood for fuel, doing construction work, and guarding the invaluable bridges. It was also instrumental in preparing at strategic points along the line many of the fortifications later utilized by the Confederate army. Ironically, this organization, which was such an obvious manifestation of state sovereignty, did nothing material to harm the Confederacy and much to help. It served much of its career under Confederate generals, and even when it was under state control it was engaged in activities of benefit to Richmond. Indeed, the regiments were probably as useful to the Confederacy as putative troops as they would have been if transferred to one of Richmond's armies.

Despite its services, the State Line left much to be desired as a military organization. To have a true state army, the governor should have kept it up to full strength and not weakened it by assigning numerous men to extra duties and factory details. The regimental commanders, most rather unsuited for their positions, should have kept stricter discipline and worked harder at promoting the preparedness of the units. General Wayne's contribution, for the most part, was positive—it was due mainly to his efforts that the regiments realized any of their potential. But his supervision of them, while not consistent or thorough enough to improve them greatly, consumed time and energy which he probably could have expended more profitably elsewhere. Since General Wayne could not devote all his time to the regiments and commanded them only briefly, it would have been better if the governor had fulfilled his initial desire to brigade the regiments under General Henry R. Jackson. If they had thus been continuously under the watchful eye of an experienced military man, they would have been the better for it. Consequently, those functions that they performed would have been better executed and their usefulness to the state and the Confederacy would have been enhanced.

Although long forgotten, "Joe Brown's Army" did fill a need for Georgia and for the Confederacy; but it was perhaps to the governor that the regiments had the greatest value. Their existence gave Brown a regular force all his own that no one in the Confederacy could commandeer. Having successfully thwarted all the moves of the Richmond government to deny him his army, Governor Brown finally surrendered the State Line to the superior force of Federal arms—a pathetic remnant, yes, but until the end his own.

APPENDIX I

The State Line Cavalry

In mid-March 1864 "the maraudings of Tories and deserters" in north Georgia—particularly in Pickens, Gilmer, and Fannin Counties—led to another State Line expedition against upcountry insurgents. For the purposes of this foray, a State Line cavalry company was created. Circumventing the legislature, the governor ordered 100 men drawn from several of Galt's companies and put on special service. All officers and men were to be given cavalry pay and allowances, but had to furnish their own horses and tack. The quartermaster department was to provide forage. The men were to be allowed 40¢ per day for the "use and risk" of the horses, as well as compensation if their mounts were killed in action.[1]

Picked as commander of the new company was Captain Francis M. Cowen, who was allowed to choose as his subordinate officers "a First and second Lieutenant and Ensign from the subalterns of the Regiment at large" and was assigned a surgeon to accompany the force. The officers and men of Companies A and C, on duty with Colonel Leon von Zinken at Marietta, were not allowed to participate.[2]

Despite the governor's impatience to have the expedition underway, it was mid-April before the cavalry contingent set out. Above Atlanta horses were so few and prices so exorbitant that most men had to be given ten days' furlough to search for a mount. They were somewhat helped, however, by the governor's decision to loan them state saddles and bridles.[3]

[1]Wayne to Galt, 18 March 1864, AGLB No. 22, GDAH; Wayne to Cowen, 2 April 1864, ibid.

[2]Wayne to Galt, 18 March 1864, ibid.; Wayne to Cowen, 2 April 1864, ibid. General Johnston was informed of Cowen's mission, and arrangements were made for the captain to return Confederate deserters to the Army of Tennessee. Wayne to Johnston, 11 April 1664, AGLB No. 23, GDAH.

[3]Cowen to Wayne, 29 March 1864, AGIC, GDAH; Wayne to Cowen, 2 April 1864, AGLB No. 22 GDAH.

When the expedition set out from Cartersville on 19 April, it was composed of seventy-nine mounted men and ten infantrymen—all armed with Enfield or Austrian rifles—and ten mule-drawn wagons. Setting up headquarters in Ellijay, Cowen noted the major activity in the area came from locals refugeeing into enemy lines—a migration Cowen wanted to stop by force. He also reported a raid on Morganton by two Tennessee bushwhackers. Additionally, forty men of the state force had stayed out all night hunting deserters, but captured only one. "They are powerful sharp here," Cowen wrote. He soon had to be warned not to interfere with families refugeeing north; neither was he to meddle with or confiscate the abandoned property of those citizens who had gone over to the enemy.[4]

In early May Cowen and seventy-five men crossed into Tennessee and raided a hamlet called Ducktown in search of deserters from Georgia rumored to be there. Cowen found that the timber had been cleared in all directions, making surprise impossible. "The ground," he added, "is perforated with tunnels and they offer great opportunities for a city of refuge in the 'lower regions' where this command 'goeth not.' " No deserters were captured, but the party did confiscate two "stolen" mules.[5]

On 3 May, the "State Scouts," as Cowen then styled them, raided the Stanley settlement near Morganton, a stronghold of bushwhackers and deserters. According to Cowen, it was "the most secluded place as well as the most romantic and picturesque" he had ever seen. It was an area of numerous streams "liberally covered with laurel, ivy, and spruce pine," cut with "deep and dark ravines." Having surprised the Stanleys, Cowen and his men were able to capture two of them after some gunplay and a hurried pursuit. They also captured two deserters, along with the horses of two others who escaped on foot.[6]

Hearing through General Wayne of Cowen's activities, the governor was "gratified to note" Cowen's energy. Brown advised him, however, not to return to Tennessee. He could keep and use any captured arms and ammunition, turning over to the quartermaster general any confiscated horses and mules.[7]

By mid-May the Confederate cavalry battalion of Colonel Andrew Young was prepared to assist Cowen. Consequently, the State Scouts' operations were to be confined to Pickens, Gordon, and Dawson Counties,

---

[4]Galt to Wayne, 19 April 1864, enclosing Galt to Cowen of the same date, AGIC, GDAH; Cowen to Wayne, 29, 31 March 1864, ibid.; Cowen to Galt, 28 April 1864, ibid.; Wayne to Galt, 5 May 1864, AGLB No. 24, GDAH.

[5]Cowen to Galt, 5 May 1864, AGIC, GDAH. The tunnels to which Cowen refers are presumably the famous Ducktown copper mines.

[6]Ibid.

[7]Wayne to Cowen, 11 May 1864, AGLB No. 24, GDAH.

along with the Pine Log section of Cherokee and the southern portion of Murray. Colonel Young was to take charge of "the rest of the upper portion of the State."[8]

This new arrangement never went into effect. The inexorable south-ward progress of the Union armies into Georgia forced Cowen and his men to abandon their territory, in which, wrote Galt on 19 May "they had re-stored in great degree quiet and confidence." According to Galt, the state cavalry only "narrowly made good their exit" from the mountains, saving their wagons and most of their baggage. Dismounted but allowed to re-main together, Cowen's men, now called the "State Mountain Infantry," served provost duty at Marietta until its evacuation.[9]

Apparently sent to serve with the Army of Tennessee, Cowen's force was caught up in the fighting around Atlanta in late July. Cowen, shot through both arms, was captured and sent prisoner to Chattanooga. There he died on 2 August, his body consigned to a nameless grave.[10]

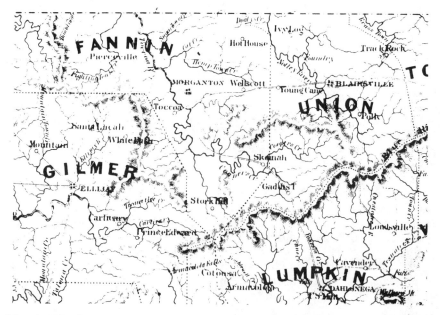

Map 4. The heart of Georgia's Tory country. Detail of J. T. Lloyd's Topo-graphical Map of Georgia, 1864. (Courtesy of Special Collections, Univer-sity of Georgia Libraries, Athens, Georgia.)

[8]Wayne to Cowen, 16 May 1864, ibid.

[9]Galt to Wayne, 19 May 1864, AGIC, GDAH; Galt to Wayne, 7 June 1864, ibid.; Cowen to Wayne, 13 June 1864, ibid.; Cowen to Wayne, 16 July 1864, ibid.

[10]F. M. Cowen file, Roll 151, Compiled Service Records.

Knowing only that Cowen was "supposed to be a prisoner in the hands of the enemy," General Wayne ordered his troopers remounted and sent to Milledgeville. There they were allowed to increase their numbers by recruiting from the Georgia Militia. Since Stoneman's Raiders had recently threatened the city, it was decided to create a permanent force for the defense of the capital, made up of the State Line cavalry, the G. M. I. Corps of Cadets, and Pruden's Artillery.[11]

Chosen as the new cavalry commander was Captain Matthew H. Talbot. A twenty-eight-year-old lawyer from Wilkes County, Talbot had served in the 9th Georgia Infantry early in the war, and then joined the staff of his kinsman, Major General W. H. T. Walker, for whom he was acting as aide-de-camp when the general was killed during the Battle of Atlanta. Soon afterwards in Milledgeville, Talbot had won the praise of General Wayne for his "great energy and action" in leading a party of volunteer cavalry in pursuit of Stoneman's Raiders.[12]

These qualities led to his appointment as cavalry commander and were likewise conspicuous as he led his men, now known as "Talbot's Scouts," during the Savannah Campaign. As part of General Wayne's motley force of convicts, cadets, and cavalry, Talbot and his men played a vital role in the holding action conducted against great odds at Ball's Ferry on the Oconee. As the adjutant general noted in his report of the engagement, "I have learned . . . that a number of graves opposite the Ferry mark in part the stubbornness of Talbot's resistance."[13]

After guarding the Ogeechee bridges during General Wayne's withdrawal to Savannah, Talbot's Scouts were divided. About sixty of them formed part of Savannah's garrison, while a forty-man detachment served once again as bridge guards, this time at the railway trestle twelve miles above Savannah.[14]

Ironically, a Confederate cavalry officer at Hardeeville, South Carolina, just up the tracks from the Savannah railroad bridge, chose this period to accuse the Scouts of thievery in central Georgia. His accusation that

[11]Special Orders, No. 103, 15 August 1864, SO, GDAH; General Orders, No. 25, 19 August 1864, GO, GDAH; John O. Ferrill to General G. W. Smith, 14 October 1864, AGLB No. 26, GDAH; Wayne to Colonel G. W. Lee, 29 August 1864, ibid.

[12]"Sketch of Matthew Henry Talbot," Civil War Miscellany—Personal Papers, GDAH (hereafter referred to as Talbot Sketch); Wayne to Brown, 4 August 1864, AGLB No. 25, GDAH.

[13]Military Operations, 18-19, 22.

[14]Ibid., 19; C. C. Jones, Jr., 89; W. H. Malone, "Memoirs," 38, Civil War Miscellany—Personal Papers, GDAH (hereafter referred to as Malone Memoirs).

a squad of the state cavalry was stealing horses in Hancock County while passing as Wheeler's Cavalry was angrily denied by Governor Brown.[15]

After Savannah's fall in late December, Talbot and his troopers returned to Milledgeville by way of Augusta, reaching the capital in early January 1865. There they remained on garrison duty until the approach of Wilson's Raiders in late April. They were then dispatched to Macon, where they appear to have participated in a final skirmish west of Macon at Bailey's Mills. Not surrendering with Macon's garrison, Talbot's Scouts returned to Milledgeville and were there paroled.[16]

---

[15]W. C. Dodson, ed., *Campaigns of Wheeler and his Cavalry, 1862-1865* (Atlanta: Hudgins Publishing Co., 1899) 399; Brown's addenda to General Joseph Wheeler's Report, 8 April 1865, GLB, GDAH (hereafter referred to as Brown's addenda).

[16]Brown's addenda; Malone Memoirs, 38; R. J. Hallett to Captain Matthew H. Talbot, 17 April 1865, Howell Cobb Order and Letter Book, Cobb-Erwin-Lamar Collection, Special Collections, University of Georgia Libraries, Athens GA; Talbot Sketch. Talbot died in 1876 and was buried in the cemetery of old Smyrna Church in Wilkes County with such forebears as Governor Matthew Talbot. Talbot Sketch.

APPENDIX II

The General Hospital, Georgia State Line

After the conclusion of the Savannah hospital controversy of the spring of 1863, the State Line always had its own hospital to care for the sick and, later, the wounded who were sent to the rear by the regimental surgeons. Supplied by the state and supervised by Dr. Aaron Pleasant Brown, the General Hospital, Georgia State Line, relocated at least two times and was apparently always housed in tents.[1]

When the Line arrived for service on the State Road in May 1863, the hospital was placed at Cartersville. In January 1864, citing difficulties in getting medical supplies and harrassment by Confederate soldiers, Colonel Galt recommended that the hospital be moved to Jonesboro. The relocation was approved and carried out in February or March of that year.[2]

Dr. Brown's hospital remained at Jonesboro until—probably—the late summer of 1864. In May 1864 it was relatively well staffed. Two surgeons, a steward, a ward master, a matron, and ten male nurses saw to the needs of the 124 patients, most of whom were suffering from dysentery, diarrhea, and other camp diseases. Three detailed men served as cooks, and two slaves were employed to do laundry work.[3]

---

[1]Brown to Dr. Brown, 30 May 1863, Hargrett Collection; Wayne to Captain Hugh M. Moore, 1 June 1863, AGLB No. 15, GDAH; Wayne to Dr. W. J. Bailey, 24 November 1863, AGLB No. 20, GDAH.

[2]Galt to Wayne, 18 January 1864, AGIC, GDAH; Hospital Pay Roll, 1 February-31 March 1864, State Line Hospital Records, Map Cabinet Drawer 1, Folder 16 (hereafter referred to as Hospital Records.), GDAH.

[3]Report of Sick in General Hospital at Jonesboro . . . May 1864, Hospital Records, GDAH; Roll of Persons employed in General Hospital, Jonesboro . . . May 1864, ibid. During the Atlanta Campaign, State Line wounded were also carried to Macon and elsewhere. During their convalescence, several members of the Line were assigned to Macon's battalion of Garrison Guards. Compiled Service Records, passim.

As Sherman's army tightened its grip on Atlanta toward summer's end in 1864, the General Hospital was moved for the last time. Its new site was a field one mile south of an Upson County hamlet called The Rock, located on the spur of the Macon and Western Railroad that led to Thomaston. Dr. Brown operated the hospital undisturbed until 23 August 1865, when he was finally found and paroled.[4]

---

[4]Dr. Brown to Brown, 10 February 1865, GBIC, GDAH; Scruggs, *Georgia Historical Markers* 466; Carrie W. Brown, Widow's Indigent Pension, 1901, Fulton County, Georgia, Confederate Pension Records, GDAH. A Georgia Historical Marker entitled "Unknown Confederate Dead" marks the site of the last General Hospital, Georgia State Line, and the graves of a dozen unknown soldiers. Scruggs, *Georgia Historical Markers* 466.

APPENDIX III

Military Justice in the Georgia State Line

During its existence, the State Line conducted a total of seven general courts-martial. Most of those tried during the proceedings were men who had deserted or absented themselves without leave. Desertion was so rampant in the Line that General Wayne conceived a novel method of dealing with the problem. In August 1863 he decided that deserters and AWOL's would simply be turned over to the conscription oficers to save the trouble and expense of trials.[1]

After about a month's experience with this new regulation, both Colonel Wilson and Lieutenant Colonel Evans of the Second Regiment informed General Wayne that the order was not having the intended effect. "The restless and impatient who desire change," wrote Evans, "leave merely to be enrolled & then are allowed to volunteer in any company they may select, receive $50 Bounty and ten days furlough. . . . They usually go to Florida under General Cobb." Evans added that the order undercut morale, since many captains, wishing to keep their ranks full, relaxed discipline for fear of losing men to desertion. Moreover, Evans asserted, some men wishing to stay with the State Line had been enrolled for overstaying sick leave or furlough. He wished punishments for AWOL's and deserters to be dealt out by the regiment, as in the past.[2]

---

[1]General Orders, No. 20, 17 May 1864, GO, GDAH; Adjutant General's General and Special Orders, 1861-1865, passim, GDAH; General Orders, No. 21, 7 August 1863, GO, GDAH; L. H. Briscoe to Major Charles J. Harris, Commandant of Conscripts, 11 February 1864, AGLB No. 22, GDAH. Deserters were those soldiers who left "their commands with an evident intention of abandoning their Company, Regiment, and duty." AWOL's were absent from their commands without such evident intention. General Orders, No. 6, 4 March 1864, GO, GDAH.

[2]Evans to Wayne, 2 September 1863, Cuyler (Wayne).

Wilson wrote in the same vein, adding that some men flouted punishment for other misconduct by deserting and being enrolled, thus escaping the "rigid accountability for all misdemeanors" necessary to good discipline. Wilson also argued, with justice, that Wayne's practice was in violation of the resolutions that governed the State Line since conscription for desertion was not allowed under the Articles of War. The colonel noted, however, that the order would be very effective if it directed that deserters and AWOL's be turned over to the Army of Tennessee, for "the boys had just as soon go to the D __ l as to General Bragg."[3]

Despite these arguments, the practice was in force until March 1864, when the order was amended. Thereafter, only AWOL's were to be conscripted; deserters were once again to be tried. No State Line deserters were sentenced to death, although Colonel Wilson commented, "I think the shooting of one or two of the Scamps in the G.S.L. would improve its status considerably."[4]

Other offenses committed in the State Line included conduct unbecoming an officer, sleeping on post, cowardice, and stealing. Nonetheless, according to the records available, the troops seem to have been relatively well behaved. The seven general courts-martial tried only twenty men on thirty-eight charges, a surprisingly low number, perhaps explained by the laxness of many of the officers, the numerous cases of men being conscripted rather than tried, and the utilization of regimental courts-martial (for which few records exist) for many lesser offenses.[5]

The most colorful State Line malefactor was Lieutenant Philip De-Priest, of Company C in Galt's regiment. During a two-week expedition against Tories and deserters in Walker County, he apparently committed an astonishing variety of offenses, including visiting "a house of *ill fame*," abducting four women and detaining them for two days, and making "advances toward unlawful intercourse" with them. DePriest was also charged with cursing and abusing a sentinel, selling one of his soldiers a canteen of whiskey and making him drunk, and conversing with and releasing a deserter from his company. Two months earlier he had supposedly gotten drunk with several members of his company at Kingston. His court-martial lasted for two weeks in mid-June 1863, and the transcript ran through fifty-six lurid pages. The court-martial was so replete with irregularities that General Wayne ordered a new trial. While DePriest had been found guilty of several counts of misconduct, his sentence had been a mere suspension from rank and forfeiture of pay for thirty days. "Mercy exercised with judgment is always commendable," Wayne noted, "but clemency

---

[3]Wilson to Wayne, 4 September 1863, AGIC, GDAH.

[4]General Orders, No. 6, 4 March 1864, GO, GDAH; Wilson to Wayne, 7 March 1864, Cuyler (Wayne).

[5]Adjutant General's General Orders, 1861-1865, passim.

ceases to be mercy when reason is abandoned." Rather than face retrial, DePriest resigned his commission and was elected a captain of the militia.[6]

The usually patient General Wayne was extremely short-tempered with the Line's officers where courts-martial were concerned. In the matter of justice he would not tolerate any of the inefficiency and lack of concern that sometimes colored the officers' other actions.

At the courts-martial, a combination of officers from both regiments sat in judgment. Wayne found some of the first trials to have been handled improperly—there had been too much imprecision and uncertainty regarding charges and specifications. The adjutant general was also displeased by the court's allowing evidence to be given without all of the court's members being present. Court officers in one case even indulged in the "extraordinary inconsistency of finding the accused guilty of a specification but not guilty of the charge." The courts, Wayne found, sometimes defeated the ends of justice through the officers' mistakes. At other times punishments were so lenient that they were more farce than deterrent.[7]

Punishments meted out to the convicted were similar to those imposed by Confederate courts-martial. In an early desertion case, for example, the man found guilty was sentenced to wear a ball and chain for ten days; for five hours each day he was to remove rubbish from the camp with a wheelbarrow.[8]

In a desertion case tried when deserters were no longer conscripted, a harsher penalty was imposed. The deserter was to serve thirty days' confinement with forfeiture of all pay and allowances during that period. He was also to be branded with the letter "D" on his right hip, but, at Colonel Galt's suggestion, the branding was not carried out.[9]

At the same court-martial another deserter—also found guilty of enlisting in Confederate service and drawing rations and clothing—was sentenced to "be bucked and gagged for one hour in the presence of the regiment and to subsist on bread and water for ten days," along with suspension of pay for two months.[10]

---

[6]General Orders, No. 14, 29 June 1863, GO, GDAH; Proceedings of a General Court-Martial convened on 8 June 1863, Courts-Martial; DePriest to Brown, 18 August 1863, GBIC, GDAH.

[7]Wayne to Galt, 28 May 1863, AGLB No. 15, GDAH; General Orders, No. 16, 27 June 1863, GO, GDAH.

[8]Wiley, *The Life of Johnny Reb, the Common Soldier of the Confederacy,* 231; General Orders, No. 16, 27 June 1863, GO, GDAH.

[9]General Orders, No. 16, 5 May 1864, GO, GDAH.

[10]Ibid.

Other punishments varied. The penalty for conduct unbecoming an officer was dismissal; for sleeping on post the sentence was five hours of hard labor for ten days.[11]

Special courts-martial, particularly regimental courts-martial, were also convened in the Georgia State Line. Presided over by three officers, such proceedings had jurisdiction only over "non-capital offenses of privates and subalterns." According to Colonel Galt, regimental courts were "more severe in punishing offences than Genl Courts." As a case in point, he cited the punishment for a young private who had twice absented himself without leave. His punishment was to be tied to a stake for six days between 8:00 A.M. and 4:00 P.M., his "Head well anointed each day with molasses." The first day of this punishment provoked an outpouring of sympathy that became "quite a mutinous demonstration." Galt had to arrest six protesters. In Wilson's regiment a private convicted of forging furloughs was sentenced by a regimental court-martial to five days on bread and water and forfeiture of one month's pay "to be applied for the benefit of the sick of his company."[12]

[11]Ibid.; General Orders, No. 16, 27 June 1863, GO, GDAH.

[12]Wiley, *The Life of Johnny Reb, the Common Soldier of the Confederacy,* 219; Galt to Wayne, 24 July 1863, Cuyler (Wayne); Wilson to Wayne, 30 August 1863, ibid.

Officers and Men
of the State Line
After the War

Ultimately, the State Line's war experiences were little different from those of Confederate regiments. When the war ended, many of the officers and men were dead, some were mortally sick, some were maimed, and some were imprisoned in the North. Most of those who returned from the war found their counties ravaged or impoverished by war. But, like other Confederate veterans, the State Line's officers and men had to wait until 1879 to receive the thanks of their state in any material form. In that year Georgia began to pay pensions to its disabled soldiers. A law passed in 1891 extended pensions to poverty-stricken veterans, as well as to veterans' widows. And eventually some men were allowed "C. S. A." stones to mark their graves.[1]

Following are brief sketches of the postwar lives of seven State Line officers and one enlisted man.

Financially "ruined by the War," General Henry C. Wayne returned to Savannah, where he ran a lumber business for a time. Later denouncing secession as "folly," he eventually became a Republican like his former commander-in-chief. Unlike Brown he remained with the party; Secretary of State Hamilton Fish and President U. S. Grant were among those who busied themselves to find Wayne government employment when his business ventures failed. Wayne remained in Savannah until his death on 15 March 1883, having lived out his postwar years "without particular distinction but respected in the community." A local newspaper's obituary

---

[1]*Civil War Records,* Georgia Department of Archives and History Publication No. 76-CW-1, 5.

noted that his "services to Georgia in the most trying hours of her history were invaluable." The general was buried in Laurel Grove Cemetery in Savannah. The inscription on his monument states, between his birth and death dates:

ENTERED U. S. ARMY 1838
RESIGNED 1860
SERVED HIS NATIVE STATE AS
ADJ. & INS. GENERAL TILL 1865.[2]

Colonel Edward Galt died before the war had been over a year. Soon after moving his family back to north Georgia, he died in Acworth on 21 January 1866, from a lung ailment apparently contracted during the war. He was buried in his family's plot in Canton.[3]

➤ Colonel Richard L. Storey farmed and also entered politics, serving as state senator for Wilkinson County in the early 1880s. He died in his home county on 19 April 1892.[4]

Lieutenant Colonel Beverly Evans reentered the practice of law in postwar Sandersville, but also farmed and served on the local board of education. He died 21 March 1897, and was buried with military honors, his former Confederate company "firing several volleys over the grave of their sleeping comrade."[5]

Lieutenant Colonel Albert Howell lived a long and varied life. In the private sector he ran an Atlanta grocery business and an icemaking concern on the Chattahoochee. He also at one time had controlling interest in the *Atlanta Constitution* and was president of the company from 1876 to 1879. He later sold out to his brother Evan, whose name—along with that of his son Clark—is prominently associated with the paper. The *Consti-*

---

[2]Henry C. Wayne to Governor Charles J. Jenkins, 6 January 1866, Henry C. Wayne Papers, GDAH; Lawrence, *Wayne,* 197, 217; Alexander A. Lawrence, ed., "Some Letters from Henry C. Wayne to Hamilton Fish," *Georgia Historical Quarterly* 43 (December 1959): 393; *Savannah Morning News,* 16 March 1883; Wayne's monument, Laurel Grove Cemetery, Savannah, Chatham County, Georgia, on-site inspection by author, 30 March 1981. In his letter to Governor Jenkins, Wayne requested back pay for services as adjutant general from 1 May 1864 to 5 December 1865 (the date of his resignation), a total of $4,791.66.

[3]"The Diary of Jennie Charlotte Smith, September 1864-May 1881," Galt Collection; Lamar H. Roberts to author, 30 March 1981. Visiting the governor's mansion at war's end, Colonel Galt had pleased Mrs. Brown by saying that her young daughter Sallie was "the very image of her uncle Colonel John M. Brown." Elizabeth Brown to "Mother and Father," 27 April 1865, Hargrett Collection.

[4]Joseph T. Maddox, *Wilkinson County, Georgia, Gravestones with Genealogical Information* (Irwinton GA: n.p., 1971) 206; Davidson, 290.

[5]Ella Mitchell, *The History of Washington County,* 125; *Sandersville Herald,* 25 March 1897.

tution's Henry W. Grady was a friend of Albert Howell; Grady once insisted on repaying $10,000 Howell lost in an investment Grady had recommended. In the public sector, Howell was an Atlanta city councilman and was engaged for the last thirty years of his life in building roads for the Atlanta Board of Public Works. He died 24 August 1927, at the age of eighty-four. The *Constitution*'s front page obituary identified him as "Battle of Atlanta Hero."[6]

Dr. Aaron P. Brown practiced medicine for a time following the war but eventually was employed by his brother's Western and Atlantic Railroad, working untill ill health forced his resignation. Predeceasing his famous elder brother by three years, Dr. Brown died in Smyrna on 23 August 1891. His wife eventually claimed a widow's indigent pension based on his State Line service.[7]

Captain Seaborn Saffold moved to Selma, Alabama, where—after abandoning a "sketchy" law practice—he became owner and editor of the *Selma Times and Messenger* in 1870. "Weighing some 300 pounds," he was described as "genial" and "impressive." Through his editorials and oratory, Saffold had become an influential figure in Reconstruction Alabama by the time of his death, 12 June 1875.[8]

Alphonza Josephus Jackson, an eighteen-year-old when he joined the State Line in February 1863, farmed after the war and eventually moved to Atlanta, where he had a grocery store on Auburn Avenue. During the last nine months of the war he had kept a diary; this, coupled with apparently excellent recall, enabled him to write two brief histories of the Second Regiment, one in 1876 and another during the mid 1890's. In later years former Private Jackson wore a Vandyke beard and looked very much the Confederate colonel. He died in Decatur, Georgia, on 16 February 1915.[9]

---

[6]*Atlanta Constitution,* 25 August 1927; Dennis Joseph Pfennig, "Evan and Clark Howell of the *Atlanta Constitution:* The Partnership (1889-1897)," (Ph. D. dissertation, University of Georgia, 1975) 6; Raymond B. Nixon, *Henry W. Grady: Spokesman of the New South* (New York: Alfred A. Knopf, 1943) 186; *Atlanta Constitution,* 25 August 1927.

[7]*Atlanta Constitution,* 25 August 1891; Carrie W. Brown, Widow's Indigent Pension, 1901, Fulton County, Georgia, Confederate Pension ecords, GDAH.

[8]*Selma (AL) Times-Journal,* 7 November 1927. Saffold was called "Major Saffold" after the war, but it is uncertain whether this was from election or self-promotion.

[9]Natalie R. Redfern to author, 23 January 1980; photograph of Jackson in old age, courtesy of Mrs. Redfern; Jackson Diary, Jackson Papers. Fact-filled, entertaining, and anecdotal, Jackson's memoirs are refreshingly free of pretension and sentimentality. They contain some very graphic descriptions of what it was like to be a common soldier of the State Line in camp, on the march, and on the battlefield. Jackson does not posture heroically in his accounts, instead blithely recalling such exploits as taking "French leave" or stealing roasting ears.

APPENDIX V

Cumulative Muster Rolls of the Georgia State Line

The following cumulative muster rolls are based upon the one hundred and sixty-three manuscript State Line muster rolls in the Georgia Department of Archives and History, Atlanta, Georgia. There are nine rolls for most of the companies of the First Regiment, none dated later than 31 May 1864. Only seven rolls exist for most of the Second Regiment's companies, none dated later than 31 January 1864. For the State Line cavalry, five muster rolls are on file, the last dated 28 February 1865.[1]

Although all legible names were transcribed from the manuscripts, no attempt was made to include the variant spellings that appeared for the names of certain men; in each such case, the predominant spelling was listed. Every effort was made to compile an accurate list, despite the illegibility of some of the manuscripts, as well as frequent instances of eccentric penmanship and phonetic spelling.

While the manuscript muster rolls yield scant information on the men of the State Line, the Georgia Archives also has typed rosters for most of the Line's companies. Prepared by the Georgia Soldier Commission, these rosters—like Lillian Henderson's *Roster of the Confederate Soldiers of Georgia, 1861-1865*—sometimes "give a brief summary of the military service of the men and sometimes the date and place of birth or death." Some sources used by the compilers, however, are of "questionable reliability."[2]

The National Archives' *Compiled Service Records of Confederate Soldiers Who Served in Organizations from the State of Georgia* yields the

---

[1]Muster Rolls, passim, GDAH. Although General Wayne designated third lieutenants "ensigns," they are seldom listed as such on the muster rolls.

[2]*Civil War Records,* Georgia Department of Archives and History Publication No. 76-CW-1, 8-9.

names of some men who joined the State Line companies during the period for which there are no muster rolls. Although much valuable information is to be found in these records, there are also a great many inaccuracies. For example, Colonel James Stapleton's Second Regiment of Carswell's Brigade, First Division, Georgia Militia, is listed as a State Line regiment, and many officers and men of the Second State Line are erroneously listed as members of Stapleton's unit. Likewise, several of Stapleton's men are listed as part of Storey's State Line. Consequently, it was decided not to add the names from these records to the muster roll lists. Instead, those names which evidence indicated belonged to men who had served in the State Line—no matter what their designation by the National Archives— were combined, without regard to regiment, alphabetized, and placed in a separate grouping after the muster rolls. When available, the soldier's rank was included with his name; company and regiment, when cited, were placed in parentheses after the name.[3]

The rolls of each regiment are preceded by lists of the regimental field and staff officers, drawn from various sources. In the cases of both regimental and company officers, a man's name is listed with each office he held, in the order in which he held it.[4]

---

[3]Compiled Service Records, passim.

[4]The most useful list of the State Line's regimental field and staff officers is found in General Orders, No. 10, 1 May 1863, GO, GDAH. Officers' names, ranks, dates of commission, and counties of residence, along with a "List of Officers arranged in the order of their Relative Rank," appear in this source. Two years of war worked changes in the officers' organization—through promotion, resignation, desertion, court-martial, and death. These changes have been gleaned from correspondence, service records, and newspaper reports.

Engraving of Georgia's state seal as it appeared on stationery and various forms during the war period. (Courtesy of Special Collections, University of Georgia Libraries, Athens, Georgia.)

First Regiment, Georgia State Line
Field and Staff Officers

Colonel:	Galt, Edward M.
Lt. Colonel:	Bryan, James
	Brown, John M.
	Howell, Albert
Major:	Brown, John M.
	Tate, William
	Scott, J. N.
Surgeon:	Brown, Maj. Aaron P.
Asst. Surgeon:	Spier, Capt. James H.
Quartermaster:	Northcutt, Capt. Jesse J.
Asst. Quartermaster:	Gordon, 2d Lt. George A.
Commissary:	Lemmon, Capt. Smith
Asst. Commissary:	McDonald, 2d Lt. J. B. W.
Adjutant:	Waters, 1st Lt. F. Emmett

Co. A., First Regiment, Georgia State Line
Catoosa County

Officers:

Capt.:	Howell, Albert		5th Sgt.:	Powers, P. J.
1st Lt.:	Day, William T.			Crumley, D. N.
2d Lt.:	Watson, Joseph G.		1st Cpl.:	Watson, F. M.
3d Lt.:	Howell, William H.			Bell, D. T.
1st Sgt.:	Johnston, R. C.		2nd Cpl.:	Posey, J. M.
	Allen, L. P.			Poole, S. N.
2nd Sgt.:	Williamson, Roy			Bell, D. L.
	Martin, Joseph			Shadburn, J. A.
	McAfee, R. E.			Ragsdale, A. B.
3rd Sgt.:	Cook, H. P.		3rd Cpl.:	Crumley, D. N.
	Pittman, W. H.			Cook, George G.
4th Sgt.:	Dunbar, J. B.		4th Cpl.:	Nix, W. A.
	McAfee, R. E.			
	Shadburn, J. A.			

("A" Company, First Regiment)

Privates:

Aiken, John W.	Austin, T. M.	Benson, Monroe
Alexander, J. A.	Bailey, J. A. W.	Benson, R. W.
Allen, A. D.	Bailey, J. M.	Benton, R. D.
Allen, John W.	Baldwin, H. A.	Black, F. M.
Allen, L. P.	Baldwin, J. J.	Boggs, T. A.
Anderson, A. G.	Baker, N.	Boyers, W.
Anderson, Charles	Ball, A. J.	Brockman, C.
Anderson, D. P.	Ball, M.	Brown, R.
Anderson, H. F.	Barker, W. H. H.	Bullard, J.
Anderson, Isaac	Bates, R. J.	Bullard, Thomas
Anderson, J.	Beck, J. A.	Burgess, A. P.
Anderson, William	Bell, David T.	Burgess, Joel

Callaway, J.
Camp, William
Cantrell, J. G.
Cash, J. M.
Cash, J. S.
Chapman, W. J.
Chapman, W. P.
Chitwood, W.
Clayton, L.
Cook, E. C.
Cook, George G.
Cook, J. M.
Collins, W.
Copeland, A.
Copeland, A. J.
Copeland, J. H.
Cross, A.
Daniel, John
Davenport, J. A.
Davis, E. M.
Day, J. R.
Dean, E.
Deaton, John D.
Dodd, J. H.
Dodd, J. M.
Dodd, James W.
Dodd, S. P.
Duckett, H. S.
Duckett, J. B.
Edmonson, J. R.
Ellenburg, John
Ellison, F. D.
Embry, J. F.
Embry, Jesse
Etris, John
Fenn, Thomas J.
Fincher, J. C.
Fowler, George
Foster, J. H.
Foster, W. G.
Freeman, B. S. (B. F.)
Gaines, J.
Gann, J.
Gilbert, J. P. (I. P.)
Glower, G. W.
Gray, J. M.
Green, A.
Grogan, G. B.
Hammond, Pink
Hammond, W. N.
Hansard, J. W.
Hansard, James
Hansard, John F.
Hansard, S. L.
Harpe, G. W.

Harris, G. C.
Hembree, D. R.
Hembree, M. P.
Hendrix, Isaac
Hendrix, J. S.
Hendrix, J. T.
Hendrix, M. M.
Hicks, H. H.
Hicks, W. D.
Hill, H. H.
Howell, C. A.
Hughes, J. T.
Hurston, A. B.
Hurt, W. J.
Hutchins, D. F.
Ivy, H.
James, O. M.
Johnson, G. P.
Johnson, J. M.
Johnson, J. R.
Johnson, R. C.
Jolly, J. M.
Jordan, E. D.
Jordan, E. P.
Jordan, W. M.
Karr, J.
Keith, S. A.
Kemp, C. T.
Kemp, William
Kendrick, J. R.
Lamb, P. J.
Land, J. M.
Lee, J. W.
Lewis, H.
Lowe, G. W.
Lowe, John S.
Lowe, Thomas J.
Lowery, W. T.
Lyle, T. P.
Majors, J. T.
Manor, J. B.
Martin, B.
Martin, J. C.
Martin, J. L.
Martin, Joseph
Martin, W.
Martin, Zachariah
Mathias, Ruben
McAfee, Robert E.
McConnell, P. W.
McCord, W. R.
McDonald, W. G.
McGinnis, A. C.
Miller, H. D.
Miller, R.

Monday, Z.
Montgomery, Samuel
Morgan, M. V.
Morgan, T. J.
Nix, John
Oliver, D. M.
Olvier, G. L.
Palmer, J. A.
Pirkle, J. L.
Pirkle, J. M.
Pittman, A. S.
Pittman, W. H.
Poe, J.
Poole, S. N.
Poss, Thomas
Poss, W. F.
Powell, J.
Power, G. H.
Power, W. C.
Queen, L. V.
Ragsdale, A. B.
Reese, L. E.
Riden, B. F.
Roberts, A. M.
Samples, J. N.
Samples, M. M.
Saterfield, W. F.
Say, C. A.
Shadburn, H. L.
Shadburn, J. A.
Shadburn, T. J.
Shadburn, W. B.
Shinn, J. D.
Smallwood, A. G.
Smith, J. M.
Smith, Willis J.
Stephens, John H.
Stephens, N. D.
Story, H. G.
Thompson, William
Tumlin, J. N.
Turner, W. H.
Turner, W. R.
Venable, R. R.
Waddial, A.
Waiter, W. J.
Waits, Alfred
Waits, Matthew
Waits, W. J.
Waitzfelder, Leopold
Wall, C. S.
Watson, F. M.
Watson, J. A.
Wellborn, J. D.
Westbrook, N. S.

Westbrook, T. M.
Wheeler, William
White, G. B.
White, Henson
White, J. H.

White, J. N.
White, J. R.
Whitner, A. B.
Williams, M. P.
Williams, O. H. P.

Wofford, E.
Wood, B. C.
Wood, B. G.
Wright, J. W.

Co. B, First Regiment, Georgia State Line
(Franklin County, "Joe Brown Defenders")

Officers:

Capt.:	Patrick, John H.	5th Sgt.:	Price, W. F.
1st Lt.:	Moseley, S. H.		Osborne, H. W.
2nd Lt.:	Osborne, D. O.		Talmadge, C. G.
3rd Lt.:	Ash, W. M.	1st Cpl.:	Osborne, H. W.
1st Sgt.:	Lester, W. G.		Macaster, David
	Fisher, L. B.		Hutcherson, T. J.
	Brown, A. H.	2nd Cpl.:	Macaster, David
2nd Sgt.:	Fisher, L. B.		Crawford, M. B.
	Brown, A. H.	3rd Cpl.:	Crawford, M. B.
	Brown, A. M.		McMurry, J. B.
3rd Sgt.:	Arendall, Nathan L.	4th Cpl.:	McMurry, J. B.
	Arnold, N. L.		Casey, F. N.
4th Sgt.:	Haddock, J. M.	Color Cpl.:	Hayes, W.
	Phillips, T. C.		Moseley, J. C.

("B" Company, First Regiment)

Privates:

Adams, W. M.
Addison, Samuel
Addison, Sanford
Aderhold, J. H. P.
Alexander, W. P.
Arendall, P. M.
Ariel, L. L.
Ayres, C. D.
Ayres, D. J.
Ayres, F. M.
Bagwell, S. F.
Bailey, Ishmael
Bird, James L.
Blackmon, F. M.
Bolding, B. T.
Bond, Livingston
Bond, S. L.
Brawner, J. H.
Brawner, J. W.
Brown, A. H.

Brown, A. M.
Bruce, M. A.
Burgess, Wiley
Burris, Joseph N.
Burris, W. A.
Casey, F. V.
Cawthon, William
Cawthorn, W. R.
Clark, Reuben J.
Clark, Tillman
Coffee, J. M.
Collins, Littleton
Comer, H. R.
Connally, J. S.
Cooper, W. A.
Crawford, E. S.
Crawford, William H.
Dortch, James S.
Dortch, John W.
Duncan, Asa B.

Duncan, Jesse
Eddleman, F. N.
Farmer, Simeon
Farrow, Andrew J.
Flood, John P.
Fowler, Jackson
Freeman, B. R.
Frix, W. S.
Garner, G. W.
Garner, Wm.
Gillespie, J. L.
Ginn, James C.
Grubbs, James R.
Haddock, J. M.
Haley, J. W.
Harbor, J. W.
Harbor, W. D.
Harbor, W. T.
Harris, J. D.
Harrison, T. A.

Harrison, W. C.
Hart, John
Hathcock, James O.
Hayes, L. H.
Hayes, W. J.
Hayes, William
Hicks, C. G.
Higgenbotham, J. H.
Holbrook, J. W.
Holland, B. F.
Hubbard, Francis
Hubbard, Levi
Hughes, M. T.
Hutcherson, T. J.
Jennings, W. W.
Kay, A. M.
Kay, J. E.
Kytle, J. C.
Landers, R. L.
Langston, A. O.
Langston, F. M.
Langston, G. B.
Langston, J. F.
Langston, Jesse
Ledbetter, G. M.
LeGrand, J. Matthew
Lester, W. G.
Looney, D. N.
Mabry, W. R.
McCarter, T. J.

McCluskey, L. M.
McClusky, L. L.
McDuffie, John
McMurry, T. E.
McWhorter, W. L.
Mitchell, Wm. T.
Mosely, J. W.
Mosly, J. C.
Neal, Francis P.
Neal, W. B.
Nicholson, D. M.
Nicholson, Wm. D.
Norris, W. J.
O'Shields, John
Payne, A. S.
Payne, H. J.
Payne, W. J.
Phillips, T. C.
Phillips, W. C.
Poole, W.
Presley, W. R.
Price, W. F.
Pulliam, J. D.
Purcell, E. L.
Ray, W. R.
Reed, G. L.
Reed, R. F.
Rice, F. N.
Richardson, J. G.
Roberts, W. H.

Seagraves, W. B.
Shackelford, M.
Shankle, S. M.
Shirley, B. F.
Shirley, B. H.
Shirley, B. N.
Skinner, F.
Smith, W. S.
Starr, L. W.
Stevenson, J. G.
Stone, Wm. H.
Talmadge, C. Y.
Tyler, J. D.
Tyler, L. C.
Vandiver, E. C.
Vandiver, W. I. P.
Vaughn, Ben.
Vaughn, Calvin
Wade, J. A. C.
Walls, E. H.
Walters, C. T.
Walters, H. M.
Walters, Lumpkin
Weldon, Wm. Shirley
Westbrook, W. G.
Wheeler, James S.
Williams, W. M.
Wilson, J. C.
Wright, L. F.
Yow, R. D.

Co. C, First Regiment, Georgia State Line
(Floyd County, "Fort Infantry")

Officers:

Capt.:	Howe, William	4th Sgt.:	Shockley, J. I., Sr.
1st Lt.:	DePriest, Philip R.	5th Sgt.:	Hamilton, Wm. T.
2nd Lt.:	Shockley, William J.	1st Cpl.:	Pettit, John D.
3rd Lt.:	Morris, Cicero H.		Floyd, William
1st Sgt.:	Harbin, John H.	2nd Cpl.:	Carter, William
2nd Sgt.:	Morris, J. G.	3rd Cpl.:	Floyd, William
3rd Sgt.:	Buchanan, W. N.		
	Pettit, John D.		

("C" Company, First Regiment)

Privates:

Adams, Thomas F.
Allen, John
Allen, W. J.
Allen, Wm. T.
Allgood, G. W.
Anthony, M. A. W.
Autry, John P.
Bagwell, Berry
Barnes, James H.
Beard, John M.
Bell, W. B.
Boatman, William
Bradberry, John W.
Bradley, J. C.
Bradley, J. H.
Brakebill, A. M.
Bramlett, N. D.
Brannon, Chas.
Brannon, R. S.
Bryant, James A.
Buchannon, W. N.
Burris, J.
Butler, John
Caldwell, Andrew J.
Caldwell, Jefferson
Camp, Wm.
Cane, Robert
Carroll, James F. M.
Castleberry, Uriah
Chambers, George
Chambers, J. T.
Chambers, T. J.
Clardy, H. L.
Cochran, R. S.
Coker, J. W.
Coker, William H.
Colston, Simon
Cook, Wm.
Cossa, Green
Dalton, Claiborne
Dalton, James
Daniel, Asa
Day, Leciel
Day, Lucius
DeFoor, Martin

Dougherty, Horatio C.
Dover, Lawson
Duke, Edward L.
Duke, Green, R.
Echols, R. W.
Estis, W. C.
Fagala, Howard
Floyd, Eli
Gilliam, Samuel T.
Gray, John
Gray, Joseph M.
Griffin, Zack J.
Hames, John
Hamilton, W. T.
Harris, Benjamin
Harris, George
Harris, W. L.
Harris, William
Jack, William A.
Keelin, Lemuel
Kelley, Jonathan
Kennedy, N. M.
Kubitsheck, W. J.
Leathers, Anson
Lloyd, James Emory
Loner, John W.
Lumpkin, Joseph H.
Martin, Enos
Martin, J. C.
Martin, Robert
Martin, Taylor
Massey, Thomas
Massey, W. T.
Mathews, James L.
Maxwell, Green L.
Maxwell, John L.
May, Benjamin F.
McClesky, John
McCullough, J. J.
McWhorter, S. W.
Meredith, Warren H.
Miller, Thomas
Morris, A. H.
Morris, A. J.
Morris, C. J.

Morrow, Wilson
Newton, A. C.
Nichols, James
Nixon, William D.
Noble, Lawrence
O'Dell, William
Oliver, George
Orr, William
Owens, W. S.
Payne, L. C. D.
Pettitt, Erwin
Phillips, E. H.
Pinson, James S.
Potter, John
Reese, George
Satterwhite, David
Sharp, James C.
Shirley, Robert H.
Shirley, Robt. H., Jr.
Shockley, J. I., Jr.
Shockly, Wm. I.
Smith, John M.
Staggs, James C.
Strickland, E.
Suggs, William A.
Summers, Lewis
Thompson, A. J.
Thompson, William R.
Thurman, W. M.
Tilley, Wm. L.
Tritt, William
Trout, H. C.
Wanslee, Nat T.
Wayne, J. A. J.
Wayne, R. C.
Webb, David
White, Patrick H.
Wiggins, Green M.
Williams, P. R.
Williams, W. C.
Wills, Ed. C.
Woodell, James P.
Wright, John W.
Wright, Joseph A.
Wright, Thomas

Co. D, First Regiment, Georgia State Line
(Lumpkin County, "Blue Ridge Rangers")

Officers:

Capt.:	Graham, Robert A.		5th Sgt.:	Mullinix, Geo. W.
1st Lt.:	McCrary, Richard H.			Watson, D. J.
2nd Lt.:	Stow, Abraham F.		1st Cpl.:	Mullinix, Elijah V.
3rd Lt.:	Jones, Martin L.			Harper, S.
1st Sgt:	Brown, Josh B.		2nd Cpl.:	Arrendale, Frank L.
	Mullinax, A. J.		4th Cpl.:	Roberts, Geo. W.
2nd Sgt.:	McCrary, James W.			Oliver, Curtis
	Reeves, John F.			Abercrombie, J. H.
3rd Sgt.:	Burns, Robert C.			Bruce, G. W.
4th Sgt.:	Martin, Harrison T.		3rd Cpl.:	Pearson, Miles G.
	Mullinax, A. J.			Swafford, J. P.
	Hatfield, G. T.			

("D" Company, First Regiment)

Privates:

Abee, Simeon	Dodd, Martin	Jackson, A. J.
Abercrombie, John H.	Dotson, James M.	Jones, James N.
Anderson, S. L.	Dowdy, Alfred J.	Kelly, Jasper
Arnhart, Wm. H.	Duckett, Dolfus E.	Lance, Samuel P. K.
Arrendale, Rice	Dyer, Samuel H.	Long, James R.
Barnes, Clement R.	Eberhart, John W.	Lyle, W. A.
Barnes, John	Eberhart, W. J.	Martin, H. T.
Beck, Wm. D.	Elliott, Berry	Mays, J. M.
Bell, Allen J.	Elrod, E. F.	McCrary, J. W.
Bond, J. C.	Elrod, E. H.	Mears, W. P.
Bonner, Wyatt A.	Elrod, J. A.	Mullinax, Andrew J.
Boone, C. J.	Elrod, John	Nelms, Jeptha P.
Brackett, B. W.	Finly, James J.	Nix, J. F.
Brown, Isaac	Finly, Waddy T.	Norrell, Wm. T.
Bruce, Callaway	Fite, S. L.	O'Kelley, A. F.
Bruce, Geo. W.	Foster, W. W.	O'Kelley, E. C.
Bryan, Berrien C.	Free, James T.	O'Kelley, Edward W.
Bryan, Marion C.	Free, Jasper	Oliver, Curtis
Burns, Robert G.	Free, Wm. C.	Prewett, James
Byers, Robert A.	Gaddis, A.	Purdy, Wm.
Caldwell, Thomas	Gaddis, Lewis C.	Ralston, H. C.
Carder, Abner	Gayden, Newton	Reid, Samuel
Carroll, Wm. P.	Gladden, Wm.	Rider, John W.
Chambers, Andrew W.	Glaze, Willis	Robinson, Wm. W.
Chester, Jesse	Gordon, Geo. A.	Roberts, G. W.
Cochran, J. W.	Hamilton, James F.	Sanders, Samuel
Cochran, N. M.	Hamilton, Wm. R.	Satterfield, John W.
Collins, Hamilton	Harper, Newsome	Seabolt, Aaron
Conn, John P.	Hatfield, Geo. T.	Seitz, Lawson
Cronan, John R.	Head, C. A. J.	Self, Elijah F.
Davis, Daniel M.	Henry, Singleton	Simmons, Elijah L.
Davis, Samuel	Howell, Brison M.	Stargel, Chas. W.
Davis, Tillman	Howell, Daniel	Stargel, Wm. C.

Stephens, A. H.
Stephens, A. W.
Stone, Columbus
Sullins, J. B.
Swafford, James P.
Tank, C. N.
Thompson, Andrew J.
Trammell, Elisha

Tumlin, A. J.
Tumlin, F. E.
Turner, W. E.
Wade, Wm.
Wadkins, P.
Warren, Robert
Watkins, Philemon
Watson, D. G.

Watson, D. J.
Wehunt, Eki
Whelchel, E. C.
Whelchel, G. D.
Whelchel, Valentine
Woody, Mulligan C.
Worley, Wm. J.
Wright, Frederick

Co. E., First Regiment, Georgia State Line
(Cobb and Fulton Counties, "State Rights Guards")

Officers:

Capt.:	Cowen, Francis M.	4th Sgt.:	Reece, L. E.
1st Lt.:	Barber, Jacob B.	5th Sgt.:	Lowe, Geo. W.
2nd Lt.:	Gunn, Francis F.	1st Cpl.:	Lowe, John S.
3rd Lt.:	Bowie, C. W.	2nd Cpl.:	Bullard, John
1st Sgt.:	Baldwin, H. A.		Talley, G. T.
2nd Sgt.:	Stanback, Joseph V.	3rd Cpl.:	Tippin, F. M.
	Gann, Berry	4th Cpl.:	Samples, John N.
3rd Sgt.:	Gann, H. T.		Simpson, W. G.

("E" Company, First Regiment)

Privates:

Abercrombie, Charles
Alexander, John R.
Alexander, Wm.
Allen, John O.
Allen, Ransom A.
Alsabrook, D. H.
Anderson, Wm. W.
Bagley, Fletcher
Bagley, J. E.
Baldwin, H. A.
Baldwin, J. J.
Baldwin, S. J.
Ballenger, A. C.
Barber, Isaiah
Barber, Josiah
Barber, Nathaniel
Barnes, W. R.
Barnett, J. B.
Beck, J. H.
Beck, Wm. A.
Benson, N. H.
Bishop, J.
Bishop, John N.
Bishop, W. L.
Bowie, J. P.
Bowling, J. H.
Braselton, Wm. G.
Brockman, C. M.
Brooke, Nathan H.
Brown, A. O.

Brown, Robert
Bullard, John
Bullard, Thomas
Cantrell, Moses
Chambers, James H.
Cochran, E. B.
Collins, Wash.
Cook, John H.
Cowen, S. D.
Cox, R. H.
Crisler, J. M.
Crisler, J. W.
Crow, S. J.
Daniel, L. N.
Daniel, J. W.
Davis, Wm.
Dodds, J. M.
Dodds, John H.
Ellis, A. M.
English, Fleming
English, Manning
English, Thomas
Eubanks, Robert S.
Fleming, W. W.
Ford, J. R.
Fowler, Geo.
Franklin, J. C.
Gaddy, P. S.
Gann, Berry
Gann, F. M.

Gann, John
Gann, Seaborn
Gann, W. G.
Glore, G. W.
Glore, J. I.
Gordon, S. H.
Griffin, Wm.
Haynie, Wm. R.
Hembree, S. G.
Hill, A. T.
James, M. H.
James, Oscar M.
Johnson, I. H.
Johnson, Noel
Jordan, E. D.
Jordan, E. P.
Jordan, S. H.
Jordan, Wm.
Knox, W. T.
Lacy, Wm. D.
Lamb, P. J.
Lamb, Peter
Landers, J. C.
Lasseter, Henry
Leak, S. W.
Loew, J. S.
Luke, S. W.
Maner, H. E.
Maner, J. B.
Maner, Wm. G.

Manning, C. J.	Pool, S. N.	Stephens, A. D.
Marion, Sylvester	Price, Wm.	Stephens, Henry
Martin, Ben.	Puckett, L. A.	Stephens, N. D.
Martin, J. H.	Reed, Daniel	Swords, F. M.
Martin, J. L.	Reed, Daniel S.	Tally, Geo. T.
Martin, James P.	Reed, Isaac	Turk, M. S.
McClain, W. G.	Reed, W. B.	Turner, B. H.
McGriff, Henry	Reeves, H. H.	Turner, W. J.
McKinney, L. W.	Rucker, Joel	Vann, A. T.
McKinney, Leonidas	Sams, C. C.	Wade, J. W.
Miller, D. T.	Sams, H. B.	Wade, Wm.
Osborne, S. K.	Simpson, Wm. G.	Watson, J. G.
Ozburn, L.	Smith, A. J.	Watson, John M., Jr.
Pace, Stephen	Smith, D. G.	Watson, John M., Sr.
Palmer, James A.	Smith, I. C.	Whelchel, J. D.
Paver, James W.	Smith, J. C.	Whelchel, J. M.
Peacock, P. A.	Smith, J. F.	White, John S.
Petty, John F.	Smith, Wm. R.	Whitfield, C. P.
Pool, J. P.	Spears, Isaac D.	Williams, Edley
Pool, John	Spier, W. H.	

Co. F, First Regiment, Georgia State Line
(Bartow County, "Georgia Blues")

Officers:

Capt.:	Nelson, Elihu G.	4th Sgt.:	Sullins, Wm. M
1st Lt.:	Dickerson, Thomas C.	5th Sgt.:	McMahan, James
2nd Lt.:	Alley, Isham	1st Cpl.:	Lindsey, John F.
3rd Lt.:	Deaton, John D.		Champion, William
1st Sgt.:	Smith, James M.	2nd Cpl.:	Keith, M. A., Jr.
2nd Sgt.:	Puckett, E. D.		Harris, S. R.
3rd Sgt.:	Puckett, A. M.	3rd Cpl.:	Deaton, Elijah
	Hardin, J. M.	4th Cpl.:	Terrell, James D.

("F" Company, First Regiment)

Privates:

Armstrong, James F.	Briant, H. D.	Champion, John
Arnold, Daniel	Brooks, Elijah	Connor, J. H.
Ashworth, John A.	Brooks, S. A.	Culver, Cleophus
Baker, B. W.	Burge, J. R. M.	Darby, James
Barton, Joshua	Butler, John	Darby, Newton
Bates, M. S.	Callahan, John W.	Darby, Oliver P.
Bogle, John Wm.	Carr, A. J.	Davis, William S.
Boyd, Robert W.	Carr, Jeptha	Dean, Henry
Bradley, J. P.	Carr, Wm. L.	Dean, Zachariah
Brannon, J. F.	Carver, T. J.	Deaton, Nathan
Brewster, O. H.	Casey, A. J.	Dempsey, L. C.

Denton, Wm. M.
Dowdy, A. P.
Dozier, Marcus
Dunnaway, J. L.
Dunnaway, John
Dunnegan, Abner
Elrod, F. A.
Evans, John W.
Fennell, Wm.
Ferguson, B. F.
Ford, John D.
Foster, J. M.
Fountain, J. W.
Fowler, Leonard C.
Freeman, G. N.
Freeman, George T.
Freeman, H. D.
Freeze, R. R.
Gassaway, S. E.
Gerrin, John
Gillstrap, R. W.
Goddard, R. T.
Gordon, A. P.
Gordon, Jarrett
Green, James
Gullidge, Eli J.
Hammond, J. B.
Haney, Thomas
Harberson, Wm.
Harbin, John
Hardy, Henry
Hardy, J. S.
Harper, Rhoderic
Harris, S. H.
Heath, V. A.

Holden, M. N.
Holland, M. W.
Howard, J. A.
Howell, Eli
Howell, J. R.
Hudson, Shadrick
Humphries, James
Jarrett, C. K.
Jefferson, R. L.
Johnson, Samuel
Johnson, W. H.
Jordan, Wm.
Keith, M. A.
Keown, T. R.
Keys, Wm.
Kilgo, Ausburn
Knox, Joseph
Lang, Stephen
Leak, Asbury
Leak, M. A.
Leonard, Wm.
Lindsey, W. M.
Lowe, Isaac M.
McCandless, Wm. M.
McCoy, Elisha
McCoy, W. A.
McFadden, A. L.
McKinnie, David
Meers, J. M.
Meirs, Joseph F.
Moon, P. L.
Moore, F. J.
Moore, F. P.
Moore, T. E.
Murphy, Wm. S.

Northcutt, L. S.
Payne, Edward
Pitts, G. W.
Prater, W. W.
Pruitt, S. J.
Ragsdale, Spencer
Reid, Robert
Rhodes, J. G.
Richie, Robert
Roberson, W. J.
Rosson, Thomas
Rowland, W.
Shaw, E. J.
Smith, E. G.
Smith, L. S.
Spear, W. H.
Stancil, Alfred
Stephenson, J. W. T.
Suggs, W. A.
Summey, Geo. L.
Thomason, James Allen
Thompson, Wm.
Tolbert, A. J.
Turner, Wm.
Walker, Daniel
Walker, John
Walls, J. S.
Waters, A. D.
White, J. M.
Wiley, G. W.
Wilson, A. D.
Wood, Powell
Worley, J. T.
Worley, W. W.
York, John

Co. G, First Regiment, Georgia State Line
(Banks and White Counties, "Chattahoochee Rangers")

Officers:

Capt.:	Stephens, Littleton	5th Sgt.:	Sargeant, E. H.
1st Lt.:	Duke, Jesse R.		Davis, S. L.
2nd Lt.:	King, James Allen	1st Cpl.:	Ritch, F. F. A.
3rd Lt.:	Morris, Wiley H.		Means, H.
1st Sgt.:	Brown, Wm. C.	2nd Cpl.:	Cason, Geo. W.
	Faulkner, N. C.		Gailey, A. C.
2nd Sgt.:	Stephens, T. J.	3rd Cpl.:	Dodd, Levi H.
3rd Sgt.:	Ayres, James M.		Reese, W. O.
	Reese, W. O.		Wilson, I. S.
4th Sgt.:	Ritch, G. H.	4th Cpl.:	Cooley, James
	Hargrove, D. W.		Harris, J. J.

("G" Company, First Regiment)

Privates:

Anderson, A.
Anderson, F. M.
Arnold, B. F.
Ausburn, H. B.
Ausburn, H. H.
Ausburn, W. T.
Bennett, W. E.
Black, J. W.
Black, T.
Blair, J. M.
Bohannan, B.
Bowen, R. C.
Bowlin, J. H.
Brooks, Kenyon
Brookshire, N. F.
Bryan, A. P.
Chapman, J. M.
Clark, G. H.
Collins, E. T.
Cooley, J. M.
Crane, B.
Cronan, J. K. P.
Crow, J. M.
Dalton, J. R.
Dalton, T. B.
Dean, W. H.
Dickerson, O. T.
Dill, A. J.
Dodd, G. B.
Dodd, L. H.
Duckett, D. C.
Echols, C. S.
Echols, Wm. E.
Edwards, J. F.

Faulkner, G. W.
Faulkner, R. M.
Ferguson, R. H.
Flanigan, A. C.
Fricks, N.
Gaddis, James
Gailey, David J.
Garrison, D. A.
Garrison, W. T.
Gilleland, F. A.
Gowder, F. M.
Gowder, R. A.
Grant, A. P.
Griffin, A. L.
Halford, W. C.
Hamilton, E.
Hargrove, J. T.
Hargrove, J. W.
Harper, C. D.
Head, B.
Henderson, A. H.
Hicks, Robert
Higgins, E. J.
Hill, J. A.
Hooper, H. W.
Howard, Samuel
Hubbard, F.
Hughes, Wm.
Hunt, Wm.
Ivie, J. L.
Ivie, W. W.
Jones, A. D.
Jones, L. P.
Jones, R. P.

Jones, R. P., Jr.
Jones, W. H.
Jones, W. T.
King, W. L.
Kinney, J. P.
Kinsey, R. L.
Kinsey, W. P.
Kytle, S.
Landers, M. M.
Laprad, E. T.
Leonard, James
Little, M. C.
Manus, J. L.
Martin, J. W.
McIntire, Felix
McWilliams, D. W.
Meadows, C. W.
Meadows, W. C.
Means, H.
Meeks, J. W.
Mize, D. W.
Monroe, J. W.
Motes, J. T.
Neese, J. W.
Nunnally, A.
Parker, L. M.
Parker, R. A.
Parsons, W. F.
Patten, Wm. M.
Payne, Phillip
Peck, A.
Perkins, G. W.
Perkins, J.
Phagans, Wm.

Pinkston, John
Porter, J. H.
Potter, G. W.
Potts, J. P.
Powers, J. H.
Redman, W. L.
Reynolds, J. A.
Ritch, G. H.
Ritch, J. R.
Ritch, W. C.
Rogers, G. I.
Roper, J. M.
Rucker, H. W.
Sargent, E. H.
Shirley, B.
Shore, W. C.

Short, A. F.
Slaton, S. H.
Smallwood, H.
Smallwood, J. K. P.
Smith, R. J.
Smith, W. W.
Speer, E. G.
Suddeth, J. A.
Suggs, J.
Tapp, T. L.
Taylor, A. J.
Taylor, G. W.
Thompson, G. M.
Tippins, De Marquis
Tippins, Dennis
Tippins, Leviticus

Tomlin, W. P.
Vickery, W. J.
Walker, W. R.
Ward, W. J.
Waters, M.
Waters, P. A.
Watson, B. H.
Watson, E.
Webb, A.
Webb, Wm.
Wells, Wm.
Wheeler, J. W.
Williams, W. K.
Williams, W. S.
Wilson, G. P.
Wilson, J. P.
Yearwood, S.

Co. H, First Regiment, Georgia State Line
(Gilmer County, "Gilmer Browns")

Officers:

Capt.: Bryan, James G.
     McAfee, Robert E.
     West, Andrew Jackson
1st Lt.: Cox, Wm.
2nd Lt.: Ellington, Wm., Jr.
1st Sgt.: Whitaker, Silas
     Allen, J. M.
2nd Sgt.: West, James Manson
     Davenport, A.
3rd Sgt.: Dalton, T. W.
4th Sgt.: Lance, Martin
     Hill, Walter

5th Sgt.: Searcy, Wm.
     Sisson, I. A.
     Sisson G. A.
1st Cpl.: Sumner, E.
2nd Cpl.: Sellers, J. D.
3rd Cpl.: Gibson, Thomas
     Mulkey, J.
4th Cpl.: Smith, G. F.
     Smith, S. W.

("H" Company, First Regiment)

Privates:

Anderson, J. R.
Ayers, M.
Baker, J.
Barnett, T. M.
Beavers, John
Bennett, A. J.
Bennett, James
Black, Daniel
Black, J. K.
Blalock, J. K.

Bowden, Thomas
Braselton, A.
Brooks, H. P.
Brooks, L. M.
Brown, Richard
Bruce, L.
Bryson, J. A.
Burrell, K.
Burrell, T.
Calhoun, B. C.

Calhoun, J. C.
Callahan, James
Carnes, J. A.
Carson, J.
Chalfinch, Hiram
Clark, C. W.
Coley, G. W.
Conner, M. L.
Cooper, J. M.
Cox, J. M.

Cox, John
Cox, Richard
Cox, W. G.
Deal, J. H.
Dillbeck, J. A.
Dillbeck, J. H.
Dispane, O.
Dobbs, Wm.
Dover, A. B.
Dover, A. E.
Ellington, B. F.
Ellington, F. J.
Elliot, L.
Evans, E.
Evans, J.
Evans, Jacin
Evans, John
Fore, H. M.
Fossett, C.
Fossett, Wm.
Foster, W. H.
Frady, J. H.
Freeman, John
Gilford, Clayton
Goss, J. W.
Gossage, Henson
Griffin, W. H.
Griffith, W. K.
Grogan, A. C.
Grogan, J. L.
Grogan, Perry W.
Grogan, W. M.
Hall, A. P.
Hall, Alfred
Hardburger, J.
Hays, Wm.
Headen, G. M.

Heath, G. W.
Hill, James
Hipp, B. M.
Holt, J. L.
Hubbard, L. S.
Jarvis, B. M.
Joice, A. E.
Jones, E. A.
Jones, Wm.
Joyce, E. A.
Kelly, Wm. L.
Kincaid, A.
Kinner, W. L.
May, J. N.
McCarter, J.
McClure, J.
McClure, R. M.
McDaniel, J. D. W.
McKinney, M.
Meace, H.
Mealer, M. A.
Moore, John
Mull, D. B.
Nelson, G. B.
Norsworthey, J. M.
Osburn, Geo. S.
Painter, S.
Parks, J. M.
Parks, M. M.
Payne, L. F.
Payne, W. C.
Perry, G.
Pettit, G. W.
Pettit, J. M.
Plemmons, S. J. P.
Plemmons, W. C.
Prince, A. A.

Pritchett, D. W.
Ray, J. R.
Read, J. C.
Riddle, D.
Riddle, J. W.
Riddle, James M.
Ridgers, Wm.
Rogers, W. K.
Roper, J. L.
Sanders, M. F.
Sanders, M. S.
Searcy, H. W.
Searcy, Wm.
Shelhorse, J. M.
Shepard, M.
Shepperd, Z.
Sisson, A.
Sluder, L.
Smith, J. H.
Starks, John
Starks, W. J.
Stone, T. P.
Teague, F. M.
Teague, R.
Thomas, James
Tippin, Landford
Underwood, W. W.
Venable, L.
Watkins, T. W.
Watkins, W. S.
Weaver, H.
Welch, Joseph
West, S. H.
Wilkins, J. T.
Williams, M. S.
Wright, R.

Co. I, First Regiment, Georgia State Line
(Whitfield County, "Galt Volunteers")

Officers:

Capt.: Norris, Robert H.
1st Lt.: Scott, James N.
2nd Lt.: Nelson, Samuel D.
3rd Lt.: Sneed, George A.
1st Sgt.: Keith, Andrew J.
2nd Sgt.: Garner, Joseph R.
3rd Sgt.: Whitner, John W.
4th Sgt.: Lynch, John T.
5th Sgt.: Miller, E. W.

1st Cpl.: Moore, Robert M.
Miller, Jacob R.
2nd Cpl.: Miller, Jacob R.
Bates, McAfee
3rd Cpl.: Craig, John G.
Maxwell, Marcus
4th Cpl.: Eades, Cicero W.
Kendrick, Aaron D.
5th Cpl.: Maulden, Alexander J.

("I" Company, First Regiment)

Privates:

Agnew, John S.
Amos, John E.
Barry, Charles W.
Bates, Andrew J.
Bates, Napoleon B.
Bates, Reuben C.
Bearden, William C.
Black, John S.
Boman, Elijah
Bradley, John A.
Bray, James
Brewer, Franklin A.
Bridges, Jeremiah
Brindle, Doctor C.
Caldwell, John
Cameron, Robert A.
Carter, Reuben
Cavender, Joseph H.
Chapman, Thomas L.
Chastain, Miles R.
Clardy, John Q.
Clements, John A.
Clements, Judson C.
Cochran, Coleman C.
Cochran, James W.
Cox, James
Craig, John G.
Crow, John C.
Cunningham, M. M.
Dantzler, L. N.
Davis, Spencer B.
Dillard, William
Dowdy, Jasper P.
Earnest, Marcellus B.
Erskew, William J.
Fagala, Lewis
Fant, Enoch M.
Farnsworth, W. P.
Fitzgerald, E. C.
Gaines, Aaron N.
Gann, James
Garner, Francis W.
Glimps, John B.
Green, James P.
Greason, Abe
Greason, Green
Griffin, Adam
Guice, William J.

Haddock, David C.
Harber, John C.
Hardcastle, William
Harland, Joshua
Harris, Moses
Haynes, V. H.
Helton, Thomas
Hodge, Robert G.
Holcombe, John M.
Holland, W. K.
Hopper, Z.
Howell, James C.
Howell, Martin S.
Hunsucker, B. C.
Jackson, Thomas
Johnson, John J.
Keith, Charles
Keith, John B.
Keith, John M.
Keith, Samuel A.
Keith, Vincent D.
Kendrick, Aaron D.
Keown, Henry C.
Key, B. L.
Keys, John M.
Langford, A. A.
Lanier, Madison
Leonard, Benjamin
Liday, J. P.
Longley, William C.
Love, James
Majors, E. G.
Malone, William B.
Mann, Young A. B.
Mashburn, Jackson B.
Massey, Leander
Masters, W. B.
Mauldin, Andrew J.
Maxwell, Caldwell
Maxwell, Marcus
Maxwell, William
McAbee, E. S.
McGhee, James M.
McLane, H. W.
Miller, James F.
Moody, A. H. S.
Moon, Robert M.
Morgan, James M.

Morgan, Pleasant
Morris, George W.
Morris, J. C.
Mote, John Q. A.
Murphy, Saul F.
Nations, Thomas
Nelson, W. T.
Offut, Robert A.
Orr, William R.
Osborne, Wylie
Owens, John M.
Oxford, C. F.
Park, James H.
Pendergrass, H. N.
Pullen, Thomas M.
Rawlins, John D.
Redwine, M. M.
Reece, Christopher C.
Reynolds, John W.
Rhodes, John W.
Richardson, Hyman L.
Richardson, John R.
Richardson, L. C.
Roberts, Andrew J.
Robertson, Robert F.
Simmons, James B.
Smalley, James C.
Staten, Samuel
Staten, Wylie B.
Stevens, Simeon
Strickland, Henry F.
Sturdivant, J. P.
Swift, Tyre G.
Taliaferro, Wylie F.
Tally, John H.
Thomas, Richard H.
Thompson, J. K. P.
Turpin, Josiah
Underwood, John
Verhine, Henry
Verhine, Richard T.
Waddell, Alford
Ware, Robert N. C.
Wetzel, Benjamin C.
Whitfield, B. H.
Wright, J. W.
Wylie, James R.

Co. K, First Regiment, Georgia State Line
(Murray and Gordon Counties, "Railroad Bridge Guards")

Officers:

Capt.:	Galt, E. M.	4th Sgt.:	Keith, J. L.
	Tate, Wm.		Kirkpatrick, J. T.
1st Lt.:	Tate, Wm.	5th Sgt.:	Stanley, Isham A.
	Fite, Isaac Marion		Kemp, Wm. Henry
2nd Lt.:	Fite, Isaac Marion	1st Cpl.:	Collins, Martin
	Parrott, Jacob E.		McGurre, Singleton
3rd Lt.:	Parrott, Jacob E.	2nd Cpl.:	Kemp, Wm. Henry
1st Sgt.:	Kendrick, William B.		Hill, Richard H.
	Jackson, Joshua	3rd Cpl.:	Prichard, James
2nd Sgt.:	Fite, Isaac Marion		Cooksey, James M.
	Brooks, E. B.	4th Cpl.:	Hill, Richard H.
3rd Sgt.:	Brooks, E. B.		Blair, J. E.
	Phillips, James A. J.	5th Cpl.:	Smith, Joseph H.

("K" Company, First Regiment)

Privates:

Allen, J. M.	Davenport, Thomas	Holcombe, Wm. D.
Anderson, H.	Dillard, Robert	Hunsucker, A. J.
Anderson, Wm.	Dobbs, James	Hunsucker, Geo. W.
Barnes, Wm. L.	Dobbs, J. P.	Hunsucker, James B.
Baucom, Sydney	Dobbs, Wm.	Hunsucker, Wm. L.
Baxter, Wm. S.	Dorsett, Thomas R.	Jarvis, Thomas J.
Benton, Wm. H. H.	Dupree, Thomas	Johnsey, H. A.
Blair, J. P.	Dupree, Wm. J.	Johnsey, J. H.
Blair, Joseph E.	Edwards, Richard W.	Johnson, I. R.
Blair, S. A.	Egan, Timothy	Johnson, J. M.
Booker, G. W.	Fite, G. T.	Johnson, John A.
Brown, Daniel J.	Fite, Partial H.	Johnson, John L.
Brown, Elbert W.	Freeman, Geo. T.	Kay, James R.
Brown, R. H.	Freeman, J. S.	Keen, James J.
Brooks, S. A.	Gibson, Isom R.	Keene, James W.
Burkhalter, John T.	Gideon, Gilead J. B.	Keith, Vincent D.
Cagle, Henry	Glore, John T.	Kemp, James S.
Callaway, E. W.	Goode, A. W.	Kemp, John B.
Cash, Joel S.	Goodwin, W. T.	Kemp, John W.
Cavender, James H.	Greeson, James W.	Kendrick, John R.
Chaffin, Edward M.	Greeson, Wm.	Keys, Wm.
Chapman, Edward E.	Griffin, Wm. A.	Kirkpatrick, Elijah G.
Chastain, Miles R.	Griffith, G. W.	Leavell, E. F.
Chitwood, Alfred	Guyton, Joshua	Leavell, Wm. J.
Chitwood, Joseph	Harber, J. N.	Lotheridge, Wm. R.
Chitwood, Wm.	Hester, Wm. H.	Mann, Joel J.
Clark, Wm. S.	Hicks, Geo. T.	Mason, Larkin W.
Clements, John A.	Hilton, Hillard G.	Maxwell, Wm.
Coffey, E. C.	Hilton, Thomas	McCrary, A. D.
Coplan, S. M.	Hodge, Robert G.	Metts, Edward
Cox, S. A.	Holcombe, C. F.	Miller, Daniel P.
Crawley, Andrew J.	Holcombe, J. M.	Miller, Samuel P.

Moody, A. H. S.
Moore, Robert M.
Morgan, Andrew J.
Morris, A. S.
Moss, Pinckney L.
Nations, James
Patton, W. C.
Payne, Edward
Randall, R. A.
Rawlins, John B.
Reeves, Henry
Rhodes, John W.
Richards, James M.
Rigsby, John W.

Robeson, T. C.
Roddy, Martin
Rogers, Hugh
Scott, James N.
Simpson, R. A.
Smith, A. B.
Smith, Alexander C.
Smith, Elijah G.
Smith, L. S.
Smith, P. L.
Stancel, Berrien D.
Stanley, Isham A.
Stephens, Zachariah
Stewart, Edward A.

Strickland, Noah
Tate, Caleb R.
Tate, Wm.
Taylor, J. W.
Taylor, Thornton
Tinsley, Wm. J.
Tipton, Thomas J.
Vandyke, Benjamin F.
Vernon, F. D.
Wade, John
Watson, Robert A.
Watson, Wm. M.
Webster, Wm. V.
Whittle, J. R.
Yarbrough, Thomas R.

Cavalry Company, First Regiment, Georgia State Line
(1) Cowen's Cavalry, March 1864-August 1864
("State Scouts," later "State Mountain Infantry")

Officers:

Capt.:	Cowen, Francis M.
1st Lt.:	Ellington, William
2nd Lt.:	Ash, W. M.
Ensign:	Deaton, J. D.
Surgeon:	Speir, Capt. James H.
Asst. Quartermaster:	Gordon, 2nd Lt. George A.
Asst. Commissary:	McDonald, 2nd Lt. J. D. W.

(2) Talbot's Scouts, August 1864-May 1865

Capt.:	Talbot, Matthew Henry
1st Lt.:	Myrick, G. T.
2nd Lt.:	Keith, C. W.
3rd Lt.:	Deaton, J. D.
1st Sgt.:	Talley, G. T.
2nd Sgt.:	Green, W. L.
1st Cpl.:	Tippins, F. M.
2nd Cpl.:	Martin, H. T.

(Cavalry Company, First Regiment)

Privates:

Agnew, J. L.
Akin, R. L.
Alexander, J. R.
Alexander, W. M.
Allen, J. M.
Anderson, H.

Arrendale, N. L.
Bales, M. J.
Ballenger, A. C.
Barnes, C. R.
Bates, M. F.
Bates, M. S.

Bates, W. T.
Beck, W. A.
Benson, N. H.
Benson, N. J. C.
Benson, W. H.
Bird, A. T.

Bishop, J. M.
Blackman, W. M.
Blow, R. H.
Bonner, W. P.
Bookout, G. F. M.
Bowden, T.
Brockman, C. M.
Bruce, M. A.
Bryant, P.
Buice, G. W.
Buice, M. A.
Burkett, L.
Carnes, J. A.
Connally, W.
Cook, G. G.
Cook, G. W. D.
Cromer, H. R.
Crow, F. J.
Cunningham, M.
Dalton, T. M.
Davis, D. M.
Davis, G. D.
Davis, J.
Deaton, E.
Dickerson, J. C.
Dodd, J. H.
Dodd, M.
Dowdy, A. P.
Duke, T. M.
Eliott, H.
Eliott, J. A.
Elrod, H.
Elrod, J. A.
Elrod, J. H.
Elrod, R. H.
Evans, W. J.
Ezell, L. D.
Fitzpatrick, Wash
Fitzpatrick, William
Foster, W. H.
Frady, J. H.
Freeman, G.
Freeze, R. R.
Garner, J. R.
George, R. R.
Godard, J.
Goolsby, J. C.
Gordan, G. A.
Gordan, J. A.
Gordan, T. R.
Grady, J. H.
Gramling, G.
Green, N. L.
Greene, J. M.
Hagan, R.

Harber, W. D.
Harbin, J.
Harbin, W. J.
Harper, W. L.
Haynes, V. H.
Haynes, R. H.
Haynie, T. M.
Haynie, W. R.
Hill, H. W.
Hill, J. A.
Hill, W.
Holcomb, J. M.
Holland, W. N.
Holland, W. R.
Hunt, J.
Hunt, J. M.
Hunt, J. P.
Hunter, A. A.
Ivey, J. L.
Jones, J. N.
Jordan, E.
Keith, C. W.
Keith, J. B.
Keith, J. L.
Keith, M. A.
Keith, R. A.
Keown, H. C.
Knowles, J. M.
Lackey, W. J.
Leverett, R.
Lewis, P. K.
Little, T. J.
Loveday, J. P.
McCanless, W. M.
McCrary, Z. T.
McDonald, J. D. W.
McKinney, L. W.
McKinney, M. W.
Manning, C. J.
Manning, W.
Marchman, J.
Marshall, H. J.
Martin, H. F.
Martin, J. P.
Mays, J. M.
Miller, D. T.
Neal, F. A.
Neal, T. P.
Neal, W. B.
Osborn, G. L.
Oxford, C. F.
Parks, M. M.
Pendleton, P. T.
Penn, R. J.
Petty, J. L.

Pitts, O.
Pool, J.
Pool, J. P.
Pool, L. N.
Pool, S. N.
Pool, T. N.
Presley, J. P.
Price, Wm.
Pritchett, D. W.
Prosser, L. C.
Purdy, W. P.
Randall, R. A.
Ray, R. A.
Reid, E.
Robertson, W. J.
Rogers, W. K.
Roper, J. H.
Roper, J. M.
Roper, J. W.
Rucker, H. N.
Rucker, H. W.
Rucker, J.
Samples, J. M.
Sams, H. B.
Scissons, J. A.
Self, J. D.
Shelhouse, J. M.
Sherlock, J.
Shirley, B. T.
Simpson, M. G.
Simpson, W. G.
Skinner, E. A.
Smith, G. F.
Speer, J. H.
Strickland, N.
Sykes, J.
Tapp, T. L.
Teague, K.
Teague, Robert
Thompson, A. J.
Turk, J. W.
Tyler, L. C.
Walton, Wm.
Watson, W. M.
Watts, J. W.
West, G. L.
Whelchel, A. M.
Whelchel, A. N.
Whelchel, E. C.
Whelchel, J. D.
Whelchel, J. M.
Whitfield, John B.
Whitfield, M. C.
Worley, W. W.
Yelvington, I. R.

Second Regiment, Georgia State Line
Field and Staff Officers

Colonel:	Storey, Richard L.
	Wilson, James
Lt. Colonel:	Evans, Beverly D.
Major:	Womble, Drury W.
Surgeon:	Blackburn, Maj. J. C. C.
	Heard, Maj. Thomas
	Douglas, Maj. Peyton W.
Asst. Surgeon:	Douglas, Capt. Peyton W.
	Bailey, Capt. James W.
Quartermaster:	Moore, Capt. Hugh M.
Asst. Quartermaster:	Daniel, 2d Lt. James R.
Commissary:	Walker, Capt. James S.
Asst. Commissary:	Garrison, 2d Lt. Patterson G.
Adjutant:	McDonald, 1st Lt. Green B.
	Slade, 1st Lt. S. D.

Co. A, Second Regiment, Georgia State Line
(Forsyth County, "State Guards")

Officers:

Capt.:	Wallace, Jesse B.	5th Sgt.:	Casey, D. P.
1st Lt.:	Thompson, J. J.	1st Cpl.:	Callaway, W. A.
2nd Lt.:	Montgomery, Wm.		Wigley, A. J.
3rd Lt.:	Talent, B. C.	2nd Cpl.:	Canning, W. E.
1st Sgt.:	Blackstock, W. N.	3rd Cpl.:	Montgomery, H. C.
2nd Sgt.:	Beaver, J. T.		Carr, Jos. A.
3rd Sgt.:	Major, D. P.	4th Cpl.:	Tate, A. M.
4th Sgt.:	White, W.	5th Cpl.:	Taylor, J. M.
	Taylor, J. M.		

("A" Company, Second Regiment)

Privates:

Allen, A. D.	Braddy, J. C.	Collett, Jacob
Armstrong, J. W.	Browning, J. C.	Coltrain, D.
Bacon, W. E.	Brownlow, J. M.	Cox, D. S.
Bailey, W. V.	Buice, E.	Cox, W. M.
Barker, W. H. H.	Butler, W. B.	Cruse, S. P.
Bennett, D. H.	Callaway, J.	Cunningham, H. L.
Black, D. M.	Callaway, Thos.	Curbon, J. N. J.
Blackstock, W. J.	Chambers, O. H. P.	Day, A. J.
Bone, W. J.	Chatham, T. B.	Day, W. M.

Edmondson, J. O.
Edwards, J. W.
Estes, Harry
Estes, Henderson
Gault, P.
Green, F.
Hammond, F. M.
Hammond, W. N.
Hampton, G. W.
Hargroves, J. W.
Harris, J. W.
Harris, O.
Harris, W. B.
Hay, G. T.
Hay, J. A.
Hendrix, M. M.
Henson, W. A.
Holcomb, A. J.
Howard, J. P.
Hurt, W. J.
Jackson, A.
Jackson, D. T.
Karr, J. A.
Key, J. L.
Lewis, H. W.

Lummus, R. W.
Martin, J. M.
Mathis, R.
Mathis, W. H.
Mays, J. T.
McGinniss, O.
Miller, Thos.
Mooney, W.
Nicholson, J. B.
Payne, A. N.
Payne, W. W.
Petty, John J. J.
Phillips, J. H.
Phillips, K. D.
Phillips, W. H.
Pinkle, W. M.
Porter, Wm.
Propes, G. M. D.
Pruett, T. W.
Puckett, N.
Puckett, P.
Puckett, S.
Ragin, J. E.
Robuck, W. E.
Roper, Jason

Roper, Jos.
Samples, J.
Samples, M. M.
Scott, John
Spencer, W.
Stephens, D.
Stephens, E.
Strickland, T.
Suddeth, J.
Swanson, W. R.
Talant, D. C.
Talant, H. C.
Talant, T. B.
Thornton, R. N.
Thornton, W. N.
Tribble, J. J.
Tucker, J. M.
Turner, J. B.
Turner, J. R.
Vaughn, H. J.
White, J. H.
White, J. N.
White, W.
Williams, H. B.
Williams, J. S.
Williams, W. P.

Co. B, Second Regiment, Georgia State Line
(Terrell and Webster Counties, "State Right Volunteers")

Officers:

Capt.: Wilson, James / Saunders, Z. F.
1st Lt.: Saunders, Z. F. / Kelly, Charles
2nd Lt.: Wall, Wm. E.
3rd Lt.: Bush, J. J. / Davis, C. O.
1st Sgt.: Allen, Thomas M. / Boyd, T. E.

2nd Sgt.: Burney, Thomas J.
3rd Sgt.: Kelly, Charles
4th Sgt.: Bush, J. P., Sr.
5th Sgt.: Johnson, Elam
1st Cpl.: Torbert, J. B.
2nd Cpl.: Morgan, J. A.
3rd Cpl.: Bush, J. P., Jr.
4th Cpl.: Bone, J. W.

("B" Company, Second Regiment)

Privates:

Abell, J. J.
Adams, P. W.
Alday, J. R.
Applewhite, J. T.
Bell, J. F.
Blackshear, J. L.
Blackshear, T. R.
Boyd, J.
Boyett, Joshua J.
Bozeman, J. H.
Bozeman, Wm. E.
Bray, J. N.
Brazile, N. E.
Britt, J. W.
Brooks, A. G.
Byrd, W.
Cammander, B. L.
Carter, J. W.
Chambless, B. F.
Chambless, W.
Chappell, Thomas A.
Cook, T. J.
Daniel, T. J.
Davis, D. B.
Dennard, J.
Duke, F. M.
Felder, Geo. D.
Foreman, J. W.
Foster, Wm. R.
Godwin, Sparkman
Graves, Albert
Griffin, James M.
Grimes, James
Harmon, Michael
Hasty, B.
Huckaby, J. G.
Huckaby, W. F.

Jack, J. B.
Johnson, N.
Johnson, N. G.
Johnston, J. C.
Jones, G. W.
Jones, J. W.
Kaigler, John
Kelley, Jackson
Kitchens, John H.
Knighton, M. C.
Lane, Benjamin
Lay, John W.
Lewis, Richard C.
Lindsey, J. S.
Little, James M.
Logan, S. G.
Matthews, Jacob N.
McDonald, R. B.
McLendon, Wiley
McLeod, Alexander
McLeod, Wm. A.
Miller, B. S.
Montgomery, G. W.
Moore, H. C.
Moses, Jesse
Mulkey, W.
Nicholson, W. F.
Odom, W. H.
Outlaw, John
Owens, John
Parker, M. J.
Passmore, Hartwell
Perryman, G. M. T.
Rainey, Egbert
Reddick, Peter W.
Ridgell, C. D.
Robertson, J.

Robinson, John
Rooks, R. R.
Rudd, S. V.
Sapp, A. J.
Sapp, Daniel
Scott, S. R.
Senn, Kinion
Shinholster, J. N.
Slaughter, H. M.
Smith, Isaiah
Spann, Henry
Stapleton, Geo.
Stephens, W. J.
Still, Martin P.
Stuart, J. G.
Sullivan, J. S.
Summerford, A.
Taylor, G. F.
Terry, John
Thompson, H. J.
Thompson, Peter
Tillman, Wm.
Torbert, Geo.
Truett, I. W.
Walker, B. R.
Walker, Daniel A.
Walker, H. D.
Warren, G. W.
Watkins, H. L.
Watson, Jackson
Webb, Wm.
Wilkerson, Charles B.
Wilkins, C. B.
Wiseman, G. W.
Wooley, Joseph

Co. C, Regiment, Georgia State Line
(Paulding County, "Paulding Guards")

Officers:

Capt.:	Northcutt, T. H.	5th Sgt.:	Northcutt, I. A.
1st Lt.:	Beall, Noble N.		McElwreath, R. P.
2nd Lt.:	Pickett, M. T.	1st Cpl.:	Adair, B.
3rd Lt.:	Roberts, S. M.		Cole, W. M.
4th Lt.:	Pickett, F. M.	2nd Cpl.:	Cole, W. M.
1st Sgt.:	Denson, J.		Sheffield, J. B.
	Edwards, S.	3rd Cpl.:	Moody, T. E.
2nd Sgt.:	Adair, J. B.		Williams, N. E.
	Harris, J. J.	4th Cpl.:	Mathews, G. P.
3rd Sgt.:	Wings, S.		Martin, John P.
	Napier, A. G.		Wings, S.
4th Sgt.:	Braswell, E.		

("C" Company, Second Regiment)

Privates:

Adair, G. W.
Adair, J. G.
Akins, J. P.
Black, Jolin N.
Bone, F. M.
Brambelow, J. J.
Brantley, O. F.
Braswell, D.
Braswell, J. T.
Brooks, T. J.
Brown, H.
Busbey, W.
Camp, B. J.
Camp, John A.
Camp, T. P.
Camp, W. M.
Cheek, G.
Chupp, J. C.
Clements, J. W.
Compton, J. D.
Davis, E.
Davis, H. M.
Davis, L.
Denson, J. F.
Dorsett, M. T.
Dunn, Jackson
Evans, W.
Frisbee, J. S.
Fuller, Jacob
Gillaland, L. G.
Gray, C. M.
Green, W. N.

Green, W. S.
Growett, N. W.
Harris, C.
Harris, H. R.
Harris, W. A.
Hollis, J. W.
Hulsey, Jesse
Johnson, J. W.
Johnson, T. J.
Kemp, J. A.
Kemp, J. F.
Kirk, John
Knight, Ira
Lathan, S.
Lawrence, J. M.
Lee, W. A.
Lindsey, M. T.
Mathews, J. A.
Matthews, G. P.
Maudling, A.
McBreyar, W.
McClung, R. B.
McCollum, C. S.
McCollum, E. S.
McEver, J. L.
McEver, W. E.
Meek, L. C.
Morgan, W. A.
Moody, W. T.
Osborn, F. M.
Parris, Jasper
Parris, S.

Pickett, J. C.
Potts, J. H.
Prewitt, J. R.
Rhodes, W. H.
Roberts, J. W.
Roberts, N.
Rodgers, J. C.
Shipp, J. P.
Simpson, J. W.
Simpson, S.
Sinzard, S.
Spinks, G. H.
Tant, T.
Tidwell, S.
Turner, J. F.
Wall, B. B.
Watson, J. A.
Watson, J. M.
Weaver, J. H.
Webb, J. M.
Webster, A.
Welch, W. H.
Wells, J.
West, James
White, A. Y.
White, J. B.
Williams, N. E.
Williams, T. H.
Wills, J. M.
Winn, T. P.
Yearwood, G. W.
Yearwood, T. P.

Co. D, Second Regiment, Georgia State Line
(Upson County, "State Volunteers")

Officers:

Capt.:	Worrill, D. W.	4th Sgt.:	Daniel, B.
	Worrill, Roderick L.	5th Sgt.:	Grisham, Geo. W.
1st Lt.:	Worrill, Roderick L.		Snelson, A. J.
	Womble, C. R.	1st Cpl.:	Williams, N. M.
2nd Lt.:	Thornton, Ruben Y.	2nd Cpl.:	Sims, S. A.
3rd Lt.:	Thornton, Henry H.		Elleby, Mark
1st Sgt.:	Legg, L. H.	3rd Cpl.:	Gross, Robert
2nd Sgt.:	Leverett, A. H.		Middlebrooks, T. J.
	McDowell, J.	4th Cpl.:	Legg, W. H.
3rd Sgt.:	Sanford, S. B.		
	Jones, J. O.		

("D" Company, Second Regiment)

Privates:

Barnes, W. A.	Fuller, J. T.	McCard, J. M.
Barnes, Wm.	Gilmer, S. M.	McCash, J. E.
Barrentine, Stephen	Gore, D. S.	McClendon, F. M.
Beard, Wm.	Graham, W. N.	Melton, Henry
Bearden, Wm.	Gray, Sherod	Middlebrooks, L. N.
Bentley, Thos.	Green, William	Middlebrooks, T. A.
Best, Christopher C.	Griffin, R. N.	Middlebrooks, W. S.
Betts, Robt.	Gross, John	Miller, William
Bowden, Enoch R.	Hambrick, R. J.	Morris, J. H.
Brawner, W. H.	Hammock, Richard	Morris, Jeff J.
Brown, J. D.	Hammock, S.	Murphey, J. A.
Brown, J. L.	Hammock, T. G.	Noell, James
Bruce, A. M.	Hancock, Richard	Parker, John T.
Bruce, Monroe	Hardaway, J. W.	Patterson, Robert
Bullock, W. C.	Hardy, Isaac	Pilkenton, Jas.
Burge, N. H.	Harris, Thos.	Rawls, Wm.
Burge, J. L.	Hartman, J. N.	Revell, H. N.
Busby, Oliver	Harvey, J. N.	Rucker, B. B.
Butler, H.	Humber, John T.	Sims, J. G.
Butler, John	James, J. C.	Smith, A. F.
Campbell, James K.	Jenkins, Larkin	Smith, Caleb
Caraway, A.	Jenkins, Starling	Smith, W. N.
Carter, John H.	Johnson, A. L.	Smith, Wm.
Castleberry, Wm. Z.	Johnston, Richard	Tarver, G. W.
Catoe, Phillip	Jones, I. L.	Teal, Andrew
Chunn, Warren	Kennedy, F.	Thompson, Z.
Collins, Charles V.	Kennedy, J. T.	Tuggle, A. M.
Daniel, Thos. N.	Kennedy, W. L.	Turner, J. R.
Dickinson, J. N.	Kent, W. P.	Turner, T. B.
Fincher, J. T.	Kent, William F. M.	Turner, W. H.
Fincher, Thomas	Lee, J. J.	Wallace, John
Fincher, W. T.	Legg, N. C.	Webster, A. S.
Fogarty, H.	Long, Richard	Wellborne, T. M.
Foster, J. H.	Long, W. D.	Williams, W. S.
Foster, J. J.	Lyles, W. Y.	Wright, John
Foster, R. B.	Manley, John	Wright, John L.
Foster, Thomas N.	McBryde, Thos.	Wright, John T.
Freeman, Stephen	McBryde, W. C.	Youngblood, G. W.

Co. E, Second Regiment, Georgia State Line
(Harris County, "Chattahoochee Guards")

Officers:

Capt.:	Neal, Thos. Jefferson	4th Sgt.:	Sizemore, R. D.
1st Lt.:	Forrest, M. I.	5th Sgt.:	Spinks, J. W.
2nd Lt.:	Porter, S. T.		Dean, S.
3rd Lt.:	Hudson, C. J.	1st Cpl.:	Attaway, J. W.
1st Sgt.:	Guice, James W.	2nd Cpl.:	Lynch, Virgil A.
2nd Sgt.:	Amos, S.	3rd Cpl.:	Watson, J. W.
3rd Sgt.:	Cook, Jas. M.	4th Cpl.:	Johnson, A.
	Spence, W.		Geesling, B. F.

("E" Company, Second Regiment)

Privates:

Alexander, J. D.	Florence, J. A.	Lott, T. W.
Allen, Rufus	Florence, T. W.	McGehee, J. V.
Anderson, A. G.	Funderburk, H. C.	Middlebrooks, J. N.
Askew, T. W.	Gandy, N.	Miller, T. A.
Austin, N.	Grant, Amzi W.	Moon, J. D.
Barret, W.	Ginn, L. S.	Moore, S.
Betts, J. R.	Harvey, B. G.	Moore, W. L.
Bonner, W.	Harvey, G. B.	Moran, W. D.
Borders, L. H.	Helton, A.	Nelson, J. B.
Brannon, S.	Hill, W. R.	Norris, Isaac
Bryant, W. L.	Holland, J.	Oxford, E. J.
Buchanan, G.	Holland, W. T.	Parker, F.
Burden, S. M.	Hood, J. W.	Perkins, I.
Cherry, G. W.	Hood, W. A.	Radney, J. T.
Christian, W. D.	Howell, J. H.	Rice, J. D.
Cooper, A. J.	Huff, W. J.	Rice, R.
Copeland, Wm. B.	Huguly, H. L.	Russell, W.
Crawford, J. M.	Hundley, W. A.	Smith, J. A.
Crawford, M. C.	Hutchinson, M.	Snellings, E.
Darrington, W.	Johnson, J. W.	Spence, F. B.
Davis, Henry	Johnston, T. C.	Thomaston, T. L.
Davis, M. J.	Joiner, A. J.	Thrailkill, J. J.
Davis, Robert	Jones, W. H.	Tillory, J. R.
Dean, E. J.	Jordan, J. J.	Waller, R. H.
Dean, E. T.	Kerlin, J. T.	White, A.
Dean, L. R.	King, T.	White, J.
Doggett, J. M.	King, W.	White, L. A.
Doggett, Wm. A.	Lee, F.	Williams, M.
Fendley, W. D.	Livingston, R. T.	Wright, N. J.

⸙Co. F, Second Regiment, Georgia State Line
(Wilkinson County, "Georgia Rangers")

Officers:

Capt.:	Hall, L. A.	2nd Sgt.:	Clements, J. D.
	Beall, A. A.		Hicks, J. R.
1st Lt.:	Hughes, N. W.	3rd Sgt.:	Payne, S. W.
	Crutchfield, J. F.		Hulsey, J. M.
2nd Lt.:	Floyd, E. M.	4th Sgt.:	Hatfield, G. H.
3rd Lt.:	Hicks, J. D.	5th Sgt.:	McRae, M. H.
	Burch, H. M.	1st Cpl.:	Spears, J.
1st Sgt.:	Burch, Henry M.	2nd Cpl.:	Johnson, R.
	Floyd, E. M.	3rd Cpl.:	Hancock, H. H.
	Ethridge, Lucien R.	4th Cpl.:	Clegg, J. P.

("F" Company, Second Regiment)

Privates:

Balkcom, J.	Fordham, E. W.	Mercer, P.
Balkcom, J. F.	Fordham, G.	Moose, W. J.
Baskin, R. H.	Fordham, W. J.	Mullins, H. J.
Batson, J. M.	Fountain, S.	Mullins, J. W.
Beall, F. H.	Fuqua, H. A. J.	Napier, A. G.
Bloodworth, W.	Gaines, R. C.	Nesbitt, T. W.
Boon, B. F.	Hall, Isaac O.	Nighton, J.
Boon, J.	Hall, L. L.	Norris, T.
Brannan, B.	Hancock, J. G.	Page, H. B.
Bright, C. M.	Hancock, W. R.	Prewit, E. J.
Brimm, J.	Hardin, L.	Redding, W. H.
Brown, T.	Harville, Wm. E.	Roach, J. W.
Browning, S.	Hicks, J. R.	Robinson, R. A.
Calhoun, J. W.	Hook, J. E.	Robinson, W. M.
Cass, L. C.	Hudson, M.	Shepherd, S. C.
Charters, Sam	Hughs, J. F.	Sikes, C. H.
Clay, E. W.	Jenkins, G.	Sikes, M.
Clerments, J. W.	Jessup, J. W.	Sikes, S.
Coleman, H.	John, W. L.	Simpson, J.
Coleman, John W.	Johnson, B.	Stark, J. W.
Coleman, Resa	Johnson, G.	Stephens, I.
Coleman, W. A.	Jones, J.	Stinson, I.
Counsal, Wm.	Kirby, S. T.	Stone, W. A.
Crosby, T. D.	Knighson, J.	Stuckey, J.
Darsey, G. W.	Lafavor, A. N.	Taylor, Isaac
Darsey, J. B.	Larkin, T. O.	Taylor, J.
Davis, M.	Lavender, J. F.	Taylor, W. M.
Donally, P.	Lee, B. F.	Thigpen, L.
Douglas, R.	Lott, J. P.	Tinley, A.
Duncan, J.	Mann, G. W.	Tonley, J. P.
Dunn, J. B.	McCarty, T. S.	Ussery, D.
Evans, J.	McMichael, E. B.	Ussery, J. B.
Ethridge, L. F.	McWilliams, S.	Valentine, J. J.
Farmer, E. N.	Meadsoms, S. S.	Vanlandingham, J. D.
Flazed, E. M.	Mercer, H. S.	Vanlandingham, J. H.

Veal, S. N.
Vinson, J. F.
Ward, J. H.

Ward, S.
Ward, T. M.
Wilkinson, T. H.

Willis, W. W.
Wyatt, E. L.
Zellner, G.

Co. G, Second Regiment, Georgia State Line
(Newton County, "Newton Guards")

Officers:

Capt.:	Maddox, Notley W.	4th Sgt.:	Cowen, Robt. T.
1st Lt.:	Weldon, Jas. O.		Dick, L. W.
2nd Lt.:	McCollum, J. R.	5th Sgt.:	Cameron, Robt. M.
3rd Lt.:	Almand, Simeon D.		Coker, W.
1st Sgt.:	Bell, Archibald S.	1st Cpl.:	Green, Geo. J.
2nd Sgt.:	McCollum, Geo. T.	2nd Cpl.:	Thompson, Samuel A.
	Thompson, C. W.	3rd Cpl.:	Brewer, Ethan M.
3rd Sgt.:	Sigman, F. M.		Harris, E. G.
	Belcher, W. D.	4th Cpl.:	Mask, Samuel B.

("G" Company, Second Regiment)

Privates:

Atkinson, J. N.
Avery, T. H.
Belcher, W. D.
Boyd, J. P.
Bradford, Wm. H.
Brand, W. E.
Brantley, W. H.
Broadnax, S. H.
Brown, J. W.
Campbell, J. C.
Christian, J. D.
Christian, James H.
Coker, Wm.
Cook, B. W.
Copeland, J. J.
Cornwell, E. L.
Cowen, R. T.
Cowen, Robert M.
Crawford, James B.
Crosley, M. G.
Cunard, W.
Dennard, J. J.
Dennard, T. W.
Dick, L. W.
Edwards, J. P.
Edwards, James J.
Eubanks, I.

Fleming. W. T.
Ford, C. W.
Freeman, J. F.
Freeman, Z. Z.
Goode, David C.
Hammock, J. M.
Harper, W.
Harris, E. G.
Harris, J. W.
Heath, L. D.
Hight, J. T.
Hinton, J.
Holland, Benj. F.
Hollingsworth, J. W.
Hooten, Moses
Hutchins, T. D.
Ivey, James W.
Ivey, Wm. H.
Jackson, Alphonza J.
Jones, R. A.
Kirkland, J. T.
Leftwich, James M.
Leftwich, John M.
Livingston, R. B.
Lockhart, J. T.
Maddox, J. H. F.
Mann, S. A.

Mask, W.
Miller, T. N.
Miller, W. G.
Mills, C. W.
Mitchell, W. R. R.
Moon, J. N.
Moore, R. H.
Morris, F. M.
Owens, D. T.
Owens, E. R.
Owens, I. J.
Patton, Geo.
Peters, H. S.
Plunkett, B. R.
Plunkett, C.
Plunkett, J.
Plunkett, Robert
Price, J. W.
Price, T. R.
Roberts, B. P.
Roberts, G.
Roberts, W. B.
Robinson, J. D.
Robinson, J. W.
Roseberry, R. G. W.
Russell, J. A.
Scott, John L.

Sharp, Henry T.	Spears, C. M.	Watkins, W.
Sigman, F. M.	Speir, W. H.	Walker, G. L.
Sims, W. J.	Streeter, J.	Webb, J. C.
Sims, W. K.	Streeter, W. F.	Webb, W. H.
Skelton, James T.	Taylor, L. F.	Weldon, James O.
Smith, D. R.	Thompson, C. W.	Wilson, J. W.
Smith, J. T.	Tuker, M.	Wright, J. R.
Smith, P. S.	Veal, A. R.	Yancey, J. E.
Sorrow, L. W.	Veal, W. S.	Yancey, Thomas J.

Co. H., Second Regiment, Georgia State Line
(Washington, Warren, and Emanuel Counties, "Joe Brown Volunteers")

Officers:

Capt.:	Evans, B. D.		5th Sgt.:	Harris, Benj. C.
	Hundley, Thos. S.			Pace, John C.
1st Lt.:	Harris, Wm. R.			O'Tyson, W. C.
2nd Lt.:	Clay, Nicholas H.		1st Cpl.:	Hall, Isaac B.
3rd Lt.:	Cason, A. H.			Pace, J. C.
1st Sgt.:	Slade, Simon D.			Hart, A.
	Lewis, Z.		2nd Cpl.:	Anderson, Wm.
2nd Sgt.:	Ivey, Benjamin			Usrey, M. D. C.
	Pace, J. C.			Collier, E. S.
3rd Sgt.:	Cason, L. A.		3rd Cpl.:	Hart, Absalom
	Downs, G. W.			Clarke, W. E.
4th Sgt.:	Harris, Benj. H.			Colvin, D. J. E.
	Curry, S. K.		4th Cpl.:	Usry, M. D. C.
	Lewis, Z.			O'Tyson, W. C.
	Bowling, W. J.			Whigham, J. W.

("H" Company, Second Regiment)

Privates:

Aldred, A. W.	Brown, S. J.	Fulghum, James
Anderson, A. S.	Bynum, C. F.	Gaines, S. W.
Avant, J. A.	Camp, Zebedee	Hanberry, Isaiah
Avery, Archy	Canady, L.	Hanberry, Jeremiah
Bennett, Calvin	Cheely, Henry	Harper, Henry
Bennett, John	Clarke, W. E.	Harrell, C. A.
Birdsong, Albert	Coleman, J. W.	Harris, B. F.
Birdsong, Asberry	Colvin, D. J. E.	Harris, J. B.
Bowling, Wm.	Curry, S. K.	Harrison, J. M.
Brantley, J. P.	Dekle, W. W.	Harrison, W. T.
Brantley, Wm. G.	Downs, G. W.	Hart, J. E.
Braswell, W. M.	Duggan, J. J.	Hart, R. J.
Brooks, Thomas	Durden, R. W.	Hattaway, Amos
Brown, H. L.	Embry, J. S.	Hattaway, John

Hodges, L. A.
Holly, E. S.
Hood, Robert
Howell, Elisha
Hubert, J. H.
Ivey, Adam
Ivey, G. W.
Jones, Braswell
Jones, Joseph
Jordan, A. F.
Kelly, Allen
Kirkland, B. F.
Kitchens, Aaron
Kitchens, J. H.
Landers, Moses
Lewis, Zachariah
Logue, Brinson
Lowe, C. C.
Marsh, S. S.
Mathews, Joseph
McCord, R. W.
Mills, J. W.
Mills, W. R.

Munford, John
Neal, John W.
Neal, T. F.
Norris, James W.
Ollif, Joseph
O'Tyson, W. C.
Overstreet, John E.
Parham, W. H.
Pate, Hilman
Pittman, John H.
Railey, Charles
Reynolds, J. W.
Rivers, J. M.
Roberts, John W.
Scott, James T.
Shirley, Wm. A.
Shirling, Wm. F.
Smith, Henry S.
Smith, Thos. S.
Smith, W. A.
Smith, W. M.
Smith, Zachariah
Stapleton, Thomas

Stephens, James
Sutton, A. L.
Swint, Joseph
Tanner, David F.
Tanner, John D.
Tanner, Miles
Tanton, Asa
Tanton, Henry
Thompson, Charles
Underwood, W. D.
Veal, J. H.
Veal, Reuben H.
Vinson, D. H.
Wales, Thomas L.
Walker, K. H.
Walton, E. W.
Warren, M. L.
Waton, J. W.
Wilaford, Barney
Wood, J. W.
Yarbrough, John
Yates, J. D.
Young, C. W.

Co. I, Second Regiment, Georgia State Line
(Carroll and Coweta Counties, "Cunningham Guards")

Officers:

Capt.:	Potts, W. A.	5th Sgt.:	Morris, J. L.
1st Lt.:	Hood, J. R.	1st Cpl.:	White, J. S.
2nd Lt.:	Smith, Gideon		Tanner, Jos.
3rd Lt.:	Richards, J. P.	2nd Cpl.:	Bunt, J. R.
1st Sgt.:	Smith, S. E.		Mann, J. W.
	Holland, F.	3rd Cpl.:	Hand, J. H.
2nd Sgt.:	Camp, A. J.		Bunt, J. R.
3rd Sgt.:	Skinner, F. M.	4th Cpl.:	Ashley, H. C.
4th Sgt.:	Richards, J. R.		
	Phillips, J. D.		

("I" Company, Second Regiment)

Privates:

Alford, Thomas
Alford, W. M.
Alford, Welborn
Allen, Augustus
Alridge, S. G.
Ayres, John
Baker, R. J.
Banester, Otis
Banester, W. T.
Barnett, J. N.
Barron, I. F.
Barron, T. J.
Bearden, Aaron
Belbo, J. B.
Benefield, W. H.
Boatright, J. A.
Boatright, W. F.
Braswell, D. M.
Braswell, I. L.
Braswell, W. F.
Brewster, W. M.
Brock, W. T.
Brown, Emanuel
Brown, J. A.
Brown, J. F.
Brown, J. H.
Brown, W. M.
Cavender, G. W.
Chaffin, J. U.
Chaffin, M. B.
Cooke, P. A.
Daniel, A. J.
Daugherty, J. S.
Dean, J. T.
Dinglar, W. A. J.
Dodson, J. M.
Douglas, W. A. I.
Duncan, M. T.
Ellison, W. L.
Enlow, A. H.
Garrison, A. J.

Gentry, W. A.
Gossett, T. J.
Gray, G. A.
Grant, W. A.
Guinnett, Stephen
Hanners, J. M.
Hardage, J. M.
Hardage, J. S.
Hays, J. C.
Head, J. R.
Hendrix, C. H.
Henry, T. L.
Holland, Ben F.
Holloway, J. W.
Holland, Tinsey
Houge, J. M.
Jackson, W. A.
Kelley, A. W.
Key, Martin
Kugler, M. P.
Landers, A. J.
Landers, J. H.
Leo, J. J.
Lowrey, Noah N.
Luster, F. M.
Lyle, W. M.
McDonald, G. B.
McGraw, E. W.
McIntosh, J. T.
McManis, M.
Miles, J. F.
Mixon, J. J.
Moody, R. W.
Moore, F. M.
Morris, W. F.
Mote, W. M.
Musick, G. W.
Nixon, C. D.
Parks, D. P.
Peace, Larry
Phillips, J. H.

Phillips, T. H.
Phillips, W. T.
Pollard, S. A.
Pollard, W. F.
Pollard, W. P.
Powell, C. H.
Prince, James
Robinson, J. W.
Robinson, Z. J.
Shadinger, John
Shirley, H. W.
Simms, Wilson
Smith, Alford
Smith, J. H.
Smith, W. M.
Spear, G. W.
Spratlin, W. F.
Sprewell, A. C.
Stephenson, J. N.
Stovall, S. J.
Swanson, A. V.
Tant, K. T.
Taylor, M. J.
Thigpen, J. H.
Thompson, A. P.
Thompson, S.
Thrasher, T. H.
Upchurch, Willis
Vines, J. K.
Vines, W. E.
Walls, W. B.
Warren, John
Warren, Lovet
Whitman, H. L.
Wilder, J. G.
Wilks, J. H.
Wilson, S. S.
Winkles, W. M.
Worthy, W. T.

Co. K, Second Regiment, Georgia State Line
(Morgan and Walton Counties, "Tom Cobb Infantry")

Officers:

Capt.:	Saffold, Seaborn J.	4th Sgt.:	Sims, David E.
1st Lt.:	Ammons, John M.		Sims, G. W.
	Copeland, Miles G.	5th Sgt.:	Anderson, J. H.
2nd Lt.:	Shaw, Sebastian		Dean, Thos. W.
3rd Lt.:	Ely, Jos. P.	1st Cpl.:	Lackey, T. W.
	Sims, David E.	2nd Cpl.:	Dean, Thomas W.
1st Sgt.:	Dye, S. H.		Maxey, E. M.
	Bell, Joseph	3rd Cpl.:	Parish, Henry C.
2nd Sgt.:	Arnold, John S.		Seals, F. A.
	Copeland, M. C.	4th Cpl.:	Hardy, J. N.
3rd Sgt.:	Bell, Joseph		Howard, J. T.
	Parish, Henry C.		

("K" Company, Second Regiment)

Privates:

Allen, D. E.
Allen, T. C.
Allen, William R.
Armstead, W. T.
Arnold, J. S.
Arnold, W. T.
Bailey, T. W.
Bean, R. E.
Bentley, Elias
Bentley, Isaac Henry
Bond, N. C.
Brown, A. H. B.
Bruce, T. P.
Bugg, W. B.
Burgis, J.
Burgis, James D.
Burgis, R. L.
Burgis, William
Burson, B. D.
Carter, J. E.
Caruthers, J. J.
Caruthers, R. J.
Chapman, M. E.
Cook, J. J.
Cooke, Cicero
Daniel, D. A.
Daniel, R. L.
Durdin, G.
Dudley, J.
Edwards, E. C.
Elrod, I. P.
Fambrough, G. B.
Fambrough, J. L.
Fambrough, W. T.
Farrar, W. T.
Freeman, R. S.
Galliher, James U.
Garrett, C. C.
Garrett, Miller
Gentry, Nicholas

George, Joseph
Ginn, T. J.
Ginn, William P.
Glass, A. J.
Grant, John G.
Gregory, James L.
Griffeth, F. P.
Griffeth, R. S.
Gunnels, A. J.
Gunnels, H. H.
Gunnels, S. T.
Haralson, J.
Hardeman, H.
Hardeman, S. A.
Harrison, Jerry
Harris, J. C.
Hogg, H. T.
Hunt, D. C.
Johnson, J. B.
Jones, Abram B.
Lester, J.
Luke, H. B.
Lynch, C. A.
Malcolm, B.
Malcolm, G.
Malcolm, W. T.
Mann, H. H.
Marable, W. A.
Marshall, LaFayette
Martin, E. W.
Maxey, J. W.
Maxey, James M.
McElhannon, J. T.
McGloughlin, J. E. H.
Meadows, D. B.
Meadows, G. A.
Moon, W. L.
Moore, F.
Moore, W.
Nicholson, Robert

Patrick, L. L.
Ponder, W. H.
Ray, D. B.
Ray, J. C.
Reeves, W.
Reid, C.
Robertson, T. J.
Sartin, A.
Seals, F. A.
Shackelford, C. G.
Sims, Doctor F.
Smith, B. A.
Smith, J. J.
Smith, Jas.
Spence, J. P.
Spence, John M.
Spence, W. M.
Stinchcomb, M. J. M.
Streeter, J.
Stroud, Thomas M.
Studdard, A.
Summerhour, J.
Taylor, John
Terrell, James B.
Thomason, Hiram Hensley (Dick)
Thompson, A. J.
Thompson, J. L.
Thompson, James M.
Threlkeld, John J.
Tiller, James R.
Twitty, W.
Wall, J. M.
Wall, John
Wall, W. F. M.
Wall, William H.
Wellmaker, Zachariah
West, J.
White, James H.
Wilson, Stephen

**Supplementary List
of Officers and Men of the Georgia State Line,
Based upon Information
from the National Archives' Compiled Service Records**
(Letter = Company / Number = Regiment)

Adcock, Wilson (1)
Ball, William (D2)
Brackeen, Josiah W. (1)
Brown, B. F. (I2)
Brown, J. T. (I2)
Brown, Leonard (1)
Brown, Shad (F2)
Brown, Shilldrake (2)
Carmichael, James D. (1)
Chapman, John A. (K1)
Clark, T. L. (B2)
Clinton, Robert G. (1)
Collins, Andrew S. (2)
Cowart, Wm.
Crawford, Samuel S.
Crumley, 2d Lt. B. W. (1)
D'Antignac, D. (E2)
Davis, Joseph (D1)
Dennis, Peter E. (F2)
Dennis, Taylor B. (B2)
Dial, George (D1)
Dickinson, Lt. J. E. (F1)
Dickinson, Sgt. J. T. (2)
Dixon, Nehemiah (E1)
Doughty, 2d Lt. W. R. (D1)
Ealy, 2d Lt. L. (K2)
Fairfield, G. M. (2)
Fitts, Tandy W. (B1)
Gilmore, Frank (1)
Hancock, John (D2)
Hardy, R. W. (F2)

Harmon, Jas. J. (F2)
Harrall, Henry (2)
Harris, Gartrell, (I2)
Harrison, Jesse J.
Harrison, Wm. P. (F1)
Hightower, James C. (G2)
Hord, T. W. (E2)
Jackson, B. W. A. (B2)
Jacobs, Wm. G. (I1)
Johnson, Thomas (1)
Jones, 2d Lt. L. M. (1)
Kent, Arch B. (2)
Kent, J. J. (C2)
Kinney, T. (D2)
Knowles, J. (B2)
Leclure, Leon (1)
Lehman, Thos. B. (1)
Little, John F.(1)
Logue, Jeremiah (E1)
Lord, William F. (1)
Loyless, Wm. A. (B2)
Lunsford, Alfred W. (1)
Madison, Joel (B2)
Maguirk, Saml. W. (1)
Marley, Capt. W. J. (1)
Martin, Sam H. (C2)
Massey, J. W. (1)
Massey, Noel J. (B2)
McCelvey, Geo. A. (2)
McIntosh, Donald (1)
Mobley, Sam R. (K2)

Morgan, William A. (1)
Morris, William F. (B2)
Nosworthy, J. T. (I2)
O'Neal, Mike (1)
Oxford, William E. (1)
Patterson, Wm. C. (1)
Puckett, William E. (1)
Rash, Robert (E2)
Rosin, A. (A2)
Rudd, S. V. (B2)
Simms, Leonard (G1)
Smith, J. (B2)
Spence, W. B. (2)
Stuckey, J. Z. (1)
Tate, 1st Lt. J. M. (1)
Taylor, E. D. (I2)
Taylor, James R. (C2)
Tomms, R. W. (C2)
Veal, A. K. (2)
Vernon, Robert M. (1)
Vickers, J. F. (K2)
Ward, Jno. M. (2)
Waters, O. (1)
Watson, Benj. F. (1)
Watson, Wm. W. (2)
Weddington, Wm. M. (C2)
Wells, Henry T. (1)
Wells, John (A2)
West, 2d Lt. J. M. (1)
Wilson, J. H. (H2)
Winchester, Coleman (1)
Woodall, J. M. (K2)

BIBLIOGRAPHY

I. Official Manuscript Sources

A. STATE OF GEORGIA MANUSCRIPTS

Adjutant General. Courts-Martial. Box 1, 3336-17. Georgia Department of Archives and History. Atlanta, Georgia.

Adjutant General Letter Books, 1861-1864. Georgia Department of Archives and History. Atlanta, Georgia.

Adjutant General's General Orders, 1861-1865. Georgia Department of Archives and History. Atlanta, Georgia.

Adjutant General's Special Orders, 1861-1864. Georgia Department of Archives and History. Atlanta, Georgia.

Commissary General. Purchases and Issues for Subsistence to Troops of State Line. Georgia Department of Archives and History. Atlanta, Georgia.

Executive Secretary Letter Books, 1862-1864. Georgia Department of Archives and History. Atlanta, Georgia.

Governor's Letter Book, 1861-1865. Georgia Department of Archives and History. Atlanta, Georgia.

Muster Rolls of the Georgia State Line. Map Cabinet Drawers 1 & 2, 8th Vault Floor, Georgia Department of Archives and History. Atlanta, Georgia.

B. CONFEDERATE MANUSCRIPTS

Compiled Service Records of Confederate Soldiers Who Served in Organizations From the State of Georgia. Microcopy No. 266, Roll 151. First Battalion, Infantry (State Guards) through First State Line. National Archives and Records Service, 1959.

Compiled Service Records of Confederate Soldiers Who Served in Organizations From the State of Georgia. Microcopy No. 266, Roll 166. Second State Line, Including Stapleton's and Storey's, and Third Infantry, A-Bo. National Archives and Records Service, 1959.

Morning Report Book, First Regiment, Georgia State Troops. Special Collections, University of Georgia Libraries. Athens, Georgia.

Report of Inspection of Brigade No. 2, Commanded by Colonel G. P. Harrison, Jr., 28 February 1863. Record Group 109, Departmental Records, Department of South Carolina, Georgia, and Florida, Box 47, Document No. 86, National Archives. Washington, D.C.

C. FEDERAL MANUSCRIPTS

U.S. Bureau of the Census, Schedule 1, Free Inhabitants, Forsyth County, Georgia, 1860.

U.S. Bureau of the Census, Schedule 1, Free Inhabitants, Franklin County, Georgia, 1860.

U.S. Bureau of the Census, Schedule 1, Free Inhabitants, Lumpkin County, Georgia, 1860.

U.S. Bureau of the Census, Schedule 1, Free Inhabitants, Morgan County, Georgia, 1860.

U.S. Bureau of the Census, Schedule 1, Free Inhabitants, Newton County, Georgia, 1860.

U.S. Bureau of the Census, Schedule 1, Free Inhabitants, Terrell County, Georgia, 1860.

U.S. Bureau of the Census, Schedule 1, Free Inhabitants, Upson County, Georgia, 1860.

U.S. Bureau of the Census, Schedule 1, Free Inhabitants, Washington County, Georgia, 1860.

U.S. Bureau of the Census, Schedule 1, Free Inhabitants, White County, Georgia, 1860.

U.S. Bureau of the Census, Schedule 1, Free Inhabitants, Whitfield County, Georgia, 1850.

U.S. Bureau of the Census, Schedule 1, Free Inhabitants, Whitfield County, Georgia, 1860.

U.S. Bureau of the Census, Schedule 2, Slave Inhabitants, Whitfield County, Georgia, 1860.

U.S. Bureau of the Census, Schedule 1, Free Inhabitants, Wilkinson County, Georgia, 1860.

II. OTHER MANUSCRIPT SOURCES

Adjutant General's Incoming Correspondence, 1861-1864. Georgia Department of Archives and History. Atlanta, Georgia.

Brown, Joseph E., Papers (microfilm). Special Collections Department, Robert W. Woodruff Library, Emory University. Atlanta, Georgia.

Brown-Connally-Spalding Collection. Georgia Department of Archives and History. Atlanta, Georgia.

Chambers, O. H. P. Letter, 2 July 1863. Civil War Miscellany—Personal Papers, Georgia Department of Archives and History. Atlanta, Georgia.

Cobb, Howell, Letter and Telegram Book, 1863-1864. Cobb-Erwin-Lamar Collection, Special Collections, University of Georgia Libraries. Athens, Georgia.

Cobb, Howell, Order and Letter Book, 1865. Cobb-Erwin-Lamar Collection, Special Collections, University of Georgia Libraries. Athens, Georgia.

Cobb, Howell, Papers. Manuscript Department, Perkins Library, Duke University. Durham, North Carolina.

Cobb County Probate Court, Returns of the Estate of F. M. Cowen, File No. 701. Marietta, Cobb County, Georgia.

Confederate Pension Applications. Georgia Department of Archives and History. Atlanta, Georgia.

Cuyler, Telamon, Collection. Adjutant General Henry C. Wayne Papers. Special Collections, University of Georgia Libraries. Athens, Georgia.

Cuyler, Telamon, Collection. Joseph E. Brown Papers. Special Collections, University of Georgia Libraries. Athens, Georgia.

Evans, Beverly, Collection. In private possession.

Fowler Family Papers. Civil War Miscellany—Personal Papers, Georgia Department of Archives and History. Atlanta, Georgia.

Galt, Edward M., Collection. In private possession.

Georgia Militia/Georgia State Line Miscellaneous File. Box 3337-10, Georgia Department of Archives and History. Atlanta, Georgia.

Georgia Ordnance—Incoming Correspondence. Georgia Department of Archives and History. Atlanta, Georgia.

Georgia State Line Hospital Records. Map Cabinet Drawer 1, Folder 15, Georgia Department of Archives and History. Atlanta, Georgia.

Governor Brown's Incoming Correspondence, 1861-1864. Georgia Department of Archives and History. Atlanta, Georgia.

Hargrett, Felix, Collection. Joseph Brown Papers (Manuscripts and Bound Typescript Letter Books, Ms. 95). Special Collections, University of Georgia Libraries. Athens, Georgia.

Jackson, A. J., Diary and Letters. Box 76-7, Microfilm Library, Georgia Department of Archives and History. Atlanta, Georgia.

Jones, Charles C., Jr., Papers. Manuscript Department, Perkins Library, Duke University. Durham, North Carolina.

Maps of the Official Survey of the Western and Atlantic Railroad . . . 1896. Georgia Surveyor General Department, Atlanta GA.

Mercer, Hugh Washington, Letters. Special Collections Department, Robert W. Woodruff Library, Emory University, Atlanta, Georgia.

"Sketch of Matthew Henry Talbot." Civil War Miscellany—Personal Papers, Georgia Department of Archives and History. Atlanta, Georgia.

Stephens, Alexander H., Papers. Special Collections, The Library, Manhattanville College. Purchase, New York.

von Zinken, Colonel Leon. Letter, 20 January 1864. Civil War Miscellany—Personal Papers, Georgia Department of Archives and History. Atlanta, Georgia.

Washington County, Superior Court Office, "Memorial of the Life and Services of Colonel Beverly D. Evans," Book of Minutes H. Sandersville, Washington County, Georgia.

Wayne, Henry C., Papers. Georgia Department of Archives and History. Atlanta, Georgia.

Wilson, James H., Manuscripts. Historical Society of Delaware. Wilmington, Delaware.

III. PRINTED PRIMARY SOURCES

A. OFFICIAL DOCUMENTS

A Proclamation. By Joseph E. Brown, Governor of Georgia. . . . [Ordering deserters to return to their commands.] Broadside, 17 January 1863.

Acts and Resolutions of the General Assembly of the State of Georgia, 1861, 1863.

Annual Report of the Adjutant and Inspector General . . . 1862-1863. Milledgeville GA: Boughton, Nisbet, Barres, & Moore, 1863.

Annual Report of the Adjutant and Inspector General . . . 1864. Milledgeville GA: Boughton, Nisbet, Barnes & Moore, 1864.

Candler, Allen D., ed. *The Confederate Records of the State of Georgia.* Vols. 1, 2, 3. Atlanta: C. P. Byrd, State Printer, 1909-1911.

Clark, R. H., Cobb, T. R. R., and Irwin, D. *The Code of the State of Georgia.* Atlanta: Crusader Book and Job Office, 1861.

Georgia House Journals, 1862, 1863 (Extra Session), 1864, 1864 (Extra Session), 1865.

Georgia State Journals, 1860, 1862, 1863 (Extra Session), 1864, 1865.

Henderson, Lillian, ed. *Roster of the Confederate Soldiers of Georgia.* 6 vols. Hapeville.

Peters, Richard, ed. *The Public Statutes at Large of the United States of America.* Boston: Charles C. Little and James Brown, 1848.

Report of House Committee on Western and Atlantic Railroad. Milledgeville GA: n.p., 1862.

Report of the Superintendent and Treasurer of the Western and Atlantic Rail Road, to his Excellency Joseph E. Brown, Governor, October 1, 1862. Atlanta: Office of the Daily Intelligencer, 1862.

Reports of the Operations of the Militia . . . . Macon GA: Boughton, Nisbet, Barnes & Moore, [1865].

Resolutions passed by the General Assembly of Georgia, authorizing the Governor to organize two regiments of state troops to be employed in the military service of the state . . . Approved Dec. 13th, 1862. [n.p., 1862].

The Constitution of the State of Georgia. [March 23, 1861. Savannah: n.p., 1861].

War of the Rebellion: Official Records of the Union and Confederate Armies. 70 volumes in 128 parts. Washington DC: Government Printing Office, 1880-1901.

B. NEWSPAPERS

Athens Southern Watchman.
Atlanta Commonwealth.
Atlanta Constitution.
Atlanta Intelligencer.
Atlanta Southern Confederacy.
Augusta Chronicle and Sentinel.
Charleston Daily Courier.
Charleston Mercury.

Dahlonega Signal.
Daily Columbus Enquirer.
Macon Daily Telegraph.
Milledgeville Confederate Union.
Milledgeville Southern Federal Union.
Milledgeville Southern Recorder.
Rome Tri-Weekly Courier.
Sandersville Central Georgian.
Selma (Ala.) Times-Journal.

C. MEMOIRS

Longstreet, James. *From Manassas to Appomattox.* Philadelphia: J. P. Lippincott Co., 1896.

Malone, W. H. "Memoirs." Civil War Miscellany—Personal Papers, Georgia Department of Archives and History, Atlanta, Georgia.

Smith, Gustavus W. "The Georgia Militia during Sherman's March to the Sea." R. U. Johnson and C. C. Buel, eds. *Battles and Leaders of the Civil War.* Vol. 4. New York: The Century Co., 1907.

Sorrel, G. Moxley, *Recollection of a Confederate Staff Officer.* New York: The Neale Publishing Co., 1905.

Wilson, James Harrison. *Under the Old Flag.* Vol. 2. New York: D. Appleton & Co., 1912.

D. OTHER PRINTED SOURCES

"The Saratoga of the Confederate States: Catoosa Springs, Catoosa County, Georgia." Pamphlet, 1861.

Wayne, Henry C. *The Sword Exercise, A Manual for Military Instruction.* Washington DC: Gideon & Co., 1850.

IV. CORRESPONDENCE AND PERSONAL INTERVIEWS

Evans, Louise. Washington County, Georgia. Interview, 6 May 1979.

Redfern, Natalie R., to author, 23 January 1980.

Roberts, Lamar H., to author, 12 July 1979.

Saffold, Mattie. Morgan County, Georgia. Interview, 27 August 1980.

V. SECONDARY SOURCES

A. BOOKS

Amlund, Curtis Arthur. *Federalism in the Southern Confederacy.* Washington DC: Public Affairs Press, 1966.

Avery, I. W. *The History of the State of Georgia from 1850 to 1881.* New York: Brown & Derby, 1881.

Beringer, Richard, et al. *Why the South Lost the Civil War.* Athens: University of Georgia Press, 1986.

Black, Robert C. III., *The Railroads of the Confederacy.* Chapel Hill: University of North Carolina Press, 1952.

Bryan, T. Conn. *Confederate Georgia.* Athens: University of Georgia Press, 1953.

Burton, E. Milby. *The Siege of Charleston, 1861-1865*. Columbia: University of South Carolina Press, 1970.

Civil War Records. Georgia Department of Archives and History Publication No. 76-CW-1.

Connelly, Thomas Lawrence. *Army of the Heartland: The Army of Tennessee, 1861-1862*. Baton Rouge: Louisiana State University Press, 1967.

Connelly, Thomas Lawrence. *Autumn of Glory: The Army of Tennessee, 1862-1865*. Baton Rouge: Louisiana State University Press, 1971.

Corley, Florence Fleming. *Confederate City: Augusta, Georgia, 1860-1865*, Columbia: University of South Carolina Press, 1960.

Coulter, E. Merton. *The Confederate States of America, 1861-1865*. Baton Rouge: Louisiana State University Press and the Littlefield Fund for Southern History, 1950.

Cullum, George W. *Biographical Register of the Officers and Graduates of the U.S. Military Academy*. Vol. 1. New York: Houghton, Mifflin Co., 1891.

Davidson, Victor. *History of Wilkinson County*. Macon, GA: J. W. Burke Co., 1930.

Davis, Burke. *Sherman's March*. New York: Random House, 1980.

Derry, Joseph Tyrone. *Georgia*. Vol. 6 in Clement A. Evans, ed., *Confederate Military History,* 12 vols. Atlanta: Confederate Publishing Co., 1899.

Dodson, W. C., ed. *Campaigns of Wheeler and His Cavalry, 1862-1865*. Atlanta: Hudgins Publishing Co., 1899.

Eaton, Clement. *A History of the Southern Confederacy*. New York: The Free Press, 1954.

Escott, Paul D. *After Secession: Jefferson Davis and the Failure of Southern Nationalism*. Baton Rouge: Louisiana State University Press, 1978.

Faulk, Odie B. *The U.S. Camel Corps, An Army Experiment*. New York: Oxford University Press, 1976.

Fielder, Herbert. *A Sketch of the Life and Times and Speeches of Joseph E. Brown*. Springfield, MA: Press of the Springfield Printing Co., 1883.

Hill, Louise Biles. *Joseph E. Brown and the Confederacy*. Chapel Hill: University of North Carolina Press, 1939.

Horn, Stanley F. *The Army of Tennessee: A Military History*. New York: The Bobbs-Merrill Co., 1941.

Hughes, Nathaniel Cheairs. *General William J. Hardee: Old Reliable*. Baton Rouge: Louisiana State University Press, 1965.

Johnson, Michael P. *Toward a Patriarchal Republic: The Secession of Georgia*. Baton Rouge: Louisiana State University Press, 1977.

Jones, Charles C., Jr. *The Siege of Savannah—Confederate Operations in Georgia*. New York: Joel Munsell, 1874.

Jones, Chas. Edgeworth. *Georgia in the War, 1861-1865*. Atlanta: Foote & Davies, 1909.

Jones, James Pickett. *Yankee Blitzkrieg: Wilson's Raid through Alabama and Georgia*. Athens: University of Georgia Press, 1976.

Kirk, Russell. *Randolph of Roanoke: A Study in Conservative Thought*. Chicago: University of Chicago Pres, 1951.

Lawrence, Alexander A. *A Present for Mr. Lincoln.* Macon GA: The Ardivan Press, 1961.

Lawrence, Alexander A. *James Moore Wayne, Southern Unionist.* Chapel Hill: University of North Carolina Press, 1943.

Lonn, Ella. *Foreigners in the Confederacy.* Gloucester MA: Peter Smith, 1965.

Maddox, Joseph T. *Wilkinson County, Georgia, Gravestones with Genealogical Information.* Irwinton GA: n.p., 1971.

Mahon, John K. *History of the Militia and the National Guard.* New York: Macmillan Publishing Co., 1983.

Marlin, Lloyd G. *The History of Cherokee County.* Atlanta: Walter W. Brown Publishing Co., 1932.

McMurry, Richard M. *John Bell Hood and the War for Southern Independence.* Lexington: The University Press of Kentucky, 1982.

McPherson, James M. *Ordeal by Fire: The Civil War and Reconstruction.* New York: Alfred A. Knopf, 1982.

Mitchell, Ella. *The History of Washington County.* Atlanta: Byrd Printing Co., 1924.

Mitchell, Joseph B. *Decisive Battles of the Civil War.* Greenwich CT: Fawcett Publications, Inc., 1955.

Montgomery, Horace. *Cracker Parties.* Baton Rouge: Louisiana State University Press, 1950.

Montgomery, Horace. *Howell Cobb's Confederate Career.* Tuscaloosa AL: Confederate Publishing Co., 1959.

Moore, Albert Burton. *Conscription and Conflict in the Confederacy.* New York: Macmillan & Co., 1924.

Myers, Robert Manson, ed. *The Children of Pride.* New Haven: Yale University Press, 1972.

Nixon, Raymond B. *Henry W. Grady: Spokesman of the New South.* New York: Alfred A. Knopf, 1943.

Nottingham, Carolyn Walker and Hannah, Evelyn. *History of Upson County, Georgia.* Macon GA: J. W. Burke Co., 1930.

Owsley, Frank Lawrence. *State Rights in the Confederacy.* Chicago: University of Chicago Press, 1925.

Parks, Joseph H. *Joseph E. Brown of Georgia.* Baton Rouge: Louisiana State University Press, 1977.

Rhodes, James Ford. *History of the United States from the Compromise of 1850 to the End of the Roosevelt Administration.* Vol. 5. New York: The Macmillan Co., 1928.

Scruggs, Carroll Proctor, ed. *Georgia Historical Markers.* Helen GA: Bay Tree Grove, 1973.

Tatum, Georgia Lee. *Disloyalty in the Confederacy.* Chapel Hill: University of North Carolina Press, 1934.

von Abele, Rudolph. *Alexander H. Stephens: A Biography.* New York: Alfred A. Knopf, 1946.

Wiley, Bell Irvin. *The Life of Johnny Reb, the Common Soldier of the Confederacy.* Baton Rouge: Louisiana State University Press, 1978.

Yearns, W. Buck, ed. *The Confederate Governors*. Athens: University of Georgia Press, 1985.

Yearns, Wilfred Buck. *The Confederate Congress*. Athens: University of Georgia Press, 1960.

B. DISSERTATIONS

Bass, James Horace. "Georgia in the Confederacy, 1861-1865." Ph. D. dissertation, University of Texas, 1932.

Guinn, Gilbert Sumter. "Coastal Defense of the Confederate Atlantic Seaboard States, 1861-1862: A Study in Political and Military Mobilization." Ph. D. dissertation, University of South Carolina, 1973.

Kaufman, Janet E. "Sentinels on the Watchtower: The Confederate Governors and the Davis Administration." Ph. D. dissertation, American University, 1977.

Pfennig, Dennis Joseph. "Evan and Clark Howell of the *Atlanta Constitution*: The Partnership (1889-1897). Ph. D. dissertation, University of Georgia, 1975.

Robbins, John Brawner. "Confederate Nationalism: Politics and Government in the Confederate South." Ph. D. dissertation, Rice University, 1964.

C. ARTICLES FROM JOURNALS AND OTHER PERIODICALS

Alvarez, Eugene. "Peter James Bracken: The Forgotten Engineer of the 'General.' " *Atlanta Historical Journal* 24 (Winter 1980): 41-50.

Bass, James Horace. "The Attack upon the Confederate Administration in Georgia in the Spring of 1864." *Georgia Historical Quarterly* 18 (September 1934): 228-47.

Black, Robert C. III., "The Railroads of Georgia in the Confederate War Effort." *Journal of Southern History* 13 (November 1947): 511-534.

Coleman, Kenneth, ed. "Ladies Volunteer Aid Association of Sandersville, Washington County, Georgia, 1861-1862." *Georgia Historical Quarterly* 52 (March 1968): 1-18.

Hay, Thomas Robson. "Joseph E. Brown, Governor of Georgia, 1857-1865." *Georgia Historical Quarterly* 13 (June 1929): 89-109.

Hitz, Alex M. "Georgia Militia Districts." *Georgia Bar Journal* 18 (February 1956): 1-7.

Holland, Lynwood M. "Georgia Military Institute, the West Point of Georgia: 1851-1864." *Georgia Historical Quarterly* 43 (September 1959): 225-247.

Johnston, Michael P. "A New Look at the Popular Vote for Delegates to the Georgia Secession Convention." *Georgia Historical Quarterly* 56 (Summer 1972): 259-75.

Lawrence, Alexander A., ed. "Some Letters from Henry C. Wayne to Hamilton Fish." *Georgia Historical Quarterly* 43 (December 1959): 391-409.

McDowell, Irvin. "Henry Constantine Wayne." *U.S. Military Academy, The Annual Association of Graduates.* N.p., n.d.: 96-98.

Niven, Alexander C. "Joseph E. Brown, Confederate Obstructionist." *Georgia Historical Quarterly* 42 (September 1958): 233-57.

Phillips, Ulrich B. "An American State-Owned Railroad." *Yale Review* 15 (November 1906): 259-82.

Wooster, Ralph A. "Notes on the Georgia Legislature of 1860." *Georgia Historical Quarterly* 45 (March 1961): 22-36.

List of Illustrations

INDEX

Unless otherwise noted, all place and county names in this index are for Georgia. With the exception of the Georgia State Line, which has its own entry, all military units or organizations raised in Georgia are indexed under "Georgia troops"; the Georgia State Line is referred to as "GSL."

Acworth, 98, 126
Albany, 110 n. 49
Allatoona Bridge, 68
Anderson, Jeff, 21
Andersonville, x
Andrews, James J., 6, 7, 10
Andrews' Raiders, 21
Army of Tennessee, vii, 66, 67, 84-95, 98, 101, 116
Atlanta, 7, 18, 67, 100; Battle of, 89-91, 95, 117; fall of, 93; siege of, 91; state gun factory in, 11
Atlanta Commonwealth, 46
Atlanta Constitution, 126-27
Atlanta Intelligencer, 75
Augusta, 103, 105, 109, 109 n. 46

Bailey's Mills, skirmish at, 118
Ball's Ferry, Battle of, 117
Bamberg SC, 105
Banks County, 42; muster rolls of GSL volunteers from, 140-41
Bartow County, 42; muster rolls of GSL volunteers from, 138-39
Beauregard, P. G. T., 45, 97
Benjamin, Judah P., 1, 13
Big Shanty, 41, 86, 94
Blackburn, J. C. C. (Maj./Surgeon, GSL), 50-51, 51 n. 25, 52-53, 53 n. 34
Blairsville, 21
Blue Mountain AL, 95
Blue Pond AL, 95
"Blue Ridge Rangers," 42. *See also* GSL, First Regiment, Co. D
Bolton, 76, 78
Bragg, Braxton, 32, 66-67, 68, 72-73, 74, 75 n. 63, 76, 94, 112, 122
Brown, Aaron P. (Maj./Surgeon, GSL), 12, 13, 13 n. 13, 32, 53, 79, 119-20, 127
Brown, Elizabeth G., 12 n. 8, 126 n. 3
Brown, George, 12-13, 32

Brown, John M. (Lt. Col., GSL), 12-13, 13-14, 32, 42, 78, 79, 87, 89-90, 91, 91 n. 23, 126 n. 23
Brown, Joseph E., 33 n. 39, 50, 57, 95 n. 35; allows GSL's transfer to Charleston, 55; and Andrews' Raid, 6; and "anti-drinking clause," 12; attempts to nullify conscription in Georgia, 24; and Bridge Guard arms, 15 n. 23; and burial of Lt. Col. Brown, 91, 91 n. 23; calls for meeting of legislature, 109, 111 n. 50; cites value of GSL, 57-58; claims Pres. Davis's acquiescence in GSL's creation, 61; confers with Toombs and Stephens, 109; and conflict with Davis administration, 3, 5 n. 13; conscription correspondence with Davis of, 24; and controversy with Col. Browne, 98-101; controversy over Richmond's troop requisition, 101; and creation of GSL, 23-26; and Dahlonega expedition, 17-18, 19, 19 n. 34, 22; and defense of Savannah (1863), 44-45, 45 n. 7; delays enforcement of second conscription act in Georgia, 24; delivers 1862 message to legislature, 23; demands guns from Gen. Wayne, 82-83; on diminution of powers, 8; discourages GSL's anti-Confederate sentiment, 48, 78-79; distrusts Davis administration, 1-2; encourages GSL proficiency, 60; encourages state-CSA cooperation, 19; exempts Bridge Guard from conscription, 16, 16 n. 25; exempts state officers from conscription, 24, 27; expands Bridge Guard, 14; and fall of Fort Pulaski, 6; and first conscription act, 7; and First Division, Georgia Volunteers, 5-6, 7-8, 9; forbids substitution

in Bridge Guard, 14; forbids substitution in GSL, 54, 55 n. 44; and Galt controversy, 81-82; and Gen. Henry R. Jackson, 8, 26; and Georgia local defense troops, viii, viii n. 2, ix, x; gives GSL clothing commutation, 51, 51 n. 27; gives permission for GSL movement into Tennessee, 106; and GSL agricultural leave requests, 62, 63; and GSL brothers, 32; and GSL cavalry, 114, 115, 118; and GSL commission seekers, 30-32; and GSL elections, 41; GSL as repudiation of conscription, 35-36; has conscription officer arrested, 73 n. 54; on importance of State Road, 61; imprisonment of, 110; informs Pres. Davis of GSL creation, 34-35; issues proclamation against deserters, 19; on local defense, 1-2, 2 n. 2, 4, 8, 9; and Marietta controversy, 79; and medical treatment in first GSL, 53; meets with Gen. Wilson, 109; on militia, 27, 34-35, 35 n. 46; offers GSL for CSA service, 76, 77, 84; orders Gen. Wayne to hold Resaca Bridge, 74; orders Gen. Wayne to inspect State Road, 67; orders GSL stationed on State Road, 56; orders leave for GSL stationed on State Road, 56; personality of, 2-3; places Gen Wayne in command of GSL, 69; policy of on conscription of GSL volunteers, 35; policy toward desertion of, 22 n. 42; political importance of state security to, 44, 44 n. 3; postwar career of, 110-11; powers provided to by CSL resolutions, 27; praises GSL, 102 n. 17; proposes raising two state regiments, 23; and Railroad Bridge Guard, 9-11; and raising of GSL, 32, 33; recruits form CSA ranks, 31; and relationship with